The Child

William Kessen, Yale University

New York • London • Sydney   John Wiley & Sons, Inc.

10 9 8

ISBN 0 471 47306 5
Library of Congress Catalog Card Number: 65-14253
Printed in the United States of America

For my father

Foreword

Perspectives in Psychology is a series of original books written for psychologists and students who are concerned with the history of ideas in psychology.

It is our intention to present fresh and thoughtful assessments of the current psychological scene in the context of relevant historical changes. Many authors of the *Perspectives* books will examine a selected slice of the history of psychology by way of selected and annotated readings. This is not to say that *Perspectives* is a uniform or systematic encyclopedia of the history of psychology. Psychologists, by disposition and training, are reluctant to work their ideas into a standard weave—homespun or exotic—and *Perspectives* represents well the happy diversity of the discipline.

Some books in the series are scholarly disquisitions on the historical antecedents of a current problem in psychological analysis; some books move—after a brief glance at historical antecedents—directly toward a discussion of contemporary psychology and its future; some books deal with the past largely as a platform for polemical exposition. And, occasionally, *Perspectives* will present an original work in psychology that escapes the historical definition altogether.

Perspectives in Psychology, by using the avenues of documented history and informed discussions of current as well as classical issues, will emphasize that psychology has a history as well as a past and that it advances as it grows.

GEORGE MANDLER
WILLIAM KESSEN

vii

Preface

This is only one of the several books that might have been drawn from the vast range of writing about children that has appeared in the last two hundred years. Several principles guiding my choice of readings in the history of child psychology are presented in the interstitial commentary; there are more general principles of selection that the reader should know about before he begins this book.

First, the passages have been selected from modern Western sources. The earliest selection was written in 1693, the latest in 1942, and all of them were written by Western Europeans or by Americans. Within these constraints, another characteristic of the readings will become apparent: they are largely theoretical. Although there is reference to observation and experiment in many of these pages, the defining theme of the book is the development of ideas about children. Not that these ideas have led toward a well-worked and consistent formal theory; on the contrary, the history of child psychology has been so much influenced by medicine, pedagogy, philosophy, the traditions of child-rearing, other branches of psychology, and by parents that theoretical diversity has been the rule. This book considers the several sources of child psychology.

The relation of child study to general psychology deserves special comment. There was a time, during the three or four decades after Preyer published his observations, when child psychology had the look of an independent discipline, but since about 1920 the study of children has been part of the wider psychological study of man, and child psychologists have been deeply involved in the contentions of schools and methods that have marked psychology for forty years. The influence has not been unidirectional with general psychology imposing its mold on the child—for psychoanalysis and Watsonian behaviorism, the child was a model for general psychology—but the connections have been so close that writing a commentary on the history of child psychology necessarily requires commentary on the larger discipline.

Another characteristic of child psychology that is brightly reflected by the readings in this book is its abiding link with practical action. Far more than other specialists in the study of man, theorists of children have been willing to give specific instructions to their fellow-citizens about how to run their lives. Shrill, pedantic, or wise, many of the important figures in the history of child study have spoken not only to their professional and academic colleagues but to parents and teachers as well. These recommendations, deriving as they did from deeply held theories of the child, are part of the story told here.

A number of people have helped me in preparing this book. I cannot hold them in any sense responsible for the outcome but I acknowledge my obligation with gratitude to Alfred Baldwin, to George Mandler, to Doris Kraeling Collins, and to my students at Yale.

New Haven, Connecticut
January, 1965

WILLIAM KESSEN

Contents

The Child

Introduction

The history of child study is a history of rediscovery. With remarkable regularity, the same themes appear, are elaborated for a while, then fade. In part, the looping of ideas about children represents the discovery by philosophers, biologists, and psychologists of their own children; the study of child behavior began anew, fresh and enthusiastic, with the birth of Doddy Darwin, Armande Binet, Polly Watson, Helen Baldwin, Jacqueline Piaget, Axel Preyer, and Friedrich Tiedemann. Each father saw his own child—that is, the child that his prejudice or theory would predict—but sharing a common object of observation bound these men of divergent times and opinions to a set of common problems about human development.

The very intransigence of the problems posed by children has also contributed to the iteration of themes; unresolved issues pop up in new form with each generation of searchers for certainty among the confusion of babies. Take the case of breast-feeding. No single example can represent the development of child psychology, but the problem of baby-feeding is an illuminating historical fragment. Perhaps the most persistent single note in the history of the child is the reluctance of mothers to suckle their babies. The running war between the mother, who does not want to nurse, and the philosopher-psychologists, who insist that they must, stretches over two thousand years; the redundancy of the argument and its slow but discernible development form a model—and a somewhat amusing one—for the history of child study. Plutarch's was not the first voice, but he was brief and the message was clear.

... the affection of wet nurses and governesses is spurious and constrained, for they love for hire. Nature itself makes it plain that mothers should themselves nurture and sustain what they have brought forth: for every animal which brings forth nature has provided a supply of milk.*

Physician and poet, the argument continued throughout antiquity, and when books were first printed in the vernacular in Western Europe, it was heard still. Heinrich von Louffenburg, in 1429, wrote in rhyme "Darumb so soll es mit geluste / saugen sein mutter bruste. . . ."

Therefore the child should delight in taking its mother's breast. On that it subsists better and without harm than on that of any other woman, because it became accustomed to it in the mother's womb . . . ,†

Scevole de Sainte-Marthe wrote in Latin dactylic hexameter, in 1584, about the joys of motherhood, the wrath of the weaned infant, and, in several forms, the importance of suckling one's own baby.

Then, if her breast maternal love contain,
Nor o'er her mind unnat'ral darkness reign,
She sure will feed the pledge herself, nor curse
The crying infant with a venal nurse;
Whose foreign blood but ill supplies
Of what th'ungrateful mother now denies:
What tenderness can e'er from her be known,
Who, for another's child, neglects her own?‡

* Plutarch, The education of children, *Selected Essays on Love, the Family, and the Good Life* (Translated by M. Hadas), New York: Mentor Books, 1957, p. 105.
† H. v. Louffenburg, *Versehung des Leibs*, Augsburg, 1491. Quoted in J. Ruhräh, *Pediatrics of the Past*, New York: Hoeber, 1925, pp. 468, 470. Louffenburg's poem was often reprinted; the copy I have seen was published in German in Erfurt in 1546.
‡ S. de St. Marthe, *Paedotrophia, or, the Art of Nursing and Rearing Children. A Poem, in Three Books* (Translated from the Latin . . . by H. W. Tytler), London: J. Nichols and others, 1797.

That man of sensitivity and great wisdom, John Comenius, asked in 1633 whether mothers of the human race were less affectionate than wolves, and he went on to remind his readers of a compelling reason for nursing one's own child.

If they suckle from their real mother rather than another, children might approach nearer to the disposition and virtues of their parents than generally happens. The philosopher Favorinus shows that the milk of animals, by some occult virtue, possesses the power of fashioning the body and mind like the form of its original. . . . Who then, unless he be blind, does not see that babies imbibe, along with the alien milk of the foster mother, morals different from those of their parents?*

In the following century, Rousseau promised a "reform of morals" when mothers "deign to nurse their own children."

. . . natural feeling will revive in every heart; there will be no lack of citizens for the state; this first step by itself will restore mutual affection.†

Although Rousseau is given credit by some historians for arousing mothers to their duty, his voice apparently did not carry across the channel. An angry physician named Davis in 1817 stated the case again in uncompromising moral tones.

The mother's breast is an infant's birthright and suckling a sacred duty, to neglect which is prejudicial to the mother and fatal to the child.‡

The exchange continued for another century, with the mothers silent, their effective protest reflected in the heat of the expert advice they got. Ingenious men tried ingenious methods—an early twentieth-century invention contained a tube that led from the mother's fully draped breast to the mouth of the child—and, for a short time, science, fashion, and the reluctant mother found a common ground in defense of the aseptic bottle. The interlude

---

* J. A. Comenius, *The School of Infancy* [1633], (Edited by E. M. Eller), Chapel Hill: University of North Carolina Press, 1956, pp. 79ff.
† J.-J. Rousseau, *Emile* [1762] (Translated by B. Foxley), London: Dent, 1911, p. 13.
‡ J. B. Davis, *A Cursory Inquiry, etc.* [1817]. Quoted in G. F. McCleary, *The Early History of the Infant Welfare Movement*, London: Lewis, 1933, p. 19.

was brief, however, and by the mid-'fifties, psychiatric arguments replaced those which were genetic, theological, and social.

The war of the breast is the oldest and best documented of the iterative themes of child study, but the return to old problems is not confined to matters of care and feeding. Three variations of a basic melody appear regularly over the entire story of the child in history, and this book is a partial account of their elaboration. Is the child a creature of nature or a creature of nurture? Is the child an active explorer or a passive receiver? Is the behavior of the child best conceived as a bundle of elements or as a set of integrated structures? The antiquity of these antinomies is testified to by Brett: ". . . the original Aristotelian point . . . , the real storm-centre of all the ages, is that the operations of the senses do not wholly account for or produce the intellectual life."* The history of child study is told around the search for the origins of mental life and the search for a mechanism of change. Unhappily for the dramatic impact of the story, the great commentators on development have always recognized the complexity and interrelatedness of the questions; we cannot speak of the wise men and the fools. Read Quintilian's first-century account of the child and hear the resonance in today's discussions.

Reasoning comes as naturally to man as flying to birds, speed to horses, and ferocity to birds of prey; . . . A proof of what I say is to be found in the fact that boys commonly show promise of many accomplishments, and when such promise dies away as they grow up, this is plainly due not to the failure of natural gifts, but to the lack of requisite care. But, it will be urged, there are degrees of talent. Undoubtedly, I reply, and there will be a corresponding variation in actual accomplishment: but that there are any who gain nothing from education, I absolutely deny.†

It is important to note at the outset, however, that much is hidden by the apparent regularity of citations from the literature of child study over two millenia. To be sure, the problems recur and

* G. S. Brett, *A History of Psychology*, 3 vol., London: George Allen, 1912–1921, Vol. II, p. 76.
† Quintilian, *Institutio Oratoria* (Translated by H. E. Butler), 4 vol., Cambridge, Mass.: Harvard University Press, 1920–1922, Vol. I, p. 19ff.

often receive familiar answers, but there is, with each new appearance of the argument, evidence of different attitudes toward children and their treatment. Ste.-Marthe's evangelism about breast-
feeding in the sixteenth century was set in a very different view
of the child from the one that surrounds pediatric and psychiatric
recommendations in the twentieth century; we shall see, in the
next chapter, that the issue of breast-feeding in the eighteenth
century was far more than a cosmetic debate. How has history
changed the child? One of the most exciting and difficult tasks
in a historical analysis of child study is to chart the rise of the child
from his older place as an ill-formed adult at the edges of the
society to his present position as cultural hero. Philippe Ariès has
recently and convincingly defended the thesis that childhood as a
phenomenon unto itself, requiring special institutions for its protection, is an invention of modern times.

In medieval society the idea of childhood did not exist; this is not
to suggest that children were neglected, forsaken, or despised. The idea
of childhood is not to be confused with affection for children: it corresponds to an awareness of the particular nature of childhood, that
particular nature which distinguishes the child from the adult, even
the young adult. In medieval society this awareness was lacking. That is
why, as soon as the child could live without the constant solicitude of
his mother, his nanny, or his cradle-rocker, he belonged to adult society.
. . . Language did not give the word "child" the restricted meaning we
give it today: people said "child" much as we say "lad" in every day
speech. The absence of definition extended to every sort of social activity: games, crafts, arms.*

This society of one age was changed through the next centuries
by the development of several new attitudes toward the child—
Ariès notes in particular the child's becoming an object to be
"coddled," the child's becoming fit for redemption, and the child's
becoming valuable enough to care for. Our story opens in Chapter
2 with two of these changes—the medical revolution and the evan-
gelical—and continues in Chapter 3 with the third—the child as a
unique and precious being.

* P. Ariès, *Centuries of Childhood* (Translated by R. Baldick), New York:
Knopf, 1962, p. 128.

There were other changes to come in history's creation of the modern child; with the publication of Darwin's *Descent of Man*, in 1871, the child became a unique part of the scientific endeavor just as he had become a unique part of society with the publication of Rousseau's *Émile*. For nearly half a century after Darwin's shattering of the mirror, the child became the best natural laboratory for the study of evolution, and the idea of *development* dominated the science of man. In Chapter 4, we shall meet the men who built child psychology with Darwin's bricks.

By 1905, the developmental movement had fallen on slow times, and the new psychology from Germany offered little for the student of children. Within the next decade, however, startling changes were to come in man's view of the child (Chapters 5 and 6). The invention of mental tests, the rise of behaviorism, and, most of all, the foundation of psychoanalysis changed the child as much as all earlier history had; he has become valuable, meaningful, and intricate in ways unknown before the twentieth century.

In sketching the outlines of a history of child study, there has been little room in these pages to tell in detail of the empirical studies of children that have been conducted over the last hundred years. Scientists, at least, remain committed to the eighteenth-century postulate of remediable ignorance and the stability of this commitment has led, slowly but steadily, to the accumulation of a body of reliable facts about children. It is our greater knowledge of the child as well as our changed attitude toward him that mark the passage of many years of study. The history of child study is a history of rediscovery; it is also a history of modest advances toward truth.

2

Precursors: Physicians and Reformers

Until late in Western history, the only experts in child care and child behavior outside the family were the midwife and the teacher. Early medical writings, from Hippocrates on, contained brief references to the child—largely on the subject of feeding—but by and large the medical care of the child was left to the traditions of the grandmothers. The little medical advice for the care of children that existed before the seventeenth century was immobilized in the canons of Hellenistic medicine and scarcely changed over fifteen hundred years. In part, the lack of interest in the child as a subject of medical inquiry and effort was required by the line of specialization that separated the functions of the midwife from those of the physician. In part, too, physicians avoided the child so long because he seemed hopelessly resistant to medical intervention. It was only yesterday in human history that the majority of children could be expected to live beyond their fifth year.

Signs of serious concern with the mortality of children began to appear early in the eighteenth century as the public records began to fill out common knowledge with the force of numbers. Even after expressing doubt about the reliability of public health data in the infancy of record-keeping, the statistics available from the eighteenth century in England and on the continent are terrifying in the inevitability of the death of children. The century had almost closed before children born in London had an even break on surviving until their fifth birthday, and before 1750 the odds were three-to-one against a child completing five years of life. Aside from the dangers of infection and disease in an age not notable for cleanliness, children of the time were subjected to the graver threat of abandonment. To meet the problem of the "dropping" of babies by mothers, foundling homes were set up in most European cities.

Foundling homes of one sort or another had existed in Western Europe at least since the eighth century but they had parochial importance until the establishment of the *Hospice des enfans trouvées* by Vincent de Paul about 1640. Moved by severe laws against infanticide and by the hope that their children might survive with the care of foundling homes, mothers from the provinces as well as from Paris began to bring their children to the Hospice. So great was the immigration of foundlings that regulations had to be enacted against the transport of infants to Paris. The abandonment of babies continued; in the mid-eighteenth century, for every three births registered in Paris, one foundling was left at the Hospice. It was too heavy a load for the understaffed institutions to carry; the foundling homes replaced the streets as locus of death. The mortality rate of foundling homes varied widely during the eighteenth century but came to tragic excess in Dublin during the last quarter of the century when, of 10,272 infants admitted to the foundling home, only 45 survived.*

The Foundling Hospital of London was founded through the philanthropy of Thomas Coram in 1740 and for several years made slow headway toward the establishment of a home for a few of the city's abandoned children. In the eighth year after the Hospital was founded a letter was written, apparently by in-

---

* Information on infant mortality is presented in several contemporary sources, notably (for London) the *Annual Register*, 1758–   . For concise reviews of the available data and for the history of foundling homes, see McCleary, *op. cit.*; also E. Caulfield, The infant welfare movement in the eighteenth century, *Annals Med. Hist.*, New Series, **2**, 1930, 480–494; 660–696. The relation between current cross-cultural mortality rates and the historical data is treated by O. W. Anderson in Age-specific mortality differentials historically and currently: Observations and implications, *Bull. Hist. Medicine*, **27**, 1953, 521–529.

vitation, to the Governors of the hospital by William Cadogan, physician. Born in 1711, Cadogan was best known to his contemporaries for a *Dissertation on Gout* in which he recommended abstinence from hard liquor as a therapy for the disease of England's rich, but his longer fame derives from this letter, which appears in the next pages. Although Cadogan was not the only man, or even the first, to call attention to the unwholesome and often lethal procedures of child care then current, his message was brief, coherent, and sensible. His *Essay on Nursing* was printed in at least ten English editions before 1800 (the first three anonymously) and was translated widely.

The shape of the society in which Cadogan writes is etched with almost unbearable clarity by Jonathan Swift in his *A Modest Proposal*. Outraged by the destitution of the Irish poor and the failure of the nation's leaders to make any adequate provision for the care of children, he proposed that, save only for a few "Breeders," the children of the poor be "offered in Sale to the *persons of Quality* and *Fortune*."

I have been assured by a very knowing *American* of my acquaintance in *London*, that a young healthy child well Nursed is at a year Old a most delicious, nourishing, and wholesome Food, whether *Stewed, Roasted, Baked,* or *Boyled,* and I make no doubt that it will equally serve in a *Fricasie,* or a *Ragoust.**

The distance of the twentieth century from the eighteenth is nowhere more succinctly put, not only because the passage suggests the horror that forced Swift to this satire, but also because, even as satire, the proposal shocks contemporary sensibility concerning children. To such an age, Cadogan wrote his letter.

Implicit in Cadogan's essay is a description of normal eighteenth-century practice. It may save modern readers some confusion to know that it was a general practice to wrap babies closely and often to encase them in girdles of stays to keep their limbs straight. The practice was so well embedded in custom that Cadogan argues against restricting infants in this way but gives up on the girdling of three- and four-year-olds. There is a remark-

* [J. Swift] *A Modest Proposal for Preventing the Children of Poor People from Being a Burthen to their Parents, or the Country, and for Making Them Beneficial to the Publick,* Dublin: S. Harding, 1729, pp. 6, 7.

ably modern tone throughout the essay—the notion that nursing is psychologically healthy for mothers as well as for children, the usefulness of self-demand, some sophisticated (and incorrect) ideas about inheritance, even the expert's universal note on the incompetence of mothers. With Cadogan's essay and associated changes in the thought of the time—changes that reflected the new conviction that amelioration was neither impossible nor sinful—the child's chances of surviving often enough to become valuable began to increase. With some exceptions that will appear later, the time was passing when a physician would write:

But there is still another reason why children are sometimes neglected, which I am sorry to mention, but of its truth I am convinced from experience. It is this: children while in their infancy, especially if the young family is numerous, and the parents in straightened circumstances, are not thought of sufficient consequence to be much attended to, unless some sudden or violent illness happens to give an alarm. This secret has sometimes come out in my hearing, even by persons who were not reckoned poor. . . .*

*   *   *

William Cadogan (1711–1797)

An Essay upon Nursing

It is with great Pleasure I see at last the Preservation of Children become the Care of Men of Sense: It is certainly a Matter that well deserves their Attention, and, I doubt not, the Publick will

[W. Cadogan], An essay upon nursing, and the management of children, from their birth to three years of age (3rd Ed.). By a Physician. London: J. Roberts, 1749. The first edition of the letter was published in 1748.

* G. Armstrong, An Account of the Diseases Most Incident to Children, etc. (New Ed.), London: T. Cadell, 1783, p. 6. The first edition appeared in 1777.

soon find the good and great Effects of it. The *Foundling Hospital* may be of more Use to the World, than was perhaps at first imagin'd by the Promoters of it; it will be a Means not only of preventing the Murder of many, but of saving more, by introducing a more reasonable and more natural Method of Nursing. In my Opinion, this Business has been too long fatally left to the Management of Women, who cannot be supposed to have proper Knowledge to fit them for such a Task, notwithstanding they look upon it to be their own Province. What I mean, is a Philosophic Knowledge of Nature, to be acquired only by learned Observation and Experience, and which therefore the Unlearned must be incapable of. They may presume upon the Examples and transmitted Customs of their Great Grand-mothers, who were taught by the Physicians of their unenlighten'd Days; when Physicians, as appears by late Discoveries, were mistaken in many things; being led away by hypothetical Reasonings to entertain very wild Conceits, in which they were greatly bewilder'd themselves, and misled others to believe, I know not what strange unaccountable Powers in certain Herbs, Roots, and Drugs; and also in some superstitious Practices and Ceremonies; for all which Notions, there being no real Foundation in Nature, they ought to be looked upon as the Effects of Ignorance, or the Artifices of designing Quacks; who found their Account, by pretending to great Knowledge in these occult Qualities, and imposing upon the Credulous. The Art of Physick has been much improv'd within this last Century; by observing and following Nature more closely, many useful Discoveries have been made, which help us to account for Things in a natural Way, that before seem'd mysterious and magical; and which have consequently made the Practice of it more conformable to Reason and good Sense. This being the Case, there is great room to fear, that those Nurses who yet retain many of these traditional Prejudices, are capitally mistaken in their Management of Children in general, and fancying that Nature has left a great deal to their Skill and Contrivance, often do much harm, where they intend to do good. Of this I shall endeavor to convince them, by shewing, how I think Children may be cloath'd, fed, and managed with much less Trouble to their Nurses, and infinitely greater Ease and Comfort to the little ones.

THE Foundlings under the Care of the Hospital, I presume, will be bred in a very plain, simple Manner: They will therefore infallibly have the more Health, Beauty, Strength, and Spirits; I might add Understanding too, as all the Faculties of the Mind are well known to depend upon the Organs of the Body; so that when these are in good Order, the thinking Part is most alert and active; the contrary, when they are disturbed or diseased. When these Advantages appear in Favour of Children so brought up, as I am confident in time they will, it may serve to convince most Nurses, Aunts, Grand-mothers, etc. how much they have hitherto been in the wrong, what Mischief is done to Children, and what Multitudes are destroyed or spoiled, as well by cramming them with Cakes, Sweetmeats, etc. till they foul their Blood, choak their Vessels, pall the Appetite, and ruin every Faculty of their Bodies; as by cockering and indulging them, to the utter Perversion of their naturally good Temper, till they become quite froward and indocile.

WHEN a Man takes upon him to contradict received Opinions and Prejudices sanctified by Time, it is expected he should bring valid Proof of what he advances. The Truth of what I say, that the Treatment of Children in general is wrong, unreasonable and unnatural, will in great measure appear, if we but consider what a puny valetudinary Race most of our People of Condition are; chiefly owing to bad Nursing, and bad Habits contracted early. But let any one, who would be fully convinced of this Matter, look over the Bills of Mortality; there he may observe, that almost half the Number of those, that fill up that black List, die under five Years of Age: So that Half the People that come into the World, go out of it again before they become of the least Use to it, or themselves. To me, this seems to deserve serious Consideration; and yet I cannot find, that any one Man of Sense, and publick Spirit, has ever attended to it at all; notwithstanding the Maxim in every one's Mouth; that a Multitude of Inhabitants is the greatest Strength and best Support of a Commonwealth. The Misconduct, to which I must impute a great Part of the Calamity, is too common and obvious to engage the Idle and Speculative, who are to be caught only by very refined Researches; and the busy Part of Mankind, where their immediate Interest is not concerned, will always overlook what they see daily: It may be thought a natural Evil, and so is submitted to without Examination. But this is by no means the Case; and where it is entirely owing to Mismanagement, and possibly may admit of a Remedy, it is ridiculous to charge it upon Nature, and suppose, that Infants are more subject to Disease and Death than grown Persons; on the contrary, they bear Pain and Disease much better, Fevers especially, (as is plain in the Case of the Small-Pox, generally most favourable to Children) and for the same Reason that a Twig is less hurt by a Storm than an Oak. In all the other Productions of Nature we see the greatest Vigor and Luxuriancy of Health, the nearer they are to the Egg or the Bud: They are indeed then most sensible of Injury, and it is Injury only that destroys them. When was there a Lamb, a Bird, or a Tree that died because it was young? These are under the immediate Nursing of unerring Nature, and they thrive accordingly. Ought it not therefore to be the Care of every Nurse and every Parent, not only to protect their Nurselings from Injury, but to be well assured that their own officious Services be not the greatest the helpless Creatures can suffer?

In the lower Class of Mankind, especially in the Country, Disease and Mortality are not so frequent, either among the Adult, or their Children. Health and Posterity are the Portion of the Poor, I mean the laborious: The Want of Superfluity confines them more within the Limits of Nature: Hence they enjoy Blessings they feel not, and are ignorant of their Cause. The Mother who has only a few Rags to cover her Child loosely, and little more than her own Breast to feed it, sees it healthy and strong, and very soon able to shift for itself; while the puny Insect, the Heir and Hope of a rich Family lies languishing under a Load of Finery, that overpowers his Limbs, abhorring and rejecting the Dainties he is crammed with, till he dies a Victim to the mistaken Care and Tenderness of his fond mother. In the Course of my Practice, I have had frequent occasion to be fully satisfied of this, and have often heard a Mother anxiously say *the Child has not been well ever since it has done puking and crying.* These Complaints, tho' not attended to, point very plainly to their Cause. Is it not very evident, that when a Child rids its Stomach several times in a Day, that it has been over-loaded? when it cries, from the Incumbrance of Confinement of its Cloaths, that it is hurt by them? While the natural Strength lasts (as every Child is born with more Health and Strength than is generally imagined) it cries at, or rejects the superfluous Load, and thrives apace: that is, grows very fat, bloated, and distended beyond measure; like a House-Lamb. But in Time, the same oppressive Cause continuing, the natural Powers are overcome, being no longer able to throw off the unequal Weight; the Child now not able to cry any more, languishes and is quiet. The Misfortune is, these Complaints are not understood; it is swaddled and cramm'd on, 'till after Gripes, Purging, etc. it sinks under both Burdens into a Convulsion Fit, and escapes any further Torture. This would be the Case with the Lamb, was it not killed when it is full fat.

THAT the present Method of Nursing is wrong, one would think needed no other Proof than the frequent Miscarriages attending it, the Death of Many, and ill Health of Those that survive. But the persuading you of it may be a needless Task; if you have ever thought about it, I doubt not but you are already convinced it is so. However, since you desire my Sentiments upon the Subject, taking it for granted you think with me, that most of our Nurses are got into a wrong Method, I will endeavor, in as few Words as possible, to tell you what I think a right one.

You perceive, Sir, by the Hints I have already dropp'd, what I am going to complain of is, that Children in general are over-cloath'd and over-fed, and fed and cloath'd improperly. To these Causes I impute almost all their Diseases. But to be a little more explicit, The first great Mistake is, that they think a new-born Infant cannot be kept too warm; from this Prejudice they load and bind it with Flannel, Wrappers, Swathes, Stays, etc. commonly called Cloaths; which all together are almost equal to its own Weight; by which means a healthy Child in a Month's Time is made so tender and chilly, it cannot bear the external Air; and if, by any Accident of a Door or Window left carelessly open too long, a refreshing Breeze be admitted into the suffocating Atmosphere of the Lying-in Bed-chamber, the Child and Mother sometimes catch irrecoverable Colds. But what is worse than this, at the End of the Month, if things go on apparently well, this

Hot-bed Plant is sent out into the Country, to be rear'd in a leaky House, that lets in Wind and Rain from every Quarter. Is it any Wonder the Child never thrives afterwards? The Truth is, a new-born Child cannot well be too cool and loose in its Dress; it wants less Cloathing than a grown Person, in proportion; because it is naturally warmer, as appears by the Thermometer; and would therefore bear the Cold of a Winter's Night, much better than any adult Person whatever. There are many Instances both ancient and modern of Infants exposed and deserted, that have lived several Days. As it was the Practice of ancient Times, in many Parts of the World, to expose all those, whom the Parents did not care to be encumber'd with; that were deformed or born under evil Stars; not to mention the many Foundlings pick'd up in *London* Streets. These Instances may serve to shew, that Nature has made Children able to bear even great Hardships, before they are made weak and sickly by their mistaken Nurses. But besides the Mischief arising from the Weight and Heat of these Swaddling-cloaths, they are put on so tight, and the Child is so cramp'd by them, that its Bowels have not room, nor the Limbs any Liberty, to act and exert themselves in the free easy Manner they ought. This is a very hurtful Circumstance, for Limbs that are not used, will never be strong, and such tender Bodies cannot bear much Pressure: The Circulation restrained by the Compression of any one Part, must produce unnatural Swellings in some other; especially as the Fibres of Infants are so easily distended. To which doubtless are owing the many Distortions and Deformities we meet with every where; chiefly among Women, who suffer more in this Particular than the Men. I would recommend the following Dress: A little Flannel Waistcoat without Sleeves, made to fit the Body, and tie loosely behind; to which there should be a Petticoat sew'd, and over this a kind of Gown of the same Material, or any other that is light, thin and flimsy. The Petticoat should not be quite so long as the Child, the Gown a few inches longer; with one Cap only on the Head, which may be made double, if it be thought not warm enough. What I mean is, that the whole Coiffure should be so contrived, that it might be put on at once, and neither bind nor press the Head at all: The Linnen as usual. This, I think, would be abundantly sufficient for the Day; laying aside all those Swathes, Bandages, Stays, and Contrivances, that are most ridiculously used to close and keep the Head in its Place, and support the Body. As if Nature, exact Nature, had produced her chief Work, a human Creature, so carelessly unfinish'd, as to want those idle Aids to make it perfect. Shoes and Stockings are very needless Incumbrances, besides that they keep the Legs wet and nasty, if they are not changed every Hour, and often cramp and hurt the Feet: A Child would stand firmer, and learn to walk much sooner without them. I think they cannot be necessary 'till it runs out in the Dirt. There should be a thin Flannel Shirt for the Night, which ought to be every way quite loose. Children in this simple, pleasant Dress, which may be readily put on and off without teazing them, would find themselves perfectly easy and happy, enjoying the free Use of their Limbs and Faculties, which they would very soon begin to employ, when they are thus left at Liberty. I would have them put into it as soon as they are born, and continued in it, till they are three Years old; when it may be changed for any other more genteel and fashionable: tho' I could wish it was not the Custom to wear Stays at all; not because I see no Beauty in the Sugar-loaf Shape, but that I am apprehensive, it is often procur'd at the Expence of the Health and Strength of the Body. There is an odd Notion enough entertained about Change, and the keeping of Children clean. Some imagine that clean Linnen and fresh Cloaths draw, and rob them of their nourishing Juices. I cannot see that they do any thing more than imbibe a little of that Moisture which their Bodies exhale. Were it as is supposed, it would be of service to them; since they are always too abundantly supplied, and therefore I think they cannot be changed too often, and would have them clean every Day; as it would free them from Stinks and Sournesses, which are not only offensive, but very prejudicial to the tender State of Infancy.

THE Feeding of Children properly is of much greater Importance to them than their Cloathing. We ought to take great Care to be right in this material Article, and that nothing be given them, but what is wholesome and good for them, and in such Quantity, as the Body calls for towards its Support and Growth; not a Grain more. Let us consider what Nature directs in the

Case: If we follow Nature, instead of leading or driving it, we cannot err. In the Business of Nursing, as well as Physick, Art is ever destructive, if it does not exactly copy this Original. When a Child is first born, there seems to be no Provision at all made for it; for the Mother's Milk seldom comes till the third Day; so that according to Nature, a Child would be left a Day and a half, or two Days, without any Food; to me a very sufficient Proof that it wants none: It is born full of Blood, full of Excrements, its Appetites not awake, nor its Senses opened; and requires this intermediate Time of Abstinence and Rest, to compose and recover the Struggle of the Birth, and the Change of Circulation, (the Blood running into new Channels,) which always put it into a little Fever. However extraordinary this may appear, I am sure it is better it were not fed at all; for it sleeps almost the whole Time, and when the Milk is ready for it, would be hungry, and suck with more Eagerness; which is often necessary, for it seldom comes freely at first. At least I would prevail thus far, that the Child be not awaked out of its Sleep to be fed, as is commonly done. This is the constant Course of Nature, which is very little attended to, and never followed. The general Practice is, as soon as a Child is born, to cram a Dab of Butter and Sugar down its Throat, a little Oil, Panada [boiled bread and sugar, sometimes spiced], Caudle [warm drink of thin gruel, mixed with wine or ale], or some such unwholesome Mess. So that they set out wrong, and the Child stands a fair Chance of being made sick from the first Hour. It is the Custom of some to give a little roast Pig to an Infant; which, it seems, is to cure it of all the Mother's Longings. I wish these Matters were a little more enquired into, for the Honour of the Sex; to which many Imperfections of this kind are imputed, which I am sure it does not lie under. When a Child sucks its own Mother, which, with a very few Exceptions, would be best for every Child, and every Mother, Nature has provided it with such wholesome and suitable Nourishment; supposing her a temperate Woman, that makes some Use of her Limbs; it can hardly do amiss. The Mother would likewise, in most hysterical, nervous Cases, establish her own Health by it, tho' she were weak and sickly before, as well as that of her offspring. For these Reasons I could wish, that every Woman that is able, whose

Fountains are not greatly disturbed or tainted, would give Suck to her child. I am very sure that forcing back the Milk, which most young Women must have in great abundance, may be of fatal Consequence: Sometimes it endangers Life, and often lays the Foundation of many incurable Diseases, The Reasons that are given for this Practice are very frivolous, and drawn from false Premises; that some Women are too weak to bear such a Drain, which would rob them of their own Nourishment. This is a very mistaken Notion; for the first general Cause of most People's Diseases is, not want of Nourishment, as is here imagined, but too great a Fulness and Redundancy of Humours; good at first, but being more than the Body can employ or consume, the whole Mass becomes corrupt, and produces many Diseases. This is confirmed by the general Practice of Physicians, who make holes in the Skin, perpetual Blisters, Issues, etc. to let out the Superfluity. I would therefore leave it to be consider'd, whether the throwing back such a Load of Humour, as a Women's first Milk, be most likely to mend her Constitution, or make her Complaints irremediable. The Mother's first Milk is purgative, and cleanses the Child of its long hoarded Excrement; no Child therefore can be deprived of it without manifest Injury. By degrees it changes its Property, becomes less purgative, and more nourishing; and is the best and only Food the Child likes, or ought to have for some time. If I could prevail, no Child should ever be cramm'd with any unnatural Mixture, 'till the Provision of Nature was ready for it; nor afterwards fed with any ungenial alien Diet whatever, the *first three Months:* for it is not well able to digest and assimilate other Aliments sooner. There is usually Milk enough with the first Child; sometimes more than it can take: It is poured forth from an exuberant, overflowing Urn, by a bountiful Hand, that never provides sparingly. The Call of Nature should be awaited for to feed it with any thing more substantial, and the Appetite ever precede the Food; not only with regard to the daily Meals, but those Changes of Diet, which opening, increasing Life requires. But this is never done in either Case, which is one of the greatest Mistakes of all Nurses. Thus far Nature, if she be not interrupted, will do the whole Business perfectly well; and there seems to be nothing left for a Nurse to do, but to keep

in warm Water. Good Bread is the lightest Thing I know;
Power of due Fermentation, in which consists the whole Art
making it, breaks and attenuates the tenacious Parts of the Flou
so as to give it these Qualities I mention, and make it the fitte:
Food for young Children. Cows Milk is also simple and light
and very good for them; but it is injudiciously prepared: it should
not be boiled, for boiling alters the Taste and Property of it, destroys its Sweetness, and makes it thicker, heavier, and less fit
to mix and assimilate with the Blood. But the chief Objection is,
that their Food is wholly vegetable; the bad consequence of
which is, that it will turn sour in their Stomachs. The first and
general Cause of all the Diseases of Infants, is manifestly this
ascescent [acid] Quality of all their Food. If any of these vegetable Preparations I have named, be kept in a Degree of Heat
equal to that of a Child's Stomach it will become sour as Vinegar
in a few Hours time. These Things are therefore very improper
to feed a Child wholly with. Some Part of its Diet should be contrived to have a contrary Tendency; such as we find only in Flesh,
which is the direct opposite to Acid, and tends to Putrefaction.
In a due Mixture of these two Extremes, correcting each other,
consists that Salubrity of Aliment our Nature seems to require.
As we are partly carniverous Animals, a Child ought not to be
fed wholly upon Vegetables. The Mother's Milk, when it is perfectly good, seems to be this true Mixture of the animal and vegetable Properties, that agrees best with the Constitution of a Child;
readily passes into good Blood, requiring but a gentle Exertion
of the Powers of Circulation to break and subdue its Particles and
make them smooth and round, and easily divisible. I would advise
therefore, that one half of Infants Diet be thin light Broths, with
a little Bread or Rice boiled in them; which last is not so ascescent
as any other kind of Meal or Flour. These Broths should be made
with the Flesh of full grown Animals, because their Juices are
more elaborate; especially if they had never been confined to be
fatted. The Juices of a young Ox, taken from the Plough, make
the finest flavour'd and most wholsome Soup. I believe it is for
the same Reason, the Flesh of all wild Animals has a lighter Taste
than that of tame, saginated [fattened] ones; and is therefore most
agreeable to the Palates of the Luxurious; but this is to be under-

:he Child clean and sweet, and to tumble and toss it ab
good deal, play with it, and keep it in good Humour.

But now the Child (I mean when it is about three Months
requires more solid Sustenance, we are to enquire what, and
much, is most proper to give it. We may be well assured, th
a great Mistake either in the Quantity or Quality of Child
Food, or both, as it is usually given them; because they are
sick by it. As to Quantity, there is a most ridiculous Error i
common Practice; for it is generally supposed, that whene
Child cries, it wants Victuals; and it is accordingly fed ten, tw
or more times in a Day and Night. This is so obvious a M
prehension, that I am surprized it should ever prevail. If a C
Wants and Motions be diligently and judiciously attended
will be found that it never cries but from Pain: Now the
Sensations of Hunger are not attended with Pain; accordin
Child (I mean this of a very young one) that is hungry,
make a hundred other Signs of its Want, before it will cr
Food. If it be healthy and quite easy in its Dress, it will h
ever cry at all. Indeed these Signs and Motions, I speak of
but rarely to be observed; because it seldom happens that
dren are ever suffered to be hungry. In a few, very few, w
I have had the Pleasure to see reasonably nursed, that were
fed above two or three times in four and twenty Hours, and
were perfectly healthy, active and happy; I have seen these
nals, which were as intelligible as if they had spoke.

There are many Faults in the Quality of their Food: It is
simple enough. Their Paps, Panadas, Gruels, etc. are gene
enriched with Sugar, Spice, and sometimes a Drop of V
neither of which they ought ever to taste. Our Bodies never
them: they are what Luxury only has introduced, to the Des
tion of the Health of Mankind. It is not enough that their Foo
simple, it should be also light. Several People, I find, are mist
in their Notions of what is light; and fancy that most kind
Pastry, Puddings, Custards, etc. are light, that is, light of Di
tion. But there is nothing heavier in this Sense than unferme
Flour and Eggs boil'd hard, which are the chief Ingredient
those Preparations. What I mean by light, to give the best I
I can of it, is any Substance that is easily separated, and sol

stood of those Creatures that feed on Corn or Herbage. The other Part of Childrens Diet may be a little Bread and Water boiled almost dry, and then mixed with fresh Milk, not boiled. This, without Sugar, Spice, or any other pretended Amendment whatever, would be perfectly light and wholesome, of sufficient Nourishment, something like Milk from the Cow, with the additional Strength and Spirit of Bread in it. Twice a Day, and not oftner, a sucking Child should be fed at first; once with the Broth, and once with the Milk thus prepared. As to the Quantity at each Time, its Appetite must be the Measure of that; its Hunger should be satisfied, but no more; for Children will always eat with some Eagerness full as much as they ought: Therefore it must be very wrong to go beyond that, and stuff them till they spue, as the common Method is. They should not be laid on their Backs to be fed, but held in a sitting Posture, that swallowing may be easier to them, and that they may the more readily discover when they have had enough. When they come to be about *six Months* old, and their Appetite and Digestion grows strong, they may be fed three times a Day; which I think they ought never to exceed their whole Lives after. By Night I would not have them fed or suckled at all, that they might at least be hungry in the Morning. It is this Night-feeding that makes them so over-fat and bloated. If they be not used to it at first, and perhaps awaked on purpose, they will never seek it; and if they are not disturbed from the Birth, in a Week's time they will get into a Habit of sleeping all, or most part of the Night very quietly; awaking possibly once or twice for a few Minutes, when they are wet and ought to be changed. If it be thought necessary to give them any thing between Meals, a little Milk and Water is best. Their Meals, and in my Opinion their sucking too, ought to be at stated Times, and the same every Day; that the stomach may have Intervals to digest, and the Appetite return. The Child would soon be quite easy and satisfied in the Habit; much more so, than when taught to expect Food at all times, and at every little Fit of Crying and Uneasiness. Let this Method be observed about a *Twelvemonth,* when, and not before, they may be weaned; not all at once, but by insensible Degrees; that they may neither feel, nor fret at the want of the Breast. This might be very easily manag'd, if they were suffer'd to suck only at certain Times. If this Plan of Nursing were literally pursued, the Children kept clean and sweet, tumbled and toss'd about a good deal, and carried out every Day in all Weathers; I am confident, that in six or eight Months time most Children would become healthy and strong, would be able to sit up on the Ground without Support, to divert themselves an Hour at a time, to the great Relief of their Nurses, would readily find the use of their Legs, and very soon shift for themselves.

IF it be asked whether I mean this of Children in general, and that weakly Ones born of unhealthy Parents should be treated in the same Manner; I answer, that it is not so common for Children to inherit the Diseases of their Parents, as is generally imagined; there is much vulgar Error in this Opinion; for People that are very unhealthy seldom have Children, especially if the bad Health be of the female Side; and it is generally late in Life when chronick Diseases take place in most Men, when the Business of Love is pretty well over: Certainly Children can have no Title to those Infirmities, which their Parents have acquired by Indolence and Intemperance long after their Birth. It is not common for People to complain of Ails they think hereditary, till they are grown up; that is, till they have contributed to them by their own Irregularities and Excesses, and then are glad to throw their own Faults back upon their Parents; and lament a bad Constitution, when they have spoiled a very good one. It is very seldom that young Children are troubled with Family Distempers: Indeed, when we find them affected with scrophulous, venereal, or high scorbutick Complaints, we may reasonably conclude the Taint to have been transmitted to them; but these Cases are very rare, in Comparison to the many others that are falsly, and without the least Foundation, imputed to Parents, when the real Cause is either in the Complainants themselves, or bad Nursing, that has fixed them early in wrong Habits. In one Sense many Diseases may be said to be hereditary, perhaps all those of male Formation; by which I mean not only Deformity and Distortion, but all those Cases where the Fibres and Vessels of one Part are weaker in Proportion than the rest; so that upon any Strain of the Body, whether of Debauch or too violent Exercise, the weak Part fails first, and disorders the whole. Thus Complaints may be produced similar to those of the Parent, owing in some measure to the Similitude of Parts, which possibly is inherited, like the Features of the Face; but yet these Diseases might never have appeared, but for the immediate acting Cause, the Violence done to the Body. Most Distempers have two Causes; the one, a particular State of the Solids and Fluids of the Body, which dispose it to receive certain Infections and Impulses; the other, the Infection or Impulse itself. Now what I contend for is, that tho' this predisponent State or Habit of the Body be heritable, yet the Diseases incident to these wretched Heirs may be avoided, by preventing the active Cause; which may be done in many Cases by a due Attention to the Non-naturals, as they are called; in plainer Words, by a regular, temperate Life: in Children, by good Nursing. Therefore I conclude, that instead of indulging and enfeebling yet more, by the common Methods, Children so unhappily born; that which I am recommending, together with the wholsome Milk of a healthy Nurse, is the best, the only Means to remedy the Evil, and by which alone they may by degrees be made healthy and strong. And thus, in a Generation or two of reasonable, temperate Persons, every Taint and Infirmity whatever, the King's Evil, and Madness not excepted, would be totally wore out.

THE plain natural Plan I have laid down, is never followed; because most Mothers, of any Condition, either cannot, or will not undertake the troublesome Task of suckling their own Children; which is troublesome only for want of proper Method; were it rightly managed, there would be much Pleasure in it, to every Woman that can prevail upon herself to give up a little of the Beauty of her Breast to feed her Offspring. There would be no fear of offending the Husband's Ears with the Noise of the squalling Brat. The Child, was it nurs'd in this Way, would be always quiet, in good Humour, ever playing, laughing, or sleeping. In my Opinion, a Man of Sense cannot have a prettier Rattle (for Rattles he must have of one kind or other) than such a young Child. I am quite at a loss to account for the general Practice of sending Infants out of Doors, to be suckled, or dry-nursed by another Woman, who has not so much Understanding, nor can have so much Affection for it, as the Parents; and how it comes to pass, that People of good Sense and easy Circumstances will not

give themselves the Pains to watch over the Health and Welfare
of their Children; that possibly would take much more with a
Shrub or a Flower; especially as the Love of Posterity is so natural to Mankind. I would earnestly recommend it to every Father
to have his Child nursed under his own Eye, to make use of his
own Reason and Sense in superintending and directing the Management of it; nor suffer it to be made one of the Mysteries of the
Bona Dea, from which the Men are to be excluded. I would advise every Mother that can, for her own sake, as well as her
Child's, to suckle it. If she be a healthy Woman, it will confirm her
Health; if weakly, in most Cases it will restore her. It need be no
Confinement to her, or Abridgment of her Time: Four times in four
and twenty Hours will be often enough to give it Suck; letting it
have as much as it will take, out of both Breasts, at each time. It
may be fed and dress'd by some handy, reasonable Servant, that
will submit to be directed; whom likewise it may sleep with. No
other Woman's Milk can be so good for her Child; and dry-nursing
I look upon to be the most unnatural and dangerous Method of
all; and, according to my Observation, not one in three survives it.
To breed a Child in this artificial Manner, requires more Knowledge of Nature, and the animal Oeconomy, than the best Nurse
was ever Mistress of, as well as more Care and Attention than is
generally bestow'd on Children: The Skill of a good Physician
would be necessary to manage it rightly. I am very glad this is not
the Method of the Hospital: I believe there is not the least
Colour of Objection to any Part of the Management of that most
useful and excellent Charity, as far as it depends upon the Direc-
tors of it. Sending the Children out to Country Nurses, under
the Care of Inspectors, is undoubtedly the best Method they
could take; but how far these Nurses and their Inspectors (who,
I suppose, are to be some good Gentlewomen in the Neighbourhood) may be persuaded out of their old Forms, to treat their
Nurselings a little more reasonably, is matter of much Doubt. I
fear they will be too tenacious of their Prejudices, as well as
opinionated of their Skill, to be easily convinced they are in the
wrong; and who shall undertake the Task? However, I despair
not of seeing a Reformation one Day or other; and to contribute
to it as much as lies in my Power, I will give you my Opinion as

to the Precautions, necessary to be taken, in the Choice of these Nurses; and likewise a few Reasons why the Children, entrusted to their Care, should be treated somewhat differently from those, who are nursed in a more natural Way, and suck their own Mothers. I make no doubt, but great Care is taken, that the Nurses, recommended to the Hospital, be clean and healthy Women. But this is not enough, the Preference should be given to the middle-aged; because they will have more Milk than the very young, and more and better than the old. This is a material Consideration, as I suppose, they have each her own Child to suckle besides: Those between twenty and thirty are certainly of the best Age. But what I think of the utmost Consequence is, that great Regard should be had to the Time of their Lying-in, and those procured, if possible, who have not been brought to bed above two or three months. The Reason of this is, that Nature intending a Child should suck about a Twelvemonth, the Milk seldom continues good much longer. About that Time, Women in general, though they give Suck, are apt to breed again; some indeed, that are very sanguine, will breed sooner; these, notwithstanding their Milk, are apt to be troubled with the *Catamenia*, [menstruation] which disturb it greatly; and therefore are not so proper to be made Nurses of. But, whether they breed or not, it is my Opinion, that after a Year's Time, or thereabouts, however it may agree with a Child that has sucked it from the first, their Milk will become stale and vapid, at least very unfit for a new-born Infant; that if it be deprived of its own Mother's Milk, ought undoubtedly to have what is most like it: the newer it is, the more suitable in all respects to its tender Nature. Yet it is a common thing for a Woman to suckle two or three Children successively with the same Milk.

A Nurse ought to have great Regard to her Diet: It is not enough that she be sober and temperate, her Food should consist of a proper Mixture of Flesh and Vegetables: She should eat one hearty Meal of Flesh-meat every Day, with a good deal of Garden-stuff, and Bread. Thin Broth or Milk would be best for her Breakfast and Supper. Her Drink should be small Beer, or Milk and Water; but upon no Account should she ever touch a Drop of Wine or strong Drink, much less any kind of spirituous

Liquors: Giving Ale or Brandy to a Nurse is, in effect, giving it the Child; and it is easy to conclude what would be the Consequence.

THE Children, likewise, thus sent out, require a particular Treatment. The Plan I would lay down, could I prevail, should be that of Nature, excluding Art and foreign Aid entirely. But when this is broke in upon, a little adventitious Skill becomes indispensibly necessary; that if we are not perfectly right in following closely the Design of Nature, we may co-operate a little, and not be totally wrong in counter-acting it, as is too often the Case. What I mean is, that every Child, not allowed the Mother's first Milk, whether it be dry-nursed, or suckled by another Woman, should be purged in a Day or two after the Birth; and this purging continued for some time; not by regular Doses of Physick, that may operate all at once; but some lenient Laxative should be contrived, and given two or three times a Day, so as to keep the Child's Body open for the first nine Days, or Fortnight; lessening the Quantity insensibly, 'till it be left off. It should be so managed, that the Operation of the artificial Physick may resemble that of the natural. This is so material, that for want of it, most Children within the first Month break out in Pimples all over; the Nurses call it the red Gum, and look upon it to be a natural thing, and that the Children will be unhealthy that have it not. So indeed they will be in all likelihood; and it is better that these Foulnesses, which become acrid and hot by remaining too long in the Body, should be discharged through the Skin, than not at all; or that they should be lodged in the Blood, or fall upon the Vitals, to lay the Foundation of numberless future Evils: but it is chiefly owing to the Neglect of this Method at first. A Child that sucks its own Mother, unless it be greatly over-fed, or kept too hot, will never be troubled with this Humour at all. If the Children that are brought to the Hospital be not above a Month old, and it be found, upon Enquiry, that they have not suck'd their own Mothers, something of this kind prescribed them would not be too late, nor improper. The following Form may be used: Take Manna [bark-juice of the ash *Fraxinus ornus*], Pulp of Cassia [pods of the pudding pipe tree *Cassia fistula*], of each half an ounce; dissolve 'em in about three ounces of thin Broth.

Let the Child take two spoonfuls three times a day, varying the Quantity according to the Effect; which at first ought to be three or four Stools in four and twenty Hours.

ORDERS should be given these Nurses to keep the Children awake by Day, as long as they are disposed to be so, and to amuse and keep them in good Humour all they can; not to lull and rock them to sleep, or to continue their Sleep too long; which is only done to save their own Time and Trouble, to the great Detriment of the Childrens Health, Spirits, and Understanding. With regard to Feeding them, as it is not likely they should have Milk enough to support two, their own, and the Hospital Child; it is best they should begin immediately according to the Method I have recommended, if they or their Inspectors can be persuaded to think it right; which, however, I would not have understood so strictly, but it might sometimes be a little varied, preserving only the Intention. I would advise, however, if it be thought proper, now and then to give them a little Bread and Butter; that the Butter be perfectly sweet and fresh, and allowed but in very small Quantity; otherwise it will be apt [to] turn bitter and rancid in the Stomach, and foul all the Juices of the Body. A Child might be allowed any kind of mellow Fruit, either raw, stewed, or baked; Roots of all Sorts, and all the Produce of the Kitchen Garden. I am sure all these things are wholsome and good for them, and every one else, notwithstanding the idle Notion of their being windy, which they are only to very debauched Stomachs; and so is Milk; but no Man's Blood wants the cleansing, refreshing Power of Milk more than his, whose Stomach, used to inflammatory things of high Relish, will not bear the first Chill of it. To Children, all this kind of Food, taken in Moderation, is perfectly grateful and salutary. Some may think that they carry into the Stomach the Eggs of future Worms; but of this I am not very apprehensive: for I believe there are few things we eat or drink, that do not convey them. But then they can never be hatch'd in a healthy Inside, where all the Juices are sweet and good, and every Gland performs its Office; the Gall in particular would destroy them: Bullocks Gall has been found to be a good and safe Vermifuge. It is my Opinion, we swallow the Eggs of many little Animals, that are never brought into Life within us, except where they find a fit Nest or Lodgment in the acid Phlegm, or vitiated Humours of the Stomach and Bowels. Were these totally discharged every Day, and the Food of yesterday employed or thrown off to the last Grain, no Worms could ever harbour in our Vitals. As soon as the Children have any Teeth, at six or eight Months they may by degrees be used to a little Flesh-meat; which they are always very fond of, much more so at first, than of any Confectionary or Pastry Wares, with which they should never debauch their Taste.

BREEDING Teeth has been thought to be, and is, fatal to many Children; but I am confident this is not from Nature: for it is no Disease, or we could not be well in Health 'till one or two and twenty, or later. Teeth are breeding the greatest Part of that Time; and it is my Opinion, the last Teeth give more Pain than the first, as the Bones and Gums, they are to pierce, are grown more firm and hard. But whatever Fever, Fits, or other dangerous Symptoms seem to attend this Operation of Nature, healthy Children have sometimes bred their Teeth without any such bad Attendants; which ought to incline us to suspect the Evil not to be natural, but rather the Effect of too great a Fulness, or the corrupt Humours of the Body put into Agitation by the stimulating Pain the Tooth causes in breaking its way out. This, I believe, never happens without some Pain, and possibly a little Fever; but if the Blood and Juices be perfectly sweet and good, and there be not too great a Redundancy of them, both will be but slight, and pass off imperceptibly, without any bad Consequence whatever. The chief Intention of the Method I am recommending is to preserve the Humours of the Body in this State; and therefore if it succeeds, Children so managed will breed their Teeth with less Pain and Danger than are commonly observed to attend this Work of Nature.

As I have said that the first and general Cause of most of the Diseases Infants are liable to, is the acid Corruption of their Food; it may not be amiss just to mention an easy and certain Remedy, or rather Preventive, if given timely, at the first Appearance of predominating Acid; which is very obvious from the green Stools, Gripes, and Purgings occasioned by it. The common Method, when these Symptoms appear, is to give the Pearl Julep, Crab's

Eye [natural concretion of calcium carbonate, sometimes obtained from crayfish stomachs], and the testaceous Powders, which, tho' they do absord the Acidities, have this Inconvenience in their Effect, that they are apt to lodge in the Body, and bring on a Costiveness, very detrimental to Infants, and therefore require a little Manna, or some gentle Purge to be given frequently to carry them off. Instead of these, I would recommend a certain fine insipid Powder, called *Magnesia alba,* which at the same time that it corrects and sweetens all Sournesses, rather more effectually than the testaceous Powders, is likewise a lenient Purgative, and keeps the Body gently open. This is the only alkaline Purge I know of, and which our Dispensatories have long wanted. I could wish it was more universally received among us, and think it well deserves the Rank in our Books of Pharmacy, which it already has in some foreign ones. I have taken it myself, and given it to others for the Heart-burn, and find it to be the best and most effectual Remedy for that Complaint. It may be given to Children from one to two drams a day, a little at a time, in all their Food, 'till the Acidities be quite overcome, and the concomitant Symptoms disappear entirely. I have often given it with good and great Effect, even when the Children have been far gone in Diseases first brought on by prevailing Acid.

THERE are some other little Niceties that, were they observed in the nursing of Children, would be of some Use to them; such as putting them soon upon their Legs, in order to forward their walking; accustoming them to use both Hands alike; for employing one more than the other, will not only make the Hand and Arm so used, but also that Side of the Body, bigger than the other. This is sometimes the Cause of Crookedness. It would likewise not be amiss to forward their speaking plain, by speaking plain distinct Words to them, instead of the Namby Pamby Stile, and giving them back their own broken inarticulate Attempts; by which Means, I believe, some Children scarcely speak intelligibly at seven Years of Age. I think they cannot be made reasonable Creatures too soon.

THESE few loose Thoughts on the Subject of Nursing Children, I send you for your private Satisfaction, if they be lucky enough to give you any. I have neither Time nor Patience to think of

Form and Order, or supporting them by affected Demonstrations taken from mechanical Principles and Powers. All I have endeavour'd is to be intelligible and useful; and therefore I have avoided, as much as possible, all Terms of Art; together with learned Quotations, as often produced out of Vanity, and to shew deep Reading, as for the sake of Proof. If you think it may be of any Use to publish this Letter, I am not unwilling it should appear; if not, do with it what you please. I deliver it up as a *Foundling* to be disposed of as you think proper. I shall only add by way of Persuasive to those who may be inclined to make Trial of the Method I recommend, that I am a Father, and have already practised it with the most desirable Success.

* * *

The history of the child did not suddenly change its course with the publication of Cadogan's *Essay*. There were setbacks of international scope—the use of children in the industrialization of Europe, for example—and there were local setbacks. In 1756, Parliament made governmental support of the London Foundling Hospital contingent on the admission of all foundlings brought to the door. In three and a half years, 13,000 children were admitted and of course the vast majority of them died. The policy was reversed in 1759, but the problem of the abandoned child remained. In France, as in England, the foundling home was supplemented by the use of hired nurses. In a report to the Queen of Hungary in 1780, the Lieutenant General of Police in Paris estimated that of 21,000 children born in the city each year, 700 were nursed by their mothers, 700 were wet-nursed at home, 2000 or 3000 children of the well-to-do were placed in suburban nursery care, and the remaining 17,000 or so were sent out into the country to be cared for by professional wet nurses.* Even with the increased interest in the preservation of infant life, dem-

* T. G. H. Drake, The wet nurse in France in the eighteenth century, *Bull. Hist. Medicine*, 8, 1940, 934–948.

onstrated by governmental agencies at the end of the eighteenth century, many children were lost in transport and in the country. The foundling and the "put-out" child will be rare in the culture which values children highly but, paradoxically, it may be that the culture in which child mortality is high does not develop a compassionate and valuing attitude toward young children. In any case, after Cadogan, there was no turning back to the doctrine of inevitable infantile death. From his day to our own, there can be traced two uninterrupted lines in medicine—the development of research that has reduced the infantile death rate from 300 or 400 per thousand births to less than 25, and the hardly less important chain of clinical pediatricians who have given advice and comfort to parents for two hundred years. The full historical account has yet to be written, but it is clear that the medical revolution of the past two centuries has permitted high valuation of the infant by saving his life.

The physicians were not alone in the eighteenth century in their concern for the child. Churchmen like Vincent de Paul had devoted themselves to the physical and moral salvation of children for centuries and, at about the time Cadogan's essay was reaching an international audience, a reform movement of heroic proportion began in England for the relief of children's suffering and for their concurrent salvation. Supported by a sense of man's essential depravity and the wisdom of starting the war with the Devil early, the work of the religious reformers grew from the need that the Industrial Revolution presented, a need that subsided only when, in the twentieth century, protection of the child became not a matter of reform but a matter of conformity.

Only a glance can be given here to the development of the child welfare movement, but the importance of the often disagreeable reformers to the present state of the child can not be overestimated. Just as the reforms of the mid-eighteenth century were giving some hope that the lot of the child might improve, the factory system began its comprehensive growth in Western Europe. With the demand for cheap labor that resulted, the child was again put in jeopardy. Under an ugly alliance of parents, officers charged with responsibility for the parish poor, and factory managers, children were sold into effective slavery. They

not infrequently worked, ate, and slept at their machines, with
neither education nor continuing adult care. For the protection of
their memories, it must be said that many of the early reformers—
particularly the Protestant churchmen—did not argue with the
righteousness of industrialization. Their goal was rather to save
the child for God, and they happily chose the way of education.
The Sunday school at its origin was not today's pale extension of
secular training; Sunday was chosen for the working child's *only*
education because it was the day on which blue laws kept the
factories closed. Robert Raikes, a Gloucester editor, was the man
who has been given credit, after some open contention over priority, for the formation of Sunday schools; he described their
beginning in a letter written in 1783.

... Some business leading me one morning into the suburbs of the city,
where the lowest of the people (who are principally employed in the
manufactory) chiefly reside, I was struck with concern at seeing a group
of children, wretchedly ragged, at play in the streets. ... "Ah! sir," said
the woman to whom I was speaking, "could you take a view of this part
of the town on a Sunday, you would be shocked indeed; for then the
street is filled with multitudes of these wretches, who, released on that
day from employment, spend their time in noise and riot, playing at
'chuck,' and cursing and swearing in a manner so horrid as to convey
to any serious mind an idea of hell rather than any other place. ..."

This conversation suggested to me that it would be at least a harmless attempt, if it were productive of no good, should some little plan
be formed to check the deplorable profanation of the Sabbath. ... I
then enquired ... if there were any decent well-disposed women in the
neighborhood who kept schools for teaching to read. I ... made an
agreement with [them] to receive as many children as I should send
upon the Sunday, whom they were to instruct in reading and in the
Church Catechism.*

The Sunday School movement flourished and, before long, had
its philosophers and theorists of child behavior. Thomas Martin,
a Wesleyan Methodist minister who served in many English
parishes during his long career, wrote, in 1818, a little book entitled (in part) *The Sunday School*, from which the next selections

---

* J. H. Harris (Ed.), *Robert Raikes: the Man and his Work*, Bristol: Arrow-
smith, 1899, pp. 305ff.

are taken. This treatise on the child did not have the impact of
Cadogan's *Essay* nor the public hearing given the work of other
reformers of the nineteenth century; but it speaks with a strong
voice on the needs of the child—and on his nature—from the perspective of a dedicated Christian reformer. More than that, it
should be remembered that English and American attitudes
toward children were long dominated by the Martins; the curious
conflict between childhood as innocence and the grim portrait
of an evil being who must be scourged to his salvation is even
now not an altogether discarded part of our heritage. It is revealing, too, to compare Martin's portrait of the child with Rousseau's;
these are the conceptions of the child (and of man) that were in
contest throughout the nineteenth century.

Martin speaks briefly of the imitativeness of children and of
the dangers of bad examples.

If a river be polluted in its source, all its streams will be impure; if
a flower be injured in its bud, its beauty will soon die away. That period
therefore must be important, when the good or evil, the wisdom or
folly, the happiness or misery of life are beginning. . . .

He is at some pains to answer the critics who fear that the education of the poor will give them ideas above their station.

. . . though education ceases to be useful, when it directs the attention
of the young, and especially of the indigent, to subjects which are
unsuited to the sphere in which they are eventually to move; yet, at
the same time, so long as it is confined to proper objects, adapted in
their nature, to be useful to them, in discharging the duties of humble
life, so long will it be desirable and beneficial.

Most of *The Sunday School* consists of advice to teachers about
the pedagogy and administration of Sunday education, but in the
few pages reprinted here, Martin presents a theory of the child
that was, with some variety of detail, woven tightly into nineteenth-century English and American life.

Thomas Martin (1780–1866)

The Characters of Childhood

Before we can proceed with either comfort or success in the instruction of children, it is desirable that we should be well acquainted with the characters of childhood and the general state of the infant mind. The want of this acquaintance will be regarded as an evil, when it is recollected, that in successful tuition, the truths which are taught, the quantity of truths which they are taught at one time, and the manner of teaching them, are all to be regulated by the strength or weakness, the capacity or incapacity of the pupil. And as the mind in a certain state of immaturity is only capable of receiving a certain quantity of ideas, it is of consequence, that the true state of the mind should be understood, and that all the measures of instruction should be adopted and regulated accordingly.

Childhood is *precipitate* and *heedless;* nor is it wise to expect from the youthful mind that calmness and recollection which are not always remarkable in persons of riper years. It is difficult to impress childhood with the importance of important things; children rush into things without regarding consequences, and often disobey without intending disobedience: and he who would judge correctly, or treat children discreetly, must take into the account the natural and characteristic heedlessness of youth, and proportion his forbearance to the peculiarities of that state of mind which so much requires it.

Childhood is *tender* and *fickle;* obduracy of mind and hardness of heart are not among the characters of this state. Children in

T. Martin, The Sunday School; or An Essay on the Character and Economy of Charitable Institutions for the Education of Children; Intended as the Manager's Companion and Teacher's Guide: To Which Are Added Sketches of Lectures, Addressed to Children. Portsea: T. Gardner, 1818, pp. 45–58.

general betray a tenderness of feeling and affection, and are soon brought to contrision and tears. Their fickleness, however, soon provides for other faults, and some new objects of desire, and new plans of diversion soon engross their minds, and are soon abandoned for something still different from the former. He therefore who deals with children should be aware of this disposition, and not cruelly torture their tenderness or resent as unnatural the fickleness and inconstancy of youth.

The youthful mind is *indistinct in its perceptions;* and in learning is rather affected with sounds, than with ideas. Hence young people often learn the theory of grammar by art, and yet are totally ignorant of all the practical uses of its rules. They often read lessons and repeat tasks without the least knowledge of the facts contained in them. There is a kind of confusion in the understanding, through the imperfect images of things presented to the mind; and a certain imbecility of intellect which renders children unable to discriminate and leaves the mind under the veil of a gloom, which can only be removed by the progressive operations of a judicious and adequate education.

It is *submissive* and *docile;* and in matters of learning, as well as in the evidences of truth, is not generally inclined to dispute legitimate authority. It is true we observe many instances of an opposite character in some, who betray a rebellious mind, and are vain enough to think themselves wiser than their teachers. It is true, instances of depravity and stupidity may occur, in which neither docility nor submission may be manifest; but these are rather to be regarded as instances of unusual evil in the disposition and temper of the mind, than as a rule by which to judge of the true and general characters of childhood, which will be found, except in such instances, submissive to the authority of parents and teachers, and disposed to receive with readiness and humility the instructions of the wise.

Childhood is *inquisitive* and *sanguine;* and if these qualities be brought under a proper control, they will often be regarded as hopeful pledges of future improvement. Children are prone to ask questions, and to propose enquiries; and sometimes their questions are original and astonishing, and though it is proper to check this propensity whenever it becomes tiresome or dangerous, yet it is equally proper to observe the greatest prudence in doing this; as an offensive and discouraging reply may induce an indifference, which is still more dangerous than the evil to be removed.

Childhood is *forgetful* and *forgiving;* the first is an evil, the second is a good. Children require again and again to be reminded of their duty and interest; and there are few things more difficult, than to make lasting impressions on their minds; trifling things too often make a more lasting impression than important ones; and both resolutions and lessons are often equally forgotten. In children however bad impressions often share the fate of good ones, and that frailty which cannot retain the good, provides for the escape of the bad. These then are the obvious characters of youth and of childhood. It is the morning of life when every thing is beginning; the dawn of wisdom, when every thing is yet to be learned; the preparation for effort, when every thing is yet to be done. It is a stage between torpidity and activity, the prelude to the scenes of life, and the birth-day of the future man. Ah, happy day! the sweetest and the fairest of life! Unruffled by perplexing cares, unembittered by a guilty conscience, and unbeclouded by dark forbodings or prevailing fears! the reign of innocence, and the heaven of earth!

In making the characters of childhood a separate article in our remarks on charitable tuition, it was intended to suggest the necessity and expediency of being acquainted with them, that the instructors of children might regulate their plans of teaching accordingly. It indicates a very imperfect knowledge of human nature, and especially of the characters of the youthful mind, to suppose, that one kind of treatment will be equally proper for children of every temperament of mind; and he who acts on this principle, in treating with children, is sure either to be unjust or unsuccessful. Some will be found dull, slow, and untractable; and others quick, volatile, and precipitate; some will be hasty, passionate, and forgetful; and some sullen, silent, and sulky; some will soon learn and soon forget, and others be found slow to receive, but sure to retain knowledge: some will be found gentle and tender-hearted, and some relentless and obdurate: some will find little or no difficulty in learning and repeating their lessons;

and others will scarcely be able, whatever be their application, to learn or repeat them at all: such, and so various are the tempers and characters of the youthful mind, and of such a variety are Sunday schools generally composed. Nothing then can be more obvious than, that a teacher should endeavour to know the tempers of his children, and to accommodate his conduct towards them accordingly.

[The advantages to teachers of understanding children are listed.]

The Dangers of Youth

And is it then possible, O thou Universal Parent, that one of these little ones should perish! Is it possible, that these fair and interesting little specimens of thy handy work should be destroyed! Is it possible, that these pledges of thy goodness, these promising comforters of our age, and these hopes of future generations,— is it possible, that these should perish! Is Satan seeking to devour! Is cruel fondness administering her cup of poison! Are all surrounding objects combining their influence to blast our hopes; and hast thou provided no means by which the impending ruin may be prevented? Blessed Father, we must owe to thee as much the safety as the reception of our children; nothing but thy power can preserve them from destruction; nothing but thy tenderness and love can prevent their perdition; and this alone is our comfort—it is not thy will, "that one of these little ones should perish."

That children, however, are exposed to danger, is capable of many a melancholy evidence; and as to prevent their running into danger is one of the avowed objects of tuition, it will be desirable for us to be made acquainted with the causes from whence this danger arises, as well as the particular nature of the evils into which childhood may be plunged. Native depravity, satanic influence, and evil example, may lead to temporal ruin, present misery, and final wrath.

Native depravity is certainly the source of all moral evil in the conduct of mankind; and as we bring with us into the world a nature replete with evil propensities, and as these propensities begin to manifest themselves as soon as the mind is capable of expression or action, so the first emotions of a mind, in such a state, will be emotions of evil, and the first efforts of powers so depraved will be evil: and hence it will be easy to trace the follies of youth, as well as the crimes of maturity, to the impurities of the heart, which is declared by the highest authority to be "Deceitful above all things, and desparately wicked."

Satanic Influence is evidently employed to pervert the youthful mind, and is another cause of the danger to which it is exposed. It is not possible to describe the manner in which infernal influence affects the mind, or to point out how the evil one gains access to the soul; but nothing is more evident than, that "He ruleth in the children of disobedience;" and that the "wicked are led captive by him at his will." Satan presents to children the temptations that are suited to their state and inclinations; suggests the innocency of complying with his will; and as he succeeded at first, so he still too often succeeds, in seducing the youthful mind by, falsely insinuating, "Ye shall not surely die."

Nor is *evil example* less dangerous to youth than the influence of Satan. Children are prone to copy the patterns set before them, to form their manners by the model of others, to adopt the expressions and imitate the amusements which they see and hear. They have not sufficient discrimination to detect, or resolution to resist that which is evil; they regard it enough to be as others, and are wont to justify their own follies by the example of their seniors. What can be more dangerous to youth, than bad company; or what more fatal to all moral rectitude and feeling than the influence of bad example! My son, if sinners entice thee consent not thou; for evil communications corrupt good manners; and the companion of fools shall be destroyed.

Temporal ruin is among the least of the dangers to which children are exposed, and which may arise from the evils we have detailed. How many instances are there around us, of persons born to fortune, and blessed with the most delightful prospects of future life, who have nevertheless by heedlessness, extravagancy, and folly, reduced themselves to penury and want! How often has a course of profligacy begun in youth, ended in rapid and irremediable ruin. The history of the prodigal son is in point, and besides many other salutary truths which it teaches, this is most prominent and impressive, that youthful depravity leads to extravagance and waste, and prodigality ends in total and irrevokable ruin.

Present Misery is entailed upon folly and sin. That youth endangers his future happiness in life, who neglects his education, and follows the course of this world. He, who in youth pursues a course of folly, is laying the foundation for future repentance and shame. He cannot be happy who lives without God, or in rebellion against him; and as children are under the influence of evil, they are by that evil rendered liable to those miseries, which sin entails upon itself.

Final wrath however is the most awful of all the dangers to which children are exposed; nor are children alone exposed to this; the wrath of God is revealed from heaven against all unrighteousness of men; and he visits sin upon children and children's children, unto the third and fourth generation. That children are exposed to to danger then cannot be doubtful. Enemies and evils exist in every direction, the disease of sin is growing, its poison is spreading through the soul, the world is seeking to deceive, and Satan to devour; childhood is equally destitute of wisdom to detect, or strength to resist. And however fair these plants may look, however pleasing the promises they may give of plenteous fruit, however dear to us are the hopes we entertain of them, let us rejoice with trembling; they are exposed to dangers; their beauty may fade away as a leaf, and all our hopes perish. This only then is our comfort, that though dangers every where surround them, and enemies threaten to destroy, "It is not the will of God that they should perish."

[A hypothetical case history is presented.]

The Claims of Children

That children have natural rights and unalienable privileges, is not a matter that is generally either doubted or denied. It is true in heathen lands and pagan countries, which are full of the habitations of cruelty, the rights of children are made to depend on the will and superstition of their savage and sanguine parents, who assume the right either to protect or abandon, to kill, or to keep alive, according to the dictates of caprice or superstition; but where civilization has obtained, and the moral government of the true God is recognized, the right and claims of children are admitted, and they become as soon as born intitled to all the privileges peculiar to the condition of man.

They have claims to protection from all the evils and dangers to which, in a state of childhood, they are particularly exposed. They have claims to all the succours and nourishments which their frailty requires and which are needful for their preservation and comfort. They have claims on *tuition* in all the duties and obligations which they are to discharge in future life, and in all those things which may be conducive to their usefulness in society. They have claims especially to be *instructed* in the great truths and duties of religion, which are to guide and comfort them at all times, and which are to produce all that public and social virtue, all that private and personal worth, and all that assurance of future and eternal bliss, which are the glory and happiness of man.

The claims of children are founded on the laws of nature and of nations, and are simplified and strengthened by the ordinances of heaven. "Can a woman forget her sucking child, that she should not have compassion on the son of her womb?" is an enquiry of as much importance in its appeal to nature as to mortality, and is equally suggested by reason and religion. The God of nature has implanted in all animals a love for their young, and this natural and universal attachment provides for the preservation of the different species of creatures which are rendered necessary to the support and accommodation of mankind. In man however heaven has not only implanted a natural affection, in common with other creatures, but hath given that affection a tenderness and rationality which renders it far superior to any other being's attachment, and far more noble and beneficial. Nothing therefore can be more certain than, that the Author of our being hath guaranteed to our children the right of participating in all the

privileges of humanity, and that they possess the most indisputable claims to every thing that we can accomplish for their
present or eternal welfare.

When the claims of children become a question of general
policy, and are regarded in their connexion with the virtue or
happiness of a nation, every principle of enlightened reason will
immediately concede them in all their natural extent. When the
claims of children are beheld by the eye of philosophy, every
dictate of true wisdom, and all that is luminous and elevated in
the liberal opinions of the wise will readily acknowledge them.
When philanthropy examines the question, her pure and expansive
ardour, her arms of love, her generous pity, and all the charms of
her character are wont to admit them. Especially, when they are
contemplated in the light of religion, and in connexion with the
thought, that children are immortal as ourselves, that they are
capable of all the felicities of an eternal world, and that they are
heirs of the manifold benedictions which heaven hath bestowed
upon us; looked at in this way, their claims assume the most com-
manding characters, and we conclude, that what policy, philosophy, philanthropy, and religion admit, must be holy, just, and
good.

It was needful, that the claims of children should have been
stated, not because the virtuous deny them, but because the
wicked are generally ignorant of, or are inclined to neglect them.
How many neglectful and unnatural parents there are who abandon their offspring to the world, and leave them exposed to all
the enemies and dangers which are peculiar to childhood; who
appear to think it enough, that they have been made the instruments of bringing them into the world, and therefore entertain
no further anxiety about them. It is difficult to designate this
monsterous offence; an offence with which brutes are not charge-
able; a crime which heaven and earth pronounces to be most foul,
strange, and unnatural; an offence alike against reason and religion, an outrage on all that entitles man to his rank in creation,
a violation of all that is agreeable and useful in social order and
intercourse, a sin against society, and a war against God. Let us
not then neglect the claims of our children; let us listen to the

silent eloquence with which they urge them; let us feel the force of their appeals, and as their claims are powerful, explicit, and indispensible, let us feel their force as we ought to feel it; and with all our affection, all our activity, and all our perseverance, concede to them all their legitimate and unalienable claims.

Some of the most beautiful and affecting intimations of divine compassion are drawn from the tenderness of parental affection, and the claims of children on its constant exercise. When Jehovah would express the kindness with which he would foster and protect his feeblest servants, he adopts this familiar explanation; "Like as a father pitieth his children, so the Lord pitieth them that fear him." Ps. ciii. 13. When the patience and forbearance of Jehovah are expressed in scripture this kind of allusion is made; "And I will spare them as a man spareth his own son that serveth him." Mal. 3. 17. There are *two* instances of allusions of this kind in the sacred records, which because of their matchless delicacy and beauty, deserve to be particularly noticed here. The first is expressed in this natural and forcible language: "Can a woman forget her sucking child, that she should not have compassion on the son of her womb? yea, they may forget, yet will I not forget thee." Isa. xlix. 15. The beauty of this divinely painted picture consists in the natural distribution of its *light* and *shade*. Its *light* presents a *Woman,* whose characteristic tenderness and affection are well known. A *Child,* always dear to the heart of a mother. A *Sucking Child,* particularly dear, because of its frailty and momentary dependence on maternal succour. A *Son,* whose virtues are its parent's hope; the *Son of her Womb,* connected with whose birth she witnessed so many pangs; for whom she offered up so many prayers; and whom she still regards as flesh of her flesh, and bone of her bone. But here the painter employs *shade;* in which is slightly intimated all those unutterable feelings, all those nameless delicacies, all those mystic emotions and tendencies of natural affection, which are not to be described; and by the power of which alone can be understood and inferred, the tenderness, the constancy, the promptitude, and the perpetuity, of that love which our Heavenly Parent displays to his children.

The second instance of this kind of allusion is contained in these beautiful words of our blessed Saviour;

If ye then, being evil, know how to give good gifts unto your children, how much more shall your Father which is in heaven give good things to them that ask him. (Matt., vii., 11).

The spirit and character of these expressions may be thus explained. Ye are evil in your tempers and dispositions; and yet evil as you are, you feel and acknowledge the claims of your children; you have knowledge enough to perceive their wants, you have love enough to supply their wants, and bounty enough to give them good gifts, because they are your children. If then you, who are evil, can do all this, how much more can God do, in whom there is no evil at all? How much more knowledge does he possess of his children's wants? How much more tenderness and love does he feel than you? How much more bounty can he display than you! And if your love will not allow you to resist the cries or deny the requests of your children, how much more attentive will your Father be to your cries, and how much less likely is he to deny your requests! He is rich, you are poor; he is constant, you are changeable; he is good, you are evil; he is a God, you are creatures; he is perfect, and you are imperfect. If you then who are poor, changeable, evil, and imperfect creatures, are kind to your children, how much more kindness shall your Father show for his children, who is rich, constant, good, and perfect? Such are the intimations of divine goodness given in the records of our salvation; in which we perceive the claims of children on their parents, and the love of parents for their children, are adapted to display its manifestations to mankind!

* * *

The history of the exchange between reformers and factory owners has been often and hysterically told in tract and novel, but the attitude toward children of the early industrial community is coldly told in the passage in 1833 of a law regulating child labor. The statute "prohibited night work to persons under 18 in cotton, woollen, and other factories, and provided that children from 9 to 13 were not to work more than 48 hours a week and those from 13 to 18 not more than 68 hours a week. Children

under 9 were not to be employed at all." It is worth noting that
the regulation was vigorously (and, considering the primitive
techniques of capitalization available, honestly) fought by the
owners for whom "juvenile labor" was "a national blessing."*
Moreover, the statute limiting the conditions of child labor did
not apply to all children's work; in the selection that follows,
Shaftesbury describes more vividly than Dickensian invention the
world of the child, working in mine and colliery, for whom the
earlier act offered no protection.

The Earl of Shaftesbury was neither physician nor philosopher;
he takes his place in the history of the child because his persistent
and knowing agitation in Parliament over many decades changed
man's conception of the child as surely as a theoretical essay or
an empirical discovery. Together with his friends in and out of
government, Shaftesbury forced the recognition that all children,
regardless of parentage, are of the same flesh, liable to the same
injuries when hurt and deserving of the same humane treatment.
He relentlessly wakened the conscience of his countrymen, particularly those in governmental power, to see the cruelties of their
society. Shaftesbury's interest in social betterment extended beyond his concern with child labor—he was heard on problems of
lunacy, education of the poor, control of opium, and sanitation—
but his continuing exposure to his colleagues of the inhumanity
of the current treatment of children changed their definition of
the child. The filthy and ignorant child who crawled in the mines
could easily be put to one side by the educated man of the time
as a different breed, even a different species, but Shaftesbury,
like all reformers and all theoreticians, began with commitment
to a postulate—for him, the postulate that these children, like all
others, were children of God and under the protection of the law.
Shaftesbury continued what the medical reformers of the previous
century had begun; the child was becoming a true human being,
valuable to society, requiring special care, and, though this point
was made only feebly in early nineteenth-century England, interesting in his own right.

* See G. H. Payne, *The Child in Human Progress*, New York: Putnam, 1916,
passim. Payne's is one of the hysterical books.

Anthony Ashley Cooper
Seventh Earl of Shaftesbury (1801-1885)

Children in Mines and Collieries

SIR,

It will not, I hope, be deemed presumptuous on my part when I rise to propound my motion to the House, and when I ask for its sympathy and patient hearing, if I add at the same time that I feel quite certain of obtaining their indulgence. The novelty of the subject, its magnitude, the deep and solemn interest which is felt throughout the country, the consideration of its vital influence on the welfare of so large a portion of our fellow subjects, will, of themselves, be sufficient to obtain your indulgence; nor can I forget, Sir, how often and how undeservedly I have experienced forbearance at the hands both of yourself and of the House.

— — —

Sir, it is not possible for any man, whatever be his station, if he have but a heart within his bosom, to read the details of this awful document [report of a special Commission] without a combined feeling of shame, terror, and indignation. But I will endeavour to dwell upon the evil itself, rather than on the parties that might be accused as, in great measure, the authors of it. An enormous mischief is discovered, and an immediate remedy is proposed; and sure I am that if those who have the power will be as ready to abate oppressions as those who have suffered will be to forgive the sense of it, we may hope to see the revival of such a good understanding between master and man, between wealth and

Shaftesbury, A. A. Cooper, Earl of, A speech on moving for leave to bring in a bill to make regulations respecting the age and sex of children and young persons employed in the mines and collieries of the United Kingdom. House of Commons: June 7, 1842. Reprinted in *Speeches of the Earl of Shaftesbury, K. G.* London: Chapman and Hall, 1868, pp. 31–58.

poverty, between ruler and ruled, as will, under God's good providence, conduce to the restoration of social comfort, and to the permanent security of the empire.

[The report of a special Commission] has shown you the ignorance and neglect of many of those who have property, and the consequent vice and suffering of those who have none; it has shown you many sad causes of pauperism; it has shown you the physical disorders which our system has engendered, and the inevitable deterioration of the British race; it has shown you in part our condition, moral, social, and religious. We know not what a day may bring forth. I know it will be said, "Vice is not new—danger is not new; this has occurred before, and will occur again." That is true; but I maintain that our danger is absolute, not comparative—our forefathers had to deal with thousands, we with millions; we must address ourselves to the evil boldly and faithfully, or it will soon acquire so enormous a magnitude, as to be insuperable by any effort either of genius or principle.

— — —

I think that the points I wish to establish should be made out by statements and evidence, rather than by any attempts at declamation. In the first place, I shall present the House with the result of the evidence respecting the age and sex of persons employed in the mines and collieries. The extent to which the employment of females prevails varies very much in different districts—in some parts of the country none but males are employed, in other places a great number of females. With respect to the age at which children are worked in mines and collieries in South Staffordshire, it is common to begin at 7 years old; in Shropshire some begin as early as 6 years of age; in Warwickshire the same; in Leicestershire nearly the same. In Derbyshire many begin at 5, many between 5 and 6 years, many at 7. In the West Riding of Yorkshire it is not uncommon for infants even of 5 years old to be sent to the pit. About Halifax and the neighbourhood children are sometimes brought to the pits at the age of 6 years, and are taken out of their beds at 4 o'clock. Bradford and Leeds, the same; in Lancashire and Cheshire, from 5 to 6. Near Oldham children are worked as low "as 4 years old, and in the small collieries towards the hills some are so young they are brought to work in their bed-gowns." In Cumberland, many at 7; in South Durham, as early as 5 years of age, and by no means uncommonly at 6.

— — —

In the south of Ireland no children at all are employed. All the underground work, which in the coalmines of England, Scotland, and Wales, is done by young children, appears in Ireland to be done by young persons between the ages of 13 and 18. Now, with respect to sex, the report states that in South Staffordshire no females are employed in underground work, nor in North Stafford-shire. In Shropshire, Warwickshire, Leicestershire, and Derby-shire, the same. In the West Riding of Yorkshire the practice of employing females underground is universal. About Halifax and the neighbourhood girls from 5 years old and upwards regularly perform the same work as boys. At Bradford and Leeds, far from uncommon. In Lancashire and Cheshire it is the general custom for girls and women to be employed. In North Lancashire, through-out the whole of the district, girls and women are regularly em-ployed underground. In Cumberland there are none, excepting in one old colliery, nor in Durham, nor in Northumberland. In the east of Scotland the employment of females is general, but in the west of Scotland extremely rare. In North Wales, some on the surface, none underground. In South Wales it is not uncommon. In Gloucestershire and Somersetshire there are none. In none of the collieries in the coal-fields of Ireland was a single instance found of a female child, nor a female of any age, being employed in any kind of work. I must observe that, with respect to that country, neither children of tender years nor females are employed in underground operations. I have often, Sir, admired the gen-erosity and warm-heartedness of the Irish people; and I must say, that if this is to be taken as a specimen of their barbarism, I would not exchange it for all the refinement and polish of the most civi-lized nations of the globe.

— — —

It must be borne in mind that it is in this district that the regular hours of a full day's labour are 14, and occasionally 16; and the children have to walk a mile or two at night without changing their clothes. In the West Riding of Yorkshire it appears that there are very few collieries with thin seams where the main roadways exceed a yard in height, and in some they do not exceed 26 or 28 inches: nay, in some the height is as little even as 22 inches; so that in such places the youngest child cannot work without the most constrained posture. The ventilation, besides, in general is very bad, and the drainage worse. In Oldham the mountain-seams are wrought in a very rude manner. There is very insufficient drainage. The ways are so low that only little boys can work in them, which they do naked, and often in mud and water, dragging sledge-tubs by the girdle and chain. In North Lancashire, "the drainage is often extremely bad: a pit of not above 20 inches seam," says a witness, "had a foot of water in it, so that he could hardly keep his head out of water." In Cumberland, it appears, the mines are tolerably dry and well ventilated, and in South Durham the same, with some exceptions. In North Durham there are some thin seams, and in Northumberland many not exceeding 2 feet, or 2 feet 2 inches. Great complaints are made by children of pains and wounds from the lowness of the roof; but the ventilation is excellent—as good, perhaps, as it can be in the present state of that science. Yet, I regret to add, the "drainage, not being so essential to the safety of the coal-mine as ventilation, has been much less attended to in this district." In East Scotland, where the side-roads do not exceed from 22 to 28 inches in height, the working-places are sometimes 100 and 200 yards distant from the main-road, so that females have to crawl backwards and forwards with their small carts in seams in many cases not exceeding 22 to 28 inches in height. The whole of these places, it appears, are in a most deplorable state as to ventilation, and the drainage is quite as bad as the ventilation. The evidence, as given by the young people and the old colliers themselves, of their sufferings, is absolutely piteous. . . . So long as a candle will burn, the labour is continued. . . .

Sir, the next subject to which I shall request your attention is the nature of the employment in these localities. Now, it appears that the practice prevails to a lamentable extent of making young persons and children of a tender age draw loads by means of the girdle and chain. This practice prevails generally in Shropshire, in Derbyshire, in the West Riding of Yorkshire, in Lancashire, in Cheshire, in the east of Scotland, in North and South Wales, and in South Gloucestershire. The child, it appears, has a girdle bound round its waist, to which is attached a chain, which passes under the legs, and is attached to the cart. The child is obliged to pass on all fours, and the chain passes under what, therefore, in that posture, might be called the hind legs; and thus they have to pass through avenues not so good as a common sewer, quite as wet, and oftentimes more contracted. This kind of labour they have to continue during several hours, in a temperature described as perfectly intolerable. By the testimony of the people themselves, it appears that the labour is exceedingly severe; that the girdle blisters their sides and causes great pain. "Sir," says an old miner, "I can only say what the mothers say, it is barbarity —absolute barbarity." Robert North says, "I went into the pit at 7 years of age. When I drew by the girdle and chain, the skin was broken and the blood ran down. . . . If we said anything, they would beat us. I have seen many draw at 6. They must do it or be beat. They cannot straighten their backs during the day. I have sometimes pulled till my hips have hurt me so that I have not known what to do with myself." In the West Riding, it appears, girls are almost universally employed as trappers and hurriers, in common with boys. The girls are of all ages, from 7 to 21. They commonly work quite naked down to the waist, and are dressed—as far as they are dressed at all—in a loose pair of trousers. These are seldom whole on either sex. In many of the collieries the adult colliers, whom these girls serve, work perfectly naked. Near Huddersfield the sub-commissioner examined a female child. He says, "I could not have believed that I should have found human nature so degraded. Mr. Holroyd, and Mr. Brook, a surgeon, confessed, that although living within a few miles, they could not have believed that such a system of unchristian cruelty could have existed." Speaking of one of the girls, he says, "She stood shivering before me from cold. The rug that hung about her waist was as black as coal, and saturated with water, the drippings of the roof." "In a pit near New Mills," says the sub-commissioner, "the chain passing high up between the legs of two girls, had worn large holes in their trousers. Any sight more disgustingly indecent or revolting can scarcely be imagined than these girls at work. No brothel can beat it."—Sir, it would be impossible to enlarge upon all these points; the evidence is most abundant, and the selection very difficult. I will, however, observe that nothing can be more graphic, nothing more touching, than the evidence of many of these poor girls themselves. Insulted, oppressed, and even corrupted, they exhibit, not unfrequently, a simplicity and a kindness that render tenfold more heart-rending the folly and cruelty of that system that has forced away these young persons, destined, in God's providence, to holier and happier duties, to occupations so unsuited, so harsh, and so degrading.

[Shaftesbury describes vividly the work of pregnant women and evidence of illness and injury in the mines.]

Here, let me observe to the House, the moral effects of the state of things which the collieries present are equally prominent and equally alarming. It begets a slave-driving system. It might, indeed, be assumed without proof; but I shall state a few cases in order to exhibit those effects to the House and the country, and to show how necessary it is, immediately, if possible, to address ourselves to the evil. A clergyman, the Rev. W. Parlane, of Tranent, says—"Children of amiable temper and conduct, at 7 years of age, often return next season from the collieries greatly corrupted, and, as an old teacher says, with most hellish dispositions." See, too, here how the system superinduces habits and feelings of ferocity that are perfectly alarming. Hannah Neale says—"My boy, 10 years old, was at work: about half a year since his toe was cut off by the bind falling; notwithstanding this, the loader made him work until the end of the day, although in the greatest pain." Isaac Tipstone says—"I was bullied by a man to do what was beyond my strength. I would not, because I could not. The man threw me down, and kicked out two of my ribs." Jonathan Watts says—"A butty has beaten a boy with a stick till he fell. He then stamped on him till the boy could scarcely stand. The boy never told, and said he would not, for he should only be served worse. Boys are pulled up and down by the ears. I have seen them beaten till the blood has flowed out of their sides. They are often punished until they can scarcely stand." John Bostock, speaking of Derby-shire, says—"The corporals used to take the burning candle-wicks after the tallow was off, light them, and burn his arms. I have known my uncle take a boy by the ears and knock his head against the wall, because his eyesight was bad, and he could not see to do his work as well as others."

— — —

Surely it is evident that to remove, or even to mitigate, these sad evils, will require the vigorous and immediate interposition of the legislature. That interposition is demanded by public reason, by public virtue, by the public honour, by the public character, and, I rejoice to add, by the public sympathy: for never, I believe, since the first disclosure of the horrors of the African slave-trade, has there existed so universal a feeling on any one subject in this country, as that which now pervades the length and breadth of the land in abhorrence and disgust of this monstrous oppression. It is demanded, moreover, I am happy to say, by many well-intentioned and honest proprietors—men who are anxious to see those ameliorations introduced which, owing to long-established prejudices, they have themselves been unable to effect. From let-ters and private communications which I have received on the subject, I know that they will hail with the greatest joy such a bill as I shall presently ask leave to introduce. In that bill I propose, in the first place, and at once, to cut off the principal evils. Much, no doubt, may be left for future legislation; but there are some of the evils of so hideous a nature that they will not admit of delay —they must be instantly removed—evils that are both disgusting and intolerable—disgusting they would be in a heathen country, and perfectly intolerable they are in one that professes to call itself Christian. The first provision, then, which I shall propose will be the total exclusion of all females from the mines and collieries of this country. I think that every principle of religion—I think that every law of nature calls for such a step; and I know of no argument that can be raised against it, unless one of a most un-worthy and of a completely selfish character. I believe, indeed, there are but very few proprietors who have any real interest in keeping women so employed; but there are some interested parties who wish to retain females in the pits, and I am anxious to state to the House and the country what the motives are for inducing or compelling those wretched females to undergo the shameful toil and degradation to which they are subjected. I will take the evidence of the working people themselves, one of whom says—"Girls and women never get coal; they always remain drawers, and are considered to be equal to half a man." Another collier says—"They prefer women to boys, as they are easier to manage, and they never get to be coal-getters, which is another good thing." Another witness says—"The temptation to employ women arises from their wages being lower than that of males."

— — —

Again, Mr. James Wright says—and here I am very anxious for the attention of the House, because I would entreat them to observe how the mischief is first engendered, and then perpetuated, by the toleration of these practices: women are allowed to work below and because they are so, the evils here stated continue without abatement; a man would complain and resist, but a woman is submissive—"I feel confident," he says, "that the exclusion of females will advantage the colliers in a physical point of view, inasmuch as the males will not work on bad roads (females are wrought only where no man can be induced to draw or work: they are mere beasts of burden).

— — —

The next point for legislation is the exclusion of all boys under 13 years of age; and this I confess may be looked upon as my weak point, for here I am likely to find the greatest opposition. I shall, however, briefly state to the House the reasons why I think it necessary to limit the admission of children into the pits to those who have arrived at the age of 13. In the first place, the Factory Act prohibits full labour under 13 years of age: in the next place, in the cotton and wool districts frequent complaints have been made of a deficiency of young persons, who, it is alleged, are called off to the print-works and coal-mines, where labour is not regulated by law. It is therefore contended that an undue advantage is thus given to these departments of industry, to the prejudice of those of wool and cotton. Now, I am extremely anxious to bring them all to this one level; and if my proposition be adopted, a due supply of children under 13 years of age will be obtained from the coal-pits, and the proprietors of wool and cotton mills, as they themselves have alleged, will be enabled to have two complete sets of workers, the demand for children under 13 years of age being thus supplied to work in two relays of 6 hours in the day each (though I should myself prefer 5), according to the provisions of the Bill introduced, but not carried, in the last session. Indeed, almost all the evidence goes to show that 14 years of age would be the proper limit required for full labour. My own feelings, I must say, lead me to that opinion; but as 13 is the age stated in the Factory Act, I am not disposed to deviate from it. If a child once goes down into a pit, he must remain in it. All who go down must work full time, and, if required, throughout the night.

— — —

Indeed, the very custom of taking those children into the mines had its origin in vice. The habits of irregularity and intoxication common among miners are the cause of it; and unhappily, from the system which prevails, those habits are transmitted from father to son. We have it in evidence that many of the miners work 8 or 9 days only in a fortnight, earn some money, and then spend the rest of their time, until those earnings are exhausted, in drinking, cock-fighting, and gambling. They then have to work again to make up for lost time; and thus it happens that they take down their wives and children into the pits with them, and make that cruel demand on female and infantile labour, which would be wholly unnecessary were they steady to their work and decently frugal in their habits. But take away the power of permitting young children to work in the pits; put an end at once to this abuse —this monstrous and shameful abuse—and, depend upon it, they will soon attain their legitimate ends in an honest way.

The next point is one of real importance: it is the necessity of making a provision that no person shall be employed in charge of an engine or an engine-house who is under the age of 21 years.

[Shaftesbury tells of fatal accidents and argues against the apprentice system.]

I ask, is all this cruelty necessary? Cannot we attain our ends by any other means? You have seen not only how needless, but how wasteful and ruinous, to themselves and their families, is the employment of females in these severe and degrading occupations: you have seen how wasteful and ruinous is the employment of children of such tender years, when we not only deprive them of all means of education, but anticipate the efforts of that strength which should be reserved for the service and defence of a future generation. Sir, I am sure that, under proper regulations, the occupation itself may be rendered both healthy and happy: indeed, all the evidence goes to show that a little expense and a little care would obviate a large proportion of the mischiefs that prevail. No employments that are necessary to mankind are deadly to man but by man's own fault: when we go beyond, and enter on the path of luxury and sensual gratification, then begins the long and grim catalogue of pestilential occupations.

[A report of crime in Manchester appears here.]

I hope, Sir, that the House will not consider that I am speaking dogmatically on these subjects—my intercourse with the working classes, both by correspondence and personal interview, has for many years been so extensive, that I think I may venture to say that I am conversant with their feelings and habits, and can state their probable movements. I do not fear any violent or general outbreaks on the part of the population: there may be a few, but not more than will be easily repressed by the ordinary force of the country. But I do fear the progress of a cancer, a perilous, and, if we much longer delay, an incurable cancer, which has seized upon the body social, moral, and political; and then in some day, when there shall be required on the part of our people an unusual energy, an unprecedented effort of virtue and patriotism, the strength of the empire will be found prostrate, for the fatal disorder will have reached its vitals.

There are, I well know, many other things to be done; but this, I must maintain, is an indispensable preliminary; for it is a mockery to talk of education to people who are engaged, as it were, in un-

ceasing toil from their cradle to their grave. I have endeavoured
for many years to attain this end by limiting the hours of labour,
and so bringing the children and young persons within the reach
of a moral and religious education. I have hitherto been dis-
appointed, and I deeply regret it, because we are daily throwing
away a noble material!—for, depend upon it, the British people
are the noblest and the most easily governed of any on the face
of the earth. Their fortitude and obedience under the severest
privations sufficiently prove it. Sure I am, that the minister of
this country, whoever he be, if he will but win their confidence
by appealing to their hearts, may bear upon his little finger the
whole weight of the reins of the British empire. And, Sir, the
sufferings of these people, so destructive to themselves, are altogether needless to the prosperity of the empire. Could it even be
proved that they were necessary, this House, I know, would pause
before it undertook to affirm the continuance of them. What could
induce you to tolerate further the existence of such abominations?

— — —

Is it not enough to announce these things to an assembly of
Christian men and British gentlemen? For twenty millions of
money you purchased the liberation of the negro; and it was a
blessed deed. You may, this night, by a cheap and harmless vote,
invigorate the hearts of thousands of your countrypeople, enable
them to walk erect in newness of life, to enter on the enjoyment
of their inherited freedom, and avail themselves (if they will accept them) of the opportunities of virtue, of morality, and religion.
These, Sir, are the ends that I venture to propose: this is the
barbarism that I seek to restore. [A member, in a preceding discussion, had said that "this kind of legislation would bring back
the barbarism of the Middle Ages."] The House will, I am sure,
forgive me for having detained them so long; and still more will
they forgive me for venturing to conclude, by imploring them, in
the words of Holy Writ, "To break off our sins by righteousness,
and our iniquities by showing mercy to the poor, if it may be a
lengthening of our tranquillity."

*   *   *

Shaftesbury did not get what he asked from Parliament. Under pressure from the "coal magnate," Lord Londonderry, who defended the proposition that for miners' children a practical education in the collieries was superior to a reading education, the apprentice system continued and boys aged ten were permitted to work in the mines. In spite of opposition, however, all girls and women were prohibited from engaging in work underground, an inspection system was established, and Shaftesbury was able to take the sacrament "in joyful and humble thankfulness to Almighty God, for the undeserved measure of success with which He has blessed my effort for the glory of His name, and the welfare of His creatures. . . ."*

* J. W. Bready, *Lord Shaftesbury and Social–Industrial Progress*, London: Allen & Unwin, 1926, p. 306.

3

Precursors: Philosophers and Teachers

Disquisitions on education are common from Solomon to Conant;
philosophers of all ages have had their say on methods of preparing the child for his life in society. The educational theories of the
ancients—theories that persisted in weakening form until our own
day—were largely based on a conception of the perfect adult or
the perfect society of adults. The task of the teacher was to arrange
circumstances so that the child was brought with understanding
and efficiency to the threshold of the adult's world. The peculiarities of childhood did not engage the interest of teachers for their
own sake; whether by using the eccentricities of the child or by
contesting them, the goal of education and the theme of the
philosophers were the reduction of childish variety to the requirements of responsible adult life. So it would always be, in a sense,
but over the last several hundred years two profound changes have
taken place in the cultural theory of the child which underlies educational practice and policy. The first change, reaching far beyond
its relevance to the child, was a renewed recognition and an enthusiasm for human variety. Montaigne in his *Essays* built a mo-
saic in praise of variety, individual detail, and the necessity of
seeing differences among men as well as their shared human form.
No longer was it enough to know the shape of the ideal adult to
prescribe the treatment of children; man could not be fit so easily
into canonical forms. Once the variety of man became interesting

and important, it was a short step to seeking the sources of variety. With this step, the study of childhood was irrevocably modified; childhood was not an unfurnished antechamber to adulthood, but a place where one might find the sources and occasions of differences among men.

The second change in the philosophy of childhood can be given neither author nor specific beginning; the assiduous and hindsighted searcher can find signs of it throughout Western history. But there can be no doubting that over the centuries there has been increasing devotion to the proposition that childhood is a time of construction. The world is not sat in by the child, it is made by him. His notions of society, or morality, of the nature of time and of man are not brought out of their instinct hiding-place by the wise and affectionate teacher; knowledge is constructed by the child from his experience of men and things. Neither evil, as Martin would have it, nor good, as some nineteenth century reformers would have it, is resident in the child. He is what he is made. A truly radical proposal is this, and the notion that man's nature depends on his history easily becomes the heart of philosophical systems and political contention. If the nature of man is defined in the experience of the child, then man can mimic God and reconstruct himself. The history of the child for three hundred years has been the history of a dialogue on the conception of childhood as construction. It is tempting to suggest that the idea of man as limited only by his experience was invented in the seventeenth century, believed in the eighteenth, made scientific in the nineteenth, and abandoned in the twentieth. But as we shall see, the issues change with the times, and contemporary man is not permitted the clarity of Locke nor the enthusiasm of Rousseau.

John Locke followed his chief work in philosophy, *Essay Concerning Human Understanding,* with a homelier book, *Some Thoughts Concerning Education.** He was moved to write these notes on the rearing of children because "I myself have been con-

---

* J. Locke, *Some Thoughts Concerning Education* (4th Ed), London: Churchill, 1699. Locke, a lifelong bachelor and a dependent of the first Earl of Shaftesbury, wrote his advice on children for his friends, the Edward Clarkes. That he was a pre-Cadogan physician is seen in his recommendations for immediate postnatal care. "If the newborn baby is in a weak condition you can blow on it the smell of chewed onions and cloves; smear its nostrils

sulted of late by so many, who profess themselves at a loss how to breed their Children; and the early corruption of Youth, is now become so general a Complaint, that he cannot be thought wholly impertinent, who brings the Consideration of this Matter on the Stage . . ." In this book, Locke presents, as physician, his renowned briefs for wet feet, cold water, and regular defecation—"People that are very *loose*, have seldom strong Thoughts, or strong bodies"—and, as philosopher, his opinions on education. Much of *Some Thoughts* is given over to matters of curriculum; Locke felt strongly that too much time was spent on antique languages in English schools and too little on natural philosophy and the practical arts. He argues well for English and dancing, but the message that survives is contained in his injunctions to parents about early training, injunctions that derive from his *Essay* and his commitment to the mind as built from sensation. Two considerations, visible in the passage that follows, make Locke seem less of a revolutionary than his espousal of an empirical epistemology would have suggested. Foremost, he clearly is committed to the ultimate Rationality of man: ". . . the great Principle and Foundation of all Vertue and Worth, is placed in this, That a Man is able to *deny himself* his own Desires, cross his own Inclinations, and purely follow what Reason directs as best, tho' the appetite lean the other way." Locke is not altogether clear about where, in the experience of sense, we may find the claims of Reason. Then too, he often glides into the assumption of rather complex mental functions to account for the changes he observes in the child. Like every associationistic psychologist to follow him, Locke slips the restraint of a purely associationistic psychology and assigns cognitive functions, even of a congenital sort, to the person. In truth, Locke is far more willing to recognize organizing mental principles than some of his heirs

---

and lips with Cinnamon water; press warm slices of meat on its head and anus; wrap in bandages soaked in red wine and place in a bath composed of water or beer and fresh butter." Quoted in K. Dewhurst, *John Locke: Physician and Philosopher. A Medical Biography*, London: Wellcome Hist. Med. Library, 1963, pp. 259ff. The quotations in the next paragraphs are from *Some Thoughts*, pp. ii–iii, 34, 43, and 1–2, in order. To see how the associationistic philosophers wrestled the problem of mental faculties, read J. M. and G. Mandler. *Thinking: From Association to Gestalt*, New York: Wiley, 1964.

in psychology; on the first page of *Some Thoughts*, he foregoes a radical empiricism.

I confess, there are some Mens Constitutions of Body and Mind so vigorous, and well framed by Nature, that they need not much Assistance from others, but by the strength of their natural Genius, they are from their Cradles carried towards what is Excellent; and by the Privilege of their happy Constitutions, are able to do Wonders. . . .

But such men are rare indeed and the more usual case is the one in which education is determinate.

The little, and almost insensible Impressions on our tender Infancies, have very important and lasting Consequences: And there 'tis, as in the Fountains of some Rivers, where a gentle Application of the Hand turns the flexible waters into Channels, that make them take quite contrary Courses, and by this little direction given them at first in the Source, they receive different Tendencies, and arrive at last, at very remote and distant Places.

Locke's ambiguity about the nature of man shows at several points in the passages that follow, but nowhere so clearly as when he speaks of "these native Propensities, these Prevalencies of Constitution." When he speaks of moral training, however, the bell rings bright—Locke's injunctions on the handling of children's "Craving" are a two-hundred-year anticipation of Watson on the spoiled child. If we were to write a modern epigraph for *Some Thoughts*, it might well be "Beware the impulse."

*   *   *

John Locke (1632–1704)

Rewards, Reputation, and Curiosity

But if you take away the Rod on one hand, and these little Encouragements [for good behavior], which they are taken with, on

J. Locke, *Some Thoughts Concerning Education* (4th Ed., Enlarged). London: A. & J. Churchill, 1699, pp. 54–66, 101–108, 118–121. The first edition was published in 1693.

the other, How then (will you say) shall Children be govern'd? Remove Hope and Fear, and there is an end of all Discipline. I grant, that Good and Evil, *Reward* and *Punishment*, are the only Motives to a rational Creature; these are the Spur and Reins, whereby all Mankind is set on work, and guided, and therefore they are to be made use of to Children too. For I advise their Parents and Governors always to carry this in their Minds, that Children are to be treated as rational Creatures.

Rewards, I grant, and *Punishments* must be proposed to Children, if we intend to work upon them. The Mistake, I imagine, is, that those that are generally made use of, are *ill chosen*. The Pains and Pleasures of the Body are, I think, of ill consequence, when made the Rewards and Punishments, whereby Men would prevail on their Children: For, as I said before, they serve but to increase and strengthen those Inclinations which 'tis our business to subdue and master. What principle of Vertue do you lay in a Child, if you will redeem his Desires of one Pleasure, by the proposal of another? This is but to enlarge his Appetite, and instruct it to wander. If a Child cries for an unwholsome and dangerous Fruit, you purchase his quiet by giving him a less hurtful Sweet-meat. This perhaps may preserve his Health; but spoils his Mind, and sets that farther out of order. For here you only change the Object; but flatter still his *Appetite*, and allow that must be satisfied; Wherein, as I have shewed, lies the root of the Mischief: And till you bring him to be able to bear a denial of that Satisfaction, the Child may at present be quiet and orderly, but the Disease is not cured. By this way of proceeding you foment and cherish in him, that which is the Spring from whence all the Evil flows, which will be sure on the next occasion to break out again with more violence, give him stronger Longings, and you more trouble.

The *Rewards* and *Punishments* then, whereby we should keep Children in order, *are* quite of another kind; and of that force, that when we can get them once to work, the business, I think, is done, and the difficulty is over. *Esteem* and *Disgrace* are, of all others, the most powerful incentives to the Mind, when once it is brought to relish them. If you can once get into Children a love of Credit, and an apprehension of Shame and Disgrace, you have put into them the true Principle, which will constantly work, and incline them to the right. But it will be asked, how shall this be done?

I confess, it does not at first appearance want some difficulty; but yet I think it worth our while, to seek the ways (and practise them when found,) to attain this, which I look on as the great Secret of Education.

First, Children (earlier perhaps than we think) are very sensible of *Praise* and Commendation. They find a Pleasure in being esteemed, and valued, especially by their Parents, and those whom they depend on. If therefore the Father *caress and commend them, when they do well; shew a cold and neglectful Countenance to them upon doing ill;* And this accompanied by a like Carriage of the Mother, and all others that are about them, it will in a little Time make them sensible of the Difference; and this if constantly observed, I doubt not but will of it self work more than Threats or Blows, which lose their Force, when once grown common, and are of no use when Shame does not attend them; and therefore are to be forborn, and never to be used, but in the Case hereafter mentioned, when it is brought to Extremity.

But *Secondly,* To make the Sense of *Esteem* or *Disgrace* sink the deeper, and be of the more weight, other *agreeable or disagreeable Things should constantly accompany these different States;* not as particular Rewards and Punishments of this or that particular Action, but as necessarily belonging to, and constantly attending one, who by his Carriage has brought himself into a State of Disgrace or Commendation. By which Way of Treating them, Children may, as much as possible, be brought to conceive, that those that are commended, and in Esteem for doing well, will necessarily be beloved and cherished by every Body, and have all other good Things as a Consequence of it; and, on the other Side, when any one by Miscarriage falls into Dis-esteem, and cares not to preserve his Credit, he will unavoidably fall under Neglect and Contempt; and in that State, the Want of what ever might satisfie or delight him, will follow. In this way, the Objects of their Desires are made assisting to Vertue; when a settled Experience from the beginning teaches Children, that the Things they delight in belong to, and are to be enjoyed by those only, who are in a State of Reputation. If by these Means you can come once to shame them out of their Faults, (for besides that, I would willingly have no Punishment,) and make them in love with the Pleasure of being well thought on, you may turn them as you please, and they will be in love with all the ways of Vertue.

The great Difficulty here, is, I imagine, from the Folly and Perverseness of Servants, who are hardly to be hinder'd from crossing herein the Design of the Father and Mother. Children, discountenanced by their Parents for any Fault, find usually a Refuge and Relief in the Caresses of those foolish Flatterers, who thereby undo whatever the Parents endeavour to establish. When the Father or Mother looks sowre on the Child, every Body else should put on the same Coldness to him, and no Body give him Countenance; till Forgiveness asked, and a Reformation of his Fault, has set him right again, and restored him to his former Credit. If this were constantly observed, I guess there would be little need of Blows, or Chiding: Their own Ease and Satisfaction would quickly teach Children to court Commendation, and avoid doing that which they found every Body condemened, and they were sure to suffer for, without being chid or beaten. This would teach them Modesty and Shame; and they would quickly come to have a natural Abhorrence for that, which, they found, made them slighted and neglected by every Body. But how this Inconvenience from Servants is to be remedied, I must leave to Parents Care and Consideration. Only I think it of great Importance; And that they are very happy, who can get discreet People about their Children.

Frequent *Beating* or *Chiding* is therefore carefully *to be avoided*. Because this sort of Correction never produces any Good, farther than it serves to raise *Shame* and Abhorrence of the Miscarriage that brought it on them. And if the greatest part of the Trouble be not the Sense that they have done amiss, and the Apprehension that they have drawn on themselves the just Displeasure of their best Friends, the Pain of Whipping will work but an imperfect Cure. It only patches up for the present, and skins it over, but reaches not to the Bottom of the Sore. Ingenuous *Shame*, and the Apprehension of Displeasure, are the only true Restraint: These alone ought to hold the Reins, and keep the Child in order. But corporal Punishments must necessarily lose that Effect, and wear out the sense of *Shame*, where they frequently return. Shame in Children has the same Place that Modesty has in Women; which cannot be kept, and often transgressed against. And as to the Apprehension of *Displeasure in the Parents,* that will come to be very insignificant, if the Marks of that Displeasure quickly cease, and a few Blows fully expiate. Parents should well consider, what Faults in their Children are weighty enough to deserve the Declaration of their Anger: But when their Displeasure is once declared, to a Degree that carries any Punishment with it, they ought not presently to lay by the Severity of their Brows, but to restore their Children to their former Grace with some Difficulty; and delay a full reconciliation, till their Conformity, and more than ordinary Merit, make good their Amendment. If this be not so ordered, *Punishment* will by Familiarity, become a mere thing of Course, and lose all its influence: Offending, being chastised, and then forgiven, will be thought as natural and necessary as Noon, Night, and Morning following one another.

Concerning Reputation, I shall only remark this one Thing more of it; That though it be not the true Principle and Measure of Vertue, (for that is the Knowledge of a Man's Duty, and the Satisfaction it is to obey his Maker, in following the Dictates of that Light God has given him, with the Hopes of Acceptation and Reward) yet it is that, which comes nearest to it: And being the Testimony and Applause that other People's Reason, as it were by a common Consent, gives to vertuous and well-ordered Actions, it is the proper Guide and Encouragement of Children, till they grow able to judge for themselves, and to find what is right, by their own Reason.

This Consideration may direct Parents, how to manage themselves in reproving and commending their Children. The rebukes and chiding, which their Faults will sometimes make hardly to be avoided, should not only be in sober, grave, and unpassionate words, but also alone and in private: But the Commendations Children deserve, they should receive before others. This doubles the Reward, by spreading their Praise; but the Backwardness Parents shew in divulging their Faults, will make them set a greater Value on their Credit themselves, and teach them to be the more careful to preserve the good opinion of others, whilst they think they have it: But when being expos'd to Shame, by publishing their Miscarriages, they give it up for lost, that Check upon them is taken off; And they will be the less careful to preserve others good Thoughts of them, the more they suspect that their Reputation with them is already blemished.

But if a right Course be taken with Children, there will not be so much need of the Application of the common Rewards and Punishments as we imagine, and as the general Practice has established. For, All their innocent Folly, Playing, and *Childish Actions, are to be* left perfectly free and *unrestrained,* as far as they can consist with the Respect due to those that are present; and that with the greatest Allowance. If these Faults of their Age, rather than of the Children themselves, were, as they should be, left only to Time and Imitation, and riper Years to cure, Children would escape a great deal of mis-applied and useless Correction; which either fails to over-power the natural Disposition of their Childhood, and so, by an ineffectual Familiarity, makes Correction in other necessary Cases of less use; or else, if it be of force to restrain the natural gaiety of that Age, it serves only to spoil the Temper both of Body and Mind. If the Noise and Bustle of their Play prove at any Time inconvenient, or unsuitable to the Place or Company they are in, (which can only be where their Parents are,) a Look or a Word from the Father or Mother, if they have established the Authority they should, will be enough either to remove, or quiet them for that Time. But this Gamesome Humour, which is wisely adapted by Nature to their Age and Temper, should rather be encouraged, to keep up their Spirits, and improve their Strength and Health, than curbed, or restrained: And the chief Art is, to make all that they have to do, Sport and Play too.

And here give me Leave to take notice of one thing I think a Fault in the ordinary Method of Education; and that is, The Charging of Children's Memories, upon all Occasions, with *Rules* and Precepts, which they often do not understand, and constantly as soon forget as given. If it be some Action you would have done, or done otherwise; whenever they forget, or do it awkardly, make them do it over and over again, till they are perfect: Whereby you will get these two Advantages; *First,* To see whether it be an Action they can do, or is fit to be expected of them. For sometimes

Children are bid to do Things, which, upon Trial, they are found not able to do; and had need be taught and exercised in, before they are required to do them. But it is much easier for a Tutor to command, than to teach. *Secondly,* Another Thing got by it will be this; That by repeating the same Action, till it be grown habitual in them, the Performance will not depend on Memory, or Reflection, the Concomitant of Prudence and Age, and not of Childhood; but will be natural in them. Thus bowing to a Gentleman when he salutes him, and looking in his Face when he speaks to him, is by constant use as natural to a well-bred Man, as breathing; it requires no Thought, no Reflection. Having this way cured in your Child any Fault, it is cured for ever: And thus one by one you may weed them out all, and plant what Habits you please.

— — —

Having thus very early set up your Authority, and by the gentler Applications of it, shamed him out of what leads towards any immoral Habit; as soon as you have observed it in him (for I would by no means have chiding used, much less Blows, till Obstinacy and Incorrigibleness make it absolutely necessary) it will be fit to consider which way the natural make of his *Mind inclines* him. Some Men by the unalterable Frame of their Constitutions are *Stout,* others *Timorous,* some *Confident,* others *Modest, Tractable* or *Obstinate, Curious* or *Careless, Quick* or *Slow.* There are not more Differences in Mens Faces, and the outward Lineaments of their Bodies, than there are in the Makes and Tempers of their Minds; Only there is this Difference, that the distinguishing Characters of the Face, and the Lineaments of the Body grow more plain and visible with Time and Age, but the peculiar *Physiognomy of the Mind* is most discernable in Children, before Art and Cunning hath taught them to hide their Deformities, and conceal their ill Inclinations under a dissembled out-side.

Begin therefore betimes nicely to observe your Son's *Temper;* and that, when he is under least restraint, in his Play, and as he thinks out of your sight. See what are his *predominant Passions,* and *prevailing Inclinations;* whether he be Fierce or Mild, Bold or Bashful, Compassionate or Cruel, Open or Reserv'd, &c. For as these are different in him, so are your Methods to be different, and your Authority must hence take measures to apply it self different ways to him. These *native Propensities,* these Prevalencies of Constitution, are not to be cured by Rules, or a direct Contest; especially those of them that are the humbler and meaner sort, which proceed from fear, and lowness of Spirit; though with Art they may be much mended, and turned to good purposes. But this, be sure, after all is done, the Byass will always hang on that side, that Nature first placed it: And if you carefully observe the Characters of his Mind, now in the first Scenes of his Life, you will ever after be able to judge which way his Thoughts lean, and what he aims at, even hereafter, when, as he grows up, the Plot thickens, and he puts on several Shapes to act it.

I told you before, that Children love *Liberty;* and therefore they should be brought to do the things are fit for them, without feeling any restraint laid upon them. I now tell you, they love something more; and that is *Dominion*: And this is the first Original of most vicious Habits, that are ordinary and natural. This Love of *Power* and Dominion shews it self very early, and that in these Two Things.

We see Children (as soon almost as they are born, I am sure long before they can speak) cry, grow peevish, sullen, and out of humour, for nothing but to have their *Wills*: They would have their Desires submitted to by others; they contend for a ready compliance from all about them; especially from those that stand near, or beneath them in Age or Degree, as soon as they come to consider others with those distinctions.

Another thing wherein they shew their love of Dominion, is, their desire to have things to be theirs; they would have *Propriety* and Possession pleasing themselves with the Power which that seems to give, and the Right they thereby have, to dispose of them, as they please. He, that has not observed these two Humours working very betimes in Children, has taken little notice of their Actions: And he, who thinks that these two Roots of almost all the Injustice and Contention, that so disturb Humane Life, are not early to be weeded out, and contrary Habits introduced, neglects the proper Season to lay the Foundations of a good and worthy Man. To do this, I imagine, these following things may somewhat conduce.

That a Child should never be suffered to have what he *craves*, much less what he *cries for*, I had said, *or so much as speaks for*. But that being apt to be mis-understood, and interpreted as if I meant, a Child should never speak to his Parents for any thing; which will perhaps be thought to lay too great a Curb on the Minds of Children, to the prejudice of that Love and Affection which should be between them and their Parents; I shall Explain my self a little more particularly. It is fit that they should have liberty to declare their Wants to their Parents, and that with all tenderness they should be hearken'd to, and supplied, at least whilst they are very little. But 'tis one thing to say, I am hungry; another to say, I would have Roast-Meat. Having declared their Wants, their natural Wants, the pain they feel from Hunger, Thirst, Cold, or any other necessity of Nature; 'tis the Duty of their Parents, and those about them, to relieve them: But Children must leave it to the choice and ordering of their Parents, what they think properest for them, and how much; and must not be permitted to chuse for themselves, and say, I would have Wine, or White-bread; the very naming of it should make them lose it.

That which Parents should take care of here, is to distinguish between the Wants of Fancy, and those of Nature, which *Horace* has well taught them to do in this Verse.

Queis humana fibi doleat natura negatis.

Those are truly Natural Wants, which Reason alone, without some other Help, is not able to fence against, nor keep from disturbing us. The Pains of Sickness and Hurts, Hunger, Thirst and Cold; want of Sleep, and Rest or Relaxation of the Part wearied with Labour, are what all Men feel, and the best dispos'd Minds cannot but be sensible of their uneasiness: And therefore ought by fit Applications to seek their removal, though not with impatience, or over-great haste, upon the first approaches of them, where Delay does not threaten some irreparable harm. The Pains, that come from the Necessities of Nature, are Monitors to us, to beware of greater Mischiefs, which they are the Forerunners of: And therefore they must not be wholly neglected, nor strain'd too far. But yet the more Children can be enur'd to Hardships of this Kind, by a wise Care to make them Stronger in Body and Mind, the better it will be for them. I need not here give any Caution to keep within the Bounds of doing them good, and to take Care, that what Children are made to suffer, should neither break their Spirits, nor injure their Health; Parents being but too apt of themselves to incline, more than they should, to the softer Side.

But whatever Compliance the Necessities of Nature may require, the Wants of Fancy Children should never be gratified in, nor suffer'd to *mention*.

——— ——— ———

Curiosity in Children . . . is but an appetite after Knowledge; and therefore ought to be encouraged in them, not only as a good sign, but as the great Instrument Nature has provided, to remove that Ignorance they were born with; and which, without this busie *Inquisitiveness*, will make them dull and useless Creatures. The ways to encourage it, and keep it active and busie, are, I suppose, these following:

1. Not to check or discountenance any *Enquiries* he shall make, nor suffer them to be laugh'd at; but to *answer* all his *Questions*, and *explain* the Matters, he desires to know, so as to make them as much intelligible to him, as suits the capacity of his Age and Knowledge. But confound not his Understanding with Explications or Notions, that are above it; or with the variety of number of Things, that are not to his present purpose. Mark what 'tis his Mind aims at in the *Question*, and not what Words he expresses it in: And when you have informed and satisfied him in that, you shall see how his Thoughts will enlarge themselves, and how by fit Answers he may be led on farther than perhaps you could imagine. For Knowledge is grateful to the Understanding, as Light to the Eyes: Children are pleased and delighted with it exceedingly, especially if they see, that their *Enquiries* are regarded, and that their desire of Knowing is encouraged and commended. And I doubt not, but one great reason, why many Children abandon themselves wholly to silly Sports, and trifle away all their time insipidly, is, because they have found their *Curiosity* bauk'd and their *Enquiries* neglected. But had they been treated with

more Kindness and Respect, and their *Questions* answered, as they should, to their satisfaction; I doubt not but they would have taken more pleasure, in learning and improving their Knowledge, wherein there would be still newness and variety, which is what they are delighted with, than in returning over and over to the same Play and Play-things.

2. To this serious answering their *Questions*, and informing their Understandings, in what they desire, as if it were a matter that needed it, should be added some peculiar ways of *Commendation*. Let others whom they esteem, be told before their faces of the knowledge, they have in such and such things; and since we are all, even from our Cradles, vain and proud Creatures, let their Vanity be flattered with Things, that will do them good; and let their Pride set them on work on something which may turn to their advantage. Upon this ground you shall find, that there cannot be a greater spur to the attaining what you would have the eldest learn, and know himself, than to set him upon *teaching* it *his younger Brothers* and Sisters.

3. As Children's *Enquiries* are not to be slighted; so also great care is to be taken, that they *never* receive *Deceitful* and *Eluding Answers*. They easily perceive when they are slighted, or deceived; and quickly learn the trick of Neglect, Dissimulation, and Falshood, which they observe others to make use of. We are not to intrench upon Truth in any Conversation, but least of all with Children; since if we play false with them, we not only deceive their Expectation, and hinder their Knowledge, but corrupt their Innocence, and teach them the worst of Vices. They are Travellers newly arrived in a strange Country, of which they know nothing: We should therefore make Conscience not to mis-lead them. And though their *Questions* seem sometimes not very material, yet they should be seriously answer'd: For however they may appear to us (to whom they are long since known) *Enquiries* not worth the making; they are of moment to those, who are wholly ignorant. Children are strangers to all we are acquainted with; and all the things they meet with, are at first unknown to them, as they once were to us: And happy are they who meet with civil People, that will comply with their Ignorance, and help them to get out of it.

If you or I now should be set down in *Japan*, with all our Prudence and Knowledge about us, a Conceit whereof makes us perhaps so apt to slight the Thoughts and *Enquiries* of Children; should we, I say, be set down in *Japan*, we should, no doubt (if we would inform our selves of what is there to be known) ask a thousand Questions, which, to a supercilious or inconsiderate *Japaner*, would seem very idle and impertinent; though to us they would be very material and of importance to be resolved; and we should be glad to find a Man so complaisant and courteous, as to satisfie our Demands, and instruct our Ignorance.

When any new thing comes in their way, Children usually ask, the common *Question* of a Stranger: *What is it?* Whereby they ordinarily mean nothing but the Name; and therefore to tell them how it is call'd, is usually the proper Answer to that Demand. The next Question usually is: *What is it for?* And to this it should be answered truly and directly: The use of the thing should be told, and the way explained, how it serves to such a Purpose, as far as their Capacities can comprehend it. And so of any other Circumstances they shall ask about it; not turning them going, till you have given them all the satisfaction they are capable of; and so leading them by your Answers into farther Questions. And perhaps to a grown Man, such Conversation will not be altogether so idle and insignificant, as we are apt to imagine. The native and untaught Suggestions of inquisitive Children, do often offer things, that may set a considering Man's Thoughts on work. And I think there is frequently more to be learn'd from the unexpected Questions of a Child, than the Discourses of Men, who talk in a road, according to the Notions they have borrowed, and the Prejudices of their Education.

4. Perhaps it may not sometimes be amiss to excite their Curiosity, by bringing strange and new things in their way, on purpose to engage their Enquiry, and give them occasion to inform themselves about them: And if by chance their Curiosity leads them to ask, what they should not know; it is a great deal better to tell them plainly, That it is a thing that belongs not to them to know, than to pop them off with a Falshood, or a frivolous Answer.

*   *   *

It is possible to see Locke as conserving his prejudices about the nature of man in a philosophical scheme too narrow to hold them comfortably, with the result that he often had to escape his restrictions with sensible evasion. No such two-mindedness troubled Jean-Jacques Rousseau. A contemporary English reviewer of *Emile* spoke for his own time and for us.

The fault most generally observed in discourses on education, is a tendency to common place. Nothing, in fact, can be more trite, than the greatest part of the observations, which have been retailed upon that subject from Quintilian to monsieur Rollin. This is however the fault, into which the ingenious author of Emilius is, of all others, in the least danger of falling. To know what the received notions are upon any subject, is to know with certainty what those of Rousseau are not.*

Rousseau knew Locke's work as he knew Hume's but the work of other men were footholds Rousseau hardly needed for his ascents into genuine novelty. The child, rescued by physicians and reformers, liberated from innate ideas by Locke and Hume, is brought to the center of human affairs by Rousseau. If the beginning of child study as a discipline of knowledge needs a date, no better candidate can be found than 1762 when, from the fury of activity that produced *The Social Contract* and *The New Heloise* as well, Rousseau published *Emile, or On Education*. It is difficult to bring this long, often diffuse work into focus briefly, but Claparède, on the bicentennial of Rousseau's birth, defended the proposition that *Emile* contained, explicitly or by clear implication, all that was good and current in child psychology. By citation and inference, he assigned to Rousseau the invention or critical development of the following principles of child behavior.

1. The Law of Genetic Succession: The child develops naturally by passing through a number of stages that succeed one another in a constant order. . . .
2. The Law of Genetico-Functional Exercise: This law really implies two, which can be stated in the following way. (a) The exercise of a function is necessary to its development. . . . (b) The

* [Anonymous] *Annual Register*, 5, 1762, p. 225.

exercise of a function is necessary to the appearance of certain
other functions. . . .

3. The Law of Functional Adaptation: That action will be elicited
which serves to satisfy the need or the interest of the moment. . . .

4. The Law of Functional Autonomy: The child is not, considered
in himself, an imperfect being; he is a being adapted to circumstances which are appropriate for him; his mental activity is
appropriate to his needs, and his mental life is integrated. . . .

5. The Law of Individuality: Every person differs more or less,
in physical and psychological characteristics, from other
people. . . .*

This program, even though embedded in a work that alter-
natively is fantasy, tract, novel, and philosophical essay, excited
all of Europe with its originality and scope, was quickly translated
into English and German (there was a hunger for philosophy at
the end of the eighteenth century that has had no match since),
and became almost at once the basis of practical reforms in educational practice. As one commentator points out wryly, "Even
Kant, . . . in his home at Königsberg, having heard of the importance of *Emile*, decided to break his day's routine, more regular
than that of the town clock, to study the burthen of its message." †

Locke was willing to empty out the child, freeing him of the
essential tendency to sin, but he continued to see the child as an
incomplete adult who required the work of rational teachers to
bring him through the plain of childhood. For many thinkers
of Locke's time, the plain was infested with snarling animals and
dangerous pits—the temptations of Satan and the perversity of
man. Locke cleared the plain, leaving a theoretically empty child
and his Rational Tutor. We have seen of course that Locke's
"empty" child of theory is filled with interesting impulse by the
good doctor. Even so, Rousseau proposed far more radical revisions
in the character of childhood. Scattered through *Emile* are sug-

---

* E. Claperède, J.-J. Rousseau et la conception fonctionelle de l'enfance,
Revue de Metaphysique et de Morale, **20**, 1912, 391–416. The laws are given
on pp. 397ff.

† H. M. Pollard, *Pioneers of Popular Education, 1760–1850*, London: Murray,
1956.

gestions of three propositions (related to the ones isolated by Claparède) that overturned human thought about the child and laid down the ground of several debates that are with us still.

Perhaps the most important of Rousseau's postulates, not unknown to the ancients and developed in part by Comenius but never before so forcibly put, maintained that childhood is natural, of nature. Childhood is not a time set aside for adults to finish God's work, to bring the child (whether filled with sin or epistemologically and morally empty) steadily into closer match with adult behavior. Childhood is a time important in itself, a time when the behavior of the child is appropriate to the demands of his needs and his world. Whenever one looks at a child, newborn, in school, adolescent, one sees a whole human being, properly put together for his particular time. It is as well to consider the ape to be an incomplete man as to consider the child to be an incomplete adult. Moreover, Rousseau pointed out that the teacher and parent had better consider the integrity of the child; the educator who proceeded blind to the nature (the naturalness, the integrity) of childhood would produce an ill-made human being

But there is more revolutionary doctrine to come. After all, the Protestant Satanists of the time could conceive of childhood as naturally evil. Rousseau suggests that no great harm to the child or to society will result if the child grows with little adult supervision and direction! The child will become increasingly fit to live in the world, not by virtue of ceaseless vigilance on the part of his governors, but because Nature has endowed him with an order of development that ensures his healthy growth. More than that, the typical interventions of parents and teachers mar and distort the natural succession of the changes of childhood; the child that Man raises is almost certain to be inferior to the child that Nature raises. Rousseau is no believer in the uselessness of adult counsel and guidance nor does he maintain that the child can learn history, mathematics, and morality without assistance; but the teacher must accept the priority of natural development—of the normal succession of stages in growth, and especially of the coherence of the child's mind at every stage—and tailor his pedagogy to the child. Locke is no more an epistemological empiricist than Rousseau is, but the differences in educational tactics are profound.

For Rousseau, the child may be morally neutral, although he thinks him morally sound, but the child has within him an inevitability of development that does not fit at all well with the views of the radical empiricists, particularly among the later psychologists. Isolated from the world, Emile encounters Nature with the help of his guide (never his governor) and grows.

In yet another innovation ascribable to Rousseau, or a restatement so clear and winning as to be novel, the beginnings of another modern debate can be seen. Not only is childhood a time of nature and the child pregnant with inevitable development (barring the perverting intervention of the usual adult didactics); the relation of child to world was, for Rousseau, an active one. The child engages his environment, using it to suit his interests. He fits his abilities to the world in play and in the solving of problems, not as a passive recipient of the tutor's instruction nor as a victim of Hume's contingencies, but as a busy, testing, motivated explorer. Knowledge is not an invention of adults poured into willing or unwilling vessels; it is joint construction of the child in nature and the natural world. From the end of the eighteenth century until our own day, the active searching child, setting his own problems, stands in contrast to the receptive one, even the one equipped with curiosity, on whom society fixes its stamp.

A glance back to Locke's words, particularly those on curiosity, will serve to lessen somewhat the disjunction between him and Rousseau, but their attitude toward the expression of impulse and the place of adult society in the construction of the child place them irreconcilably apart. Moreover, it is not unfair to see in these men the antique and continuing argument between the psychologist who sees abstract truth and fits it to man and the psychologist who sees man and his variety too clearly to fit him to truth. The abstract thinker and theorist inevitably advances our ability to predict, even to understand, behavior, but the Montaignes, Rousseaus, and Halls do not let the theorist relax, presenting him always with the exceptional instance, the unpredicted event, the child untabulated.

*   *   *

Jean-Jacques Rousseau (1712–1778)

The Child in Nature

God makes all things good; man meddles with them and they become evil. He forces one soil to yield the products of another, one tree to bear another's fruit. He confuses and confounds time, place, and natural condition. He mutilates his dog, his horse, and his slave. He destroys and defaces all things; he loves all that is deformed and monstrous; he will have nothing as nature made it, not even man himself, who must learn his paces like a saddlehorse, and be shaped to his master's taste like the trees in his garden.

— — —

We are born capable of learning, but knowing nothing, perceiving nothing. The mind, bound up within imperfect and half grown organs, is not even aware of its own existence. The movements and cries of the new-born child are purely reflex, without knowledge or will.

Suppose a child born with the size and strength of manhood, entering upon life full grown like Pallas from the brain of Jupiter; such a child-man would be a perfect idiot, an automaton, a statue without motion and almost without feeling; he would see and hear nothing, he would recognise no one, he could not turn his eyes towards what he wanted to see; not only would he perceive no external object, he would not even be aware of sensation through the several sense-organs. His eye would not perceive colour, his ear sounds, his body would be unaware of contact with neigh-

J.-J. Rousseau, *Emile, or On Education* (Translated by Barbara Foxley). London: Dent, 1911, pp. 5, 28–29, 55–61, 70–74, 89–98, 124–127, 134–135, 147–148, 172–179. The first French edition was published in 1762; the first English edition in 1763.

bouring bodies, he would not even know he had a body, what his hands handled would be in his brain alone; all his sensations would be united in one place, they would exist only in the common "sensorium," he would have only one idea, that of self, to which he would refer all his sensations; and this idea, or rather this feeling, would be the only thing in which he excelled an ordinary child.

This man, full grown at birth, would also be unable to stand on his feet, he would need a long time to learn how to keep his balance; perhaps he would not even be able to try to do it, and you would see the big strong body left in one place like a stone, or creeping and crawling like a young puppy.

He would feel the discomfort of bodily needs without knowing what was the matter and without knowing how to provide for these needs. There is no immediate connection between the muscles of the stomach and those of the arms and legs to make him take a step towards food, or stretch a hand to seize it, even were he surrounded with it; and as his body would be full grown and his limbs well developed he would be without the perpetual restlessness and movement of childhood, so that he might die of hunger without stirring to seek food. However little you may have thought about the order and development of our knowledge, you cannot deny that such a one would be in the state of almost primitive ignorance and stupidity natural to man before he has learnt anything from experience or from his fellows.

We know then, or we may know, the point of departure from which we each start towards the usual level of understanding; but who knows the other extreme? Each progresses more or less according to his genius, his taste, his needs, his talents, his zeal, and his opportunities for using them. No philosopher, so far as I know, has dared to say to man, "Thus far shalt thou go and no further." We know not what nature allows us to be, none of us has measured the possible difference between man and man. Is there a mind so dead that this thought has never kindled it, that has never said in his pride, "How much have I already done, how much more may I achieve? Why should I lag behind my fellows?"

As I said before, man's education begins at birth; before he can speak or understand he is learning. Experience precedes instruction; when he recognises his nurse he has learnt much. The knowledge of the most ignorant man would surprise us if we had followed his course from birth to the present time. If all human knowledge were divided into two parts, one common to all, the other peculiar to the learned, the latter would seem very small compared with the former. But we scarcely heed this general experience, because it is acquired before the age of reason. Moreover, knowledge only attracts attention by its rarity, as in algebraic equations common factors count for nothing. Even animals learn much. They have senses and must learn to use them; they have needs, they must learn to satisfy them; they must learn to eat, walk, or fly. Quadrupeds which can stand on their feet from the first cannot walk for all that; from their first attempts it is clear that they lack confidence. Canaries who escape from their cage are unable to fly, having never used their wings. Living and feeling creatures are always learning. If plants could walk they would need senses and knowledge, else their species would die out. The child's first mental experiences are purely affective, he is only aware of pleasure and pain; it takes him a long time to acquire the definite sensations which show him things outside himself, but before these things present and withdraw themselves, so to speak, from his sight, taking size and shape for him, the recurrence of emotional experiences is beginning to subject the child to the rule of habit.

— — —

Treat your scholar according to his age. Put him in his place from the first, and keep him in it, so that he no longer tries to leave it. Then before he knows what goodness is, he will be practising its chief lesson. Give him no orders at all, absolutely none. Do not even let him think that you claim any authority over him. Let him only know that he is weak and you are strong, that his condition and yours puts him at your mercy; let this be perceived, learned, and felt. Let him early find upon his proud neck, the heavy yoke which nature has imposed upon us, the heavy yoke of necessity, under which every finite being must bow. Let him find this necessity in things, not in the caprices of man; let the curb be force, not authority. If there is something he should not do, do not forbid him, but prevent him without explanation or reasoning; what you give him, give it at his first word without prayers or entreaties, above all without conditions. Give willingly, refuse unwillingly, but let your refusal be irrevocable; let no entreaties move you; let your "No," once uttered, be a wall of brass, against which the child may exhaust his strength some five or six times, but in the end he will try no more to overthrow it.

Thus you will make him patient, equable, calm, and resigned, even when he does not get all he wants; for it is in man's nature to bear patiently with the nature of things but not with the ill-will of another. A child never rebels against, "There is none left," unless he thinks the reply is false. Moreover, there is no middle course; you must either make no demands on him at all, or else you must fashion him to perfect obedience. The worst education of all is to leave him hesitating between his own will and yours, constantly disputing whether you or he is master; I would rather a hundred times that he were master.

It is very strange that ever since people began to think about education they should have hit upon no other way of guiding children than emulation, jealousy, envy, vanity, greediness, base cowardice, all the most dangerous passions, passions ever ready to ferment, ever prepared to corrupt the soul even before the body is full-grown. With every piece of precocious instruction which you try to force into their minds you plant a vice in the depths of their hearts; foolish teachers think they are doing wonders when they are making their scholars wicked in order to teach them what goodness is, and then they tell us seriously, "Such is man." Yes, such is man, as you have made him. Every means has been tried except one, the very one which might succeed—well-regulated liberty. Do not undertake to bring up a child if you cannot guide him merely by the laws of what can or cannot be. The limits of the possible and the impossible are alike unknown to him, so they can be extended or contracted around him at your will. Without a murmur he is restrained, urged on, held back, by the hands of necessity alone; he is made adaptable and teachable by the mere force of things, without any chance for vice to spring up in him; for passions do not arise so long as they have accomplished nothing.

Give your scholar no verbal lessons; he should be taught by experience alone; never punish him, for he does not know what it is to do wrong; never make him say, "Forgive me," for he does not know how to do you wrong. Wholly unmoral in his actions, he can do nothing morally wrong, and he deserves neither punishment nor reproof.

— — —

May I venture at this point to state the greatest, the most important, the most useful rule of education? It is: Do not save time, but lose it. I hope that every-day readers will excuse my paradoxes; you cannot avoid paradox if you think for yourself, and whatever you may say I would rather fall into paradox than into prejudice. The most dangerous period in human life lies between birth and the age of twelve. It is the time when errors and vices spring up, while as yet there is no means to destroy them; when the means of destruction are ready, the roots have gone too deep to be pulled up. If the infant sprang at one bound from its mother's breast to the age of reason, the present type of education would be quite suitable, but its natural growth calls for quite a different training. The mind should be left undisturbed till its faculties have developed; for while it is blind it cannot see the torch you offer it, nor can it follow through the vast expanse of ideas a path so faintly traced by reason that the best eyes can scarcely follow it.

Therefore the education of the earliest years should be merely negative. It consists, not in teaching virtue or truth, but in preserving the heart from vice and from the spirit of error. If only you could let well alone, and get others to follow your example; if you could bring your scholar to the age of twelve strong and healthy, but unable to tell his right hand from his left, the eyes of his understanding would be open to reason as soon as you began to teach him. Free from prejudices and free from habits, there would be nothing in him to counteract the effects of your labours. In your hands he would soon become the wisest of men; by doing nothing to begin with, you would end with a prodigy of education.

Reverse the usual practice and you will almost always do right. Fathers and teachers who want to make the child, not a child but a man of learning, think it never too soon to scold, correct, reprove, threaten, bribe, teach, and reason. Do better than they; be reasonable, and do not reason with your pupil, more especially do not try to make him approve what he dislikes; for if reason is always connected with disagreeable matters, you make it distasteful to him, you discredit it at an early age in a mind not yet ready to understand it. Exercise his body, his limbs, his senses, his strength, but keep his mind idle as long as you can. Distrust all opinions which appear before the judgment to discriminate between them. Restrain and ward off strange impressions; and to prevent the birth of evil do not hasten to do well, for goodness is only possible when enlightened by reason. Regard all delays as so much time gained; you have achieved much, you approach the boundary without loss. Leave childhood to ripen in your children. In a word, beware of giving anything they need to-day if it can be deferred without danger to to-morrow.

There is another point to be considered which confirms the suitability of this method: it is the child's individual bent, which must be thoroughly known before we can choose the fittest moral training. Every mind has its own form, in accordance with which it must be controlled; and the success of the pains taken depends largely on the fact that he is controlled in this way and no other. Oh, wise man, take time to observe nature; watch your scholar well before you say a word to him; first leave the germ of his character free to show itself, do not constrain him in anything, the better to see him as he really is.

— — —

Zealous teachers, be simple, sensible, and reticent; be in no hurry to act unless to prevent the actions of others. Again and again I say, reject, if it may be, a good lesson for fear of giving a bad one. Beware of playing the tempter in this world, which nature intended as an earthly paradise for men, and do not attempt to give the innocent child the knowledge of good and evil; since you cannot prevent the child learning by what he sees outside himself, restrict your own efforts to impressing those examples on his mind in the form best suited for him.

The explosive passions produce a great effect upon the child when he sees them; their outward expression is very marked; he is struck by this and his attention is arrested. Anger especially is so noisy in its rage that it is impossible not to perceive it if you are within reach. You need not ask yourself whether this is an opportunity for a pedagogue to frame a fine disquisition. What! no fine disquisition, nothing, not a word! Let the child come to you; impressed by what he has seen, he will not fail to ask you questions. The answer is easy; it is drawn from the very things which have appealed to his senses. He sees a flushed face, flashing eyes, a threatening gesture, he hears cries; everything shows that the body is ill at ease. Tell him plainly, without affectation or mystery, "This poor man is ill, he is in a fever." You may take the opportunity of giving him in a few words some idea of disease and its effects; for that too belongs to nature, and is one of the bonds of necessity which he must recognise. By means of this idea, which is not false in itself, may he not early acquire a certain aversion to giving way to excessive passions, which he regards as diseases; and do you not think that such a notion, given at the right moment, will produce a more wholesome effect than the most tedious sermon? But consider the after effects of this idea; you have authority, if ever you find it necessary, to treat the rebellious child as a sick child; to keep him in his room, in bed if need be, to diet him, to make him afraid of his growing vices, to make him hate and dread them without ever regarding as a punishment the strict measures you will perhaps have to use for his recovery. If it happens that you yourself in a moment's heat depart from the calm and self-control which you should aim at, do not try to conceal your fault, but tell him frankly, with a gentle reproach, "My dear, you have hurt me."

Moreover, it is a matter of great importance that no notice should be taken in his presence of the quaint sayings which result from the simplicity of the ideas in which he is brought up, nor should they be quoted in a way he can understand. A foolish laugh may destroy six months' work and do irreparable damage for life. I cannot repeat too often that to control the child one must often control oneself.

— — —

The apparent ease with which children learn is their ruin. You fail to see that this very facility proves that they are not learning. Their shining, polished brain reflects, as in a mirror, the things you show them, but nothing sinks in. The child remembers the words and the ideas are reflected back; his hearers understand them, but to him they are meaningless.

Although memory and reason are wholly different faculties, the one does not really develop apart from the other. Before the age of reason the child receives images, not ideas; and there is this difference between them: images are merely the pictures of external objects, while ideas are notions about those objects determined by their relations. An image when it is recalled may exist by itself in the mind, but every idea implies other ideas. When we image we merely perceive, when we reason we compare. Our sensations are merely passive, our notions or ideas spring from an active principle which judges. . . .

I maintain, therefore, that as children are incapable of judging, they have no true memory. They retain sounds, form, sensation, but rarely ideas, and still more rarely relations. You tell me they acquire some rudiments of geometry, and you think you prove your case; not so, it is mine you prove; you show that far from being able to reason themselves, children are unable to retain the reasoning of others; for if you follow the method of these little geometricians you will see they only retain the exact impression of the figure and the terms of the demonstration. They cannot meet the slightest new objection; if the figure is reversed they can do nothing. All their knowledge is on the sensation-level, nothing has penetrated to their understanding. Their memory is little better than their other powers, for they always have to learn over again, when they are grown up, what they learnt as children.

I am far from thinking, however, that children have no sort of reason. On the contrary, I think they reason very well with regard to things that affect their actual and sensible well-being. But people are mistaken as to the extent of their information, and they attribute to them knowledge they do not possess, and make them reason about things they cannot understand. Another mistake is to try to turn their attention to matters which do not concern them in the least, such as their future interest, their happiness when they are grown up, the opinion people will have of them when they are men—terms which are absolutely meaningless when addressed to creatures who are entirely without foresight. But all the forced studies of these poor little wretches are directed towards matters utterly remote from their minds. You may judge how much attention they can give to them.

The pedagogues, who make a great display of the teaching they give their pupils, are paid to say just the opposite; yet their actions show that they think just as I do. For what do they teach? Words! words! words! Among the various sciences they boast of teaching their scholars, they take good care never to choose those which might be really useful to them, for then they would be compelled to deal with things and would fail utterly; the sciences they choose are those we seem to know when we know their technical terms—heraldry, geography, chronology, languages, etc., studies so remote from man, and even more remote from the child, that it is a wonder if he can ever make any use of any part of them.

You will be surprised to find that I reckon the study of languages among the useless lumber of education; but you must remember that I am speaking of the studies of the earliest years, and whatever you may say, I do not believe any child under twelve or fifteen ever really acquired two languages.

— — —

In any study whatsoever the symbols are of no value without the idea of the things symbolized. Yet the education of the child is confined to those symbols, while no one ever succeeds in making him understand the thing signified. You think you are teaching him what the world is like; he is only learning the map; he is taught the names of towns, countries, rivers, which have no existence for him except on the paper before him. I remember seeing a geography somewhere which began with: "What is the world?"—"A sphere of cardboard." That is the child's geography. I maintain that after two years' work with the globe and cosmography, there is not a single ten-year-old child who could find his way from Paris to Saint Denis by the help of the rules he has learnt. I maintain that not one of these children could find his way by the map

about the paths on his father's estate without getting lost. These
are the young doctors who can tell us the position of Pekin, Ispa-
han, Mexico, and every country in the world.

— — —

As a man's first natural impulse is to measure himself with his
environment, to discover in every object he sees those sensible
qualities which may concern himself, so his first study is a kind of
experimental physics for his own preservation. He is turned away
from this and sent to speculative studies before he has found his
proper place in the world. While his delicate and flexible limbs
can adjust themselves to the bodies upon which they are intended
to act, while his senses are keen and as yet free from illusions,
then is the time to exercise both limbs and senses in their proper
business. It is the time to learn to perceive the physical relations
between ourselves and things. Since everything that comes into
the human mind enters through the gates of sense, man's first
reason is a reason of sense-experience. It is this that serves as a
foundation for the reason of the intelligence; our first teachers in
natural philosophy are our feet, hands, and eyes. To substitute
books for them does not teach us to reason, it teaches us to use the
reason of others rather than our own; it teaches us to believe much
and know little.

Before you can practise an art you must first get your tools; and
if you are to make good use of those tools, they must be fashioned
sufficiently strong to stand use. To learn to think we must therefore exercise our limbs, our senses, and our bodily organs, which
are the tools of the intellect; and to get the best use out of these
tools, the body which supplies us with them must be strong and
healthy. Not only is it quite a mistake that true reason is developed
apart from the body, but it is a good bodily constitution which
makes the workings of the mind easy and correct.

While I am showing how the child's long period of leisure should
be spent, I am entering into details which may seem absurd. You
will say, "This is a strange sort of education, and it is subject to
your own criticism, for it only teaches what no one needs to learn.
Why spend your time in teaching what will come of itself without

care or trouble? Is there any child of twelve who is ignorant of all you wish to teach your pupil, while he also knows what his master has taught him."

Gentlemen, you are mistaken. I am teaching my pupil an art the acquirement of which demands much time and trouble, an art which your scholars certainly do not possess; it is the art of being ignorant; for the knowledge of any one who only thinks he knows, what he really does know is a very small matter. You teach science; well and good; I am busy fashioning the necessary tools for its acquisition. Once upon a time, they say the Venetians were displaying the treasures of the Cathedral of Saint Mark to the Spanish ambassador; the only comment he made was, "Qui non c'e la radice." When I see a tutor showing off his pupil's learning I am always tempted to say the same to him.

Every one who has considered the matter of life among the ancients, attributes the strength of body and mind by which they are distinguished from the men of our own day to their gymnastic exercises. The stress laid by Montaigne upon this opinion, shows that it had made a great impression on him; he returns to it again and again. Speaking of a child's education he says, "To strengthen the mind you must harden the muscles; by training the child to labour you train him to suffering; he must be broken in to the hardships of gymnastic exercises to prepare him for the hardships of dislocations, colics, and other bodily ills." The philosopher Locke, the worthy Rollin, the learned Fleury, the pedant De Crouzas, differing as they do so widely from one another, are agreed in this one matter of sufficient bodily exercise for children. This is the wisest of their precepts, and the one which is certain to be neglected. I have already dwelt sufficiently on its importance, and as better reasons and more sensible rules cannot be found than those in Locke's book, I will content myself with referring to it, after taking the liberty of adding a few remarks of my own.

The limbs of a growing child should be free to move easily in his clothing; nothing should cramp their growth or movement; there should be nothing tight, nothing fitting closely to the body, no belts of any kind. The French style of dress, uncomfortable and unhealthy for a man, is especially bad for children. The stagnant humours, whose circulation is interrupted, putrify in a state of inaction, and this process proceeds more rapidly in an inactive and sedentary life; they become corrupt and give rise to scurvy; this disease, which is continually on the increase among us, was almost unknown to the ancients, whose way of dressing and living protected them from it. The hussar's dress, far from correcting this fault, increases it, and compresses the whole of the child's body, by way of dispensing with a few bands. The best plan is to keep children in frocks as long as possible and then to provide them with loose clothing, without trying to define the shape which is only another way of deforming it. Their defects of body and mind may all be traced to the same source, the desire to make men of them before their time.

— — —

A child is smaller than a man; he has not the man's strength or reason, but he sees and hears as well or nearly as well; his sense of taste is very good, though he is less fastidious, and he distinguishes scents as clearly though less sensuously. The senses are the first of our faculties to mature; they are those most frequently overlooked or neglected.

To train the senses it is not enough merely to use them; we must learn to judge by their means, to learn to feel, so to speak; for we cannot touch, see, or hear, except as we have been taught.

There is a mere natural and mechanical use of the senses which strengthens the body without improving the judgment. It is all very well to swim, run, jump, whip a top, throw stones; but have we nothing but arms and legs? Have we not eyes and ears as well; and are not these organs necessary for the use of the rest? Do not merely exercise the strength, exercise all the senses by which it is guided; make the best use of every one of them, and check the results of one by the other. Measure, count, weigh, compare. Do not use force till you have estimated the resistance; let the estimation of the effect always precede the application of the means. Get the child interested in avoiding insufficient or superfluous efforts. If in this way you train him to calculate the effects of all his movements, and to correct his mistakes by experience, is it not clear that the more he does the wiser he will become?

Take the case of moving a heavy mass; if he takes too long a lever, he will waste his strength; if it is too short, he will not have strength enough; experience will teach him to use the very stick he needs. This knowledge is not beyond his years. Take, for example, a load to be carried; if he wants to carry as much as he can, and not to take up more than he can carry, must he not calculate the weight by the appearance? Does he know how to compare masses of like substance and different size, or to choose between masses of the same size and different substances? he must set to work to compare their specific weights. I have seen a young man, very highly educated, who could not be convinced, till he had tried it, that a bucket full of blocks of oak weighed less than the same bucket full of water.

All our senses are not equally under our control. One of them, touch, is always busy during our waking hours; it is spread over the whole surface of the body, like a sentinel ever on the watch to warn us of anything which may do us harm. Whether we will or not, we learn to use it first of all by experience, by constant practice, and therefore we have less need for special training for it. Yet we know that the blind have a surer and more delicate sense of touch than we, for not being guided by the one sense, they are forced to get from the touch what we get from sight. Why, then, are not we trained to walk as they do in the dark, to recognise what we touch, to distinguish things about us; in a word, to do at night and in the dark what they do in the daytime without sight? We are better off than they while the sun shines; in the dark it is their turn to be our guide. We are blind half our time, with this difference: the really blind always know what to do, while we are afraid to stir in the dark. We have lights, you say. What! always artificial aids. Who can insure that they will always be at hand when required. I had rather Emile's eyes were in his finger tips, than in the chandler's shop.

— — —

The chief drawback to this early education is that it is only appreciated by the wise; to vulgar eyes the child so carefully educated is nothing but a rough little boy. A tutor thinks rather of the advantage to himself than to his pupil; he makes a point of showing that there has been no time wasted; he provides his pupil with goods which can be readily displayed in the shop window, accomplishments which can be shown off at will; no matter whether they are useful, provided they are easily seen. Without choice or discrimination he loads his memory with a pack of rubbish. If the child is to be examined he is set to display his wares; he spreads them out, satisfies those who behold them, packs up his bundle and goes his way. My pupil is poorer, he has no bundle to display, he has only himself to show. Now neither child nor man can be read at a glance. Where are the observers who can at once discern the characteristics of this child? There are such people, but they are few and far between; among a thousand fathers you will scarcely find one.

Too many questions are tedious and revolting to most of us and especially to children. After a few minutes their attention flags, they cease to listen to your everlasting questions and reply at random. This way of testing them is pedantic and useless; a chance word will often show their sense and intelligence better than much talking, but take care that the answer is neither a matter of chance nor yet learnt by heart. A man must needs have a good judgment if he is to estimate the judgment of a child.

I heard the late Lord Hyde tell the following story about one of his friends. He had returned from Italy after a three years' absence, and was anxious to test the progress of his son, a child of nine or ten. One evening he took a walk with the child and his tutor across a level space where the schoolboys were flying their kites. As they went, the father said to his son, "Where is the kite that casts this shadow?" Without hesitating and without glancing upwards the child replied, "Over the high road." "And indeed," said Lord Hyde, "the high road was between us and the sun." At these words, the father kissed his child, and having finished his examination he departed. The next day he sent the tutor the papers settling an annuity on him in addition to his salary.

What a father! and what a promising child! The question is exactly adapted to the child's age, the answer is perfectly simple; but see what precision it implies in the child's judgment. Thus did the pupil of Aristotle master the famous steed which no squire had ever been able to tame.

— — —

Remember that this is the essential point in my method—Do not teach the child many things, but never to let him form inaccurate or confused ideas. I care not if he knows nothing provided he is not mistaken, and I only acquaint him with truths to guard him against the errors he might put in their place. Reason and judgment come slowly, prejudices flock to us in crowds, and from these he must be protected. But if you make science itself your object, you embark on an unfathomable and shoreless ocean, an ocean strewn with reefs from which you will never return. When I see a man in love with knowledge, yielding to its charms and flitting from one branch to another unable to stay his steps, he seems to me like a child gathering shells on the sea-shore, now picking them up, then throwing them aside for others which he sees beyond them, then taking them again, till overwhelmed by their number and unable to choose between them, he flings them all away and returns empty handed.

Time was long during early childhood; we only tried to pass our time for fear of using it ill; now it is the other way; we have not time enough for all that would be of use. The passions, remember, are drawing near, and when they knock at the door your scholar will have no ear for anything else. The peaceful age of intelligence is so short, it flies so swiftly, there is so much to be done, that it is madness to try to make your child learned. It is not your business to teach him the various sciences, but to give him a taste for them and methods of learning them when this taste is more mature. That is assuredly a fundamental principle of all good education.

This is also the time to train him gradually to prolonged attention to a given object; but this attention should never be the result of constraint, but of interest or desire; you must be very careful that it is not too much for his strength, and that it is not carried to the point of tedium. Watch him, therefore, and whatever happens, stop before he is tired, for it matters little what he learns; it does matter that he should do nothing against his will.

If he asks questions let your answers be enough to whet his curiosity but not enough to satisfy it; above all, when you find him talking at random and overwhelming you with silly questions instead of asking for information, at once refuse to answer; for it is clear that he no longer cares about the matter in hand, but wants to make you a slave to his questions. Consider his motives rather than his words. This warning, which was scarcely needed before, becomes of supreme importance when the child begins to reason.

— — —

I hate books; they only teach us to talk about things we know nothing about. Hermes, they say, engraved the elements of science on pillars lest a deluge should destroy them. Had he imprinted them on men's hearts they would have been preserved by tradition. Well-trained minds are the pillars on which human knowledge is most deeply engraved.

Is there no way of correlating so many lessons scattered through so many books, no way of focussing them on some common object, easy to see, interesting to follow, and stimulating even to a child? Could we but discover a state in which all man's needs appear in such a way as to appeal to the child's mind, a state in which the ways of providing for these needs are as easily developed, the simple and stirring portrayal of this state should form the earliest training of the child's imagination.

Eager philosopher, I see your own imagination at work. Spare yourself the trouble; this state is already known, it is described, with due respect to you, far better than you could describe it, at least with greater truth and simplicity. Since we must have books, there is one book which, to my thinking, supplies the best treatise on an education according to nature. This is the first book Emile will read; for a long time it will form his whole library, and it will always retain an honoured place. It will be the text to which all our talks about natural science are but the commentary. It will serve to test our progress towards a right judgment, and it will always be read with delight, so long as our taste is unspoilt. What is this wonderful book? Is it Aristotle? Pliny? Buffon? No; it is *Robinson Crusoe*.

Robinson Crusoe on his island, deprived of the help of his fellow-men, without the means of carrying on the various arts, yet finding food, preserving his life, and procuring a certain amount of comfort; this is the thing to interest people of all ages, and it can be made attractive to children in all sorts of ways. We shall thus make a reality of that desert island which formerly served as an illustration. The condition, I confess, is not that of a social being, nor is it in all probability Emile's own condition, but he should use it as a standard of comparison for all other conditions. The surest way to raise him above prejudice and to base his judgments on the true relations of things, is to put him in the place of a solitary man, and to judge all things as they would be judged by such a man in relation to their own utility.

This novel, stripped of irrelevant matter, begins with Robinson's shipwreck on his island, and ends with the coming of the ship which bears him from it, and it will furnish Emile with material, both for work and play, during the whole period we are considering. His head should be full of it, he should always be busy with his castle, his goats, his plantations. Let him learn in detail, not from books but from things, all that is necessary in such a case. Let him think he is Robinson himself; let him see himself clad in skins, wearing a tall cap, a great cutlass, all the grotesque get-up of Robinson Crusoe, even to the umbrella which he will scarcely need. He should anxiously consider what steps to take; will this or that be wanting. He should examine his hero's conduct; has he omitted nothing; is there nothing he could have done better? He should carefully note his mistakes, so as not to fall into them himself in similar circumstances, for you may be sure he will plan out just such a settlement for himself. This is the genuine castle in the air of this happy age, when the child knows no other happiness but food and freedom.

— — —

How swiftly life passes here below! The first quarter of it is gone before we know how to use it; the last quarter finds us incapable of enjoying life. At first we do not know how to live; and when we know how to live it is too late. In the interval between these two useless extremes we waste three-fourths of our time sleeping, working, sorrowing, enduring restraint and every kind of suffering. Life is short, not so much because of the short time it lasts, but because we are allowed scarcely any time to enjoy it. In vain is there a long interval between the hour of death and that of birth; life is still too short, if this interval is not well spent.

We are born, so to speak, twice over; born into existence, and born into life; born a human being, and born a man. Those who regard woman as an imperfect man are no doubt mistaken, but they have external resemblance on their side. Up to the age of puberty children of both sexes have little to distinguish them to the eye, the same face and form, the same complexion and voice, everything is the same; girls are children and boys are children; one name is enough for creatures so closely resembling one another. Males whose development is arrested preserve this resemblance all their lives; they are always big children; and women who never lose this resemblance seem in many respect never to be more than children.

But, speaking generally, man is not meant to remain a child. He leaves childhood behind him at the time ordained by nature; and this critical moment, short enough in itself, has far-reaching consequences.

As the roaring of the waves precedes the tempest, so the murmur of rising passions announces this tumultuous change; a suppressed excitement warns us of the approaching danger. A change of temper, frequent outbreaks of anger, a perpetual stirring of the mind, make the child almost ungovernable. He becomes deaf to the voice he used to obey; he is a lion in a fever; he distrusts his keeper and refuses to be controlled.

With the moral symptoms of a changing temper there are perceptible changes in appearance. His countenance develops and takes the stamp of his character; the soft and sparse down upon his checks becomes darker and stiffer. His voice grows hoarse or rather he loses it altogether. He is neither a child nor a man and cannot speak like either of them. His eyes, those organs of the soul which till now were dumb, find speech and meaning; a kindling fire illumines them, there is still a sacred innocence in their ever brightening glance, but they have lost their first meaningless expression; he is already aware that they can say too much; he is beginning to learn to lower his eyes and blush, he is becoming sensitive, though he does not know what it is that he feels; he is uneasy without knowing why. All this may happen gradually and give you time enough; but if his keenness becomes impatience, his eagerness madness, if he is angry and sorry all in a moment, if he weeps without cause, if in the presence of objects which are beginning to be a source of danger his pulse quickens and his eyes sparkle, if he trembles when a woman's hand touches his, if he is troubled or timid in her presence, O Ulysses, wise Ulysses! have a care! The passages you closed with so much pains are open; the winds are unloosed; keep your hand upon the helm or all is lost.

This is the second birth I spoke of; then it is that man really enters upon life; henceforth no human passion is a stranger to him. Our efforts so far have been child's play, now they are of the greatest importance. This period when education is usually finished is just the time to begin; but to explain this new plan properly, let us take up our story where we left it.

Our passions are the chief means of self-preservation; to try to destroy them is therefore as absurd as it is useless; this would be to overcome nature, to reshape God's handiwork. If God bade man annihilate the passions he has given him, God would bid him be and not be; He would contradict himself. He has never given such a foolish commandment, there is nothing like it written on the heart of man, and what God will have a man do, He does not leave to the words of another man, He speaks Himself; His words are written in the secret heart.

Now I consider those who would prevent the birth of the passions almost as foolish as those who would destroy them, and those who think this has been my object hitherto are greatly mistaken.

But should we reason rightly, if from the fact that passions are natural to man, we inferred that all the passions we feel in ourselves and behold in others are natural? Their source, indeed, is natural; but they have been swollen by a thousand other streams; they are a great river which is constantly growing, one in which we can scarcely find a single drop of the original stream. Our natural passions are few in number; they are the means to freedom, they tend to self-preservation. All those which enslave and destroy us have another source; nature does not bestow them on us; we seize on them in her despite.

The origin of our passions, the root and spring of all the rest, the only one which is born with man, which never leaves him as long as he lives, is self-love; this passion is primitive, instinctive, it precedes all the rest, which are in a sense only modifications of it. In this sense, if you like, they are all natural. But most of these modifications are the result of external influences, without which they would never occur, and such modifications, far from being advantageous to us, are harmful. They change the original purpose and work against its end; then it is that man finds himself outside nature and at strife with himself.

Self-love is always good, always in accordance with the order of nature. The preservation of our own life is specially entrusted to each one of us, and our first care is, and must be, to watch over our own life; and how can we continually watch over it, if we do not take the greatest interest in it?

Self-preservation requires, therefore, that we shall love ourselves; we must love ourselves above everything, and it follows directly from this that we love what contributes to our preservation. Every child becomes fond of its nurse; Romulus must have loved the she-wolf who suckled him. At first this attachment is quite unconscious; the individual is attracted to that which contributes to his welfare and repelled by that which is harmful; this is merely blind instinct. What transforms this instinct into feeling, the liking into love, the aversion into hatred, is the evident intention of helping or hurting us. We do not become passionately attached to objects without feeling, which only follow the direction given them; but those from which we expect benefit or injury from their internal disposition, from their will. Those we see acting freely for or against us, inspire us with like feelings to those they exhibit towards us. Something does us good, we seek after it; but we love the person who does us good; something harms us and we shrink from it, but we hate the person who tries to hurt us.

The child's first sentiment is self-love, his second, which is derived from it, is love of those about him; for in his present state of weakness he is only aware of people through the help and attention received from them. At first his affection for his nurse and his governess is mere habit. He seeks them because he needs them and because he is happy when they are there; it is rather perception than kindly feeling. It takes a long time to discover not merely that they are useful to him, but that they desire to be useful to him, and then it is that he begins to love them.

So a child is naturally disposed to kindly feeling because he sees that every one about him is inclined to help him, and from this experience he gets the habit of a kindly feeling towards his species; but with the expansion of his relations, his needs, his dependence, active or passive, the consciousness of his relations to others is awakened, and leads to the sense of duties and preferences. Then the child becomes masterful, jealous, deceitful, and vindictive. If he is not compelled to obedience, when he does not see the usefulness of what he is told to do, he attributes it to caprice, to an intention of tormenting him, and he rebels. If people give in to him, as soon as anything opposes him he regards it as rebellion, as a determination to resist him; he beats the chair or table for disobeying him. Self-love, which concerns itself only with ourselves, is content to satisfy our own needs; but selfishness, which is always comparing self with others, is never satisfied and never can be; for this feeling, which prefers ourselves to others, requires that they should prefer us to themselves, which is impossible. Thus the tender and gentle passions spring from self-love, while the hateful and angry passions spring from selfishness. So it is the fewness of his needs, the narrow limits within which he can compare himself with others, that makes a man really good; what makes him really bad is a multiplicity of needs and dependence on the opinions of others. It is easy to see how we can apply this principle and guide every passion of children and men towards good or evil. True, man cannot always live alone, and it will be hard therefore to remain good; and this difficulty will increase of necessity as his relations with others are extended. For this reason, above all, the dangers of social life demand that the necessary skill and care shall be devoted to guarding the human heart against the depravity which springs from fresh needs.

Man's proper study is that of his relation to his environment. So long as he only knows that environment through his physical nature, he should study himself in relation to things; this is the business of his childhood; when he begins to be aware of his moral nature, he should study himself in relation to his fellow-men; this is the business of his whole life, and we have now reached the time when that study should be begun.

As soon as a man needs a companion he is no longer an isolated creature, his heart is no longer alone. All his relations with his species, all the affections of his heart, come into being along with this. His first passion soon arouses the rest.

* * *

The turmoil of Rousseau and the conditions that produced him had consequences in politics, literature, and education. The bridge between *Emile* and the community of educators was built by the second remarkable Swiss in our story of the child, Johann Heinrich Pestalozzi. Moved to political and social agitation by the promise of Rousseau's vision, Pestalozzi's enduring contribution to the history of the child is a series of books he wrote on early education. Pestalozzi had no doubts about the innate goodness of children, and he preached with enthusiasm and occasional clarity his belief that men in society corrupt the child's essential purity. He drew from this belief an implication of wide influence—that it was both possible and morally enjoined to educate the poor.

Even more strongly than Rousseau, Pestalozzi was committed to the relevance of education at the knee; for him, the mother is not only the first but also the most important educator of the child. In *How Gertrude Teaches her Children,* a group of letters to his friend Gessner, Pestalozzi intentionally goes far beyond what a mother may realistically be expected to achieve even under the best of circumstances. Nonetheless, his emphasis on early education reflected his conviction that the child could be truly educated only through the use of his active intellectual and moral strivings. For Pestalozzi, knowledge was a creation of the self and he built his theory of the child around the notion of *Anschauung,* the intuition or apperception or appreciation of the world that represented the active principle of mind (his translator uses the far-too-weak word "observation"). Pestalozzi had no confidence that this active tendency would develop naturally in the child; he feared its erosion in the usual educational procedures of the day and founded his own educational system on techniques designed to foster and support *Anschauung.* His decision that the elements of knowledge were form, number, and language led him to the invention of teaching devices and exercises that were to become part of the Pestalozzian Method. After both Fichte and von Humboldt, the Prussian Minister of Education, became convinced of the wisdom and efficacy of Pestalozzi's procedures, the Nature school of Education rose to a position of dominance in Europe.

The details of Pestalozzi's pedagogical methods, however, are not tied irrevocably to his view of the child. Within his lifetime he saw that his drills were almost as dull and inhibiting of the child's invention of knowledge as were the classical pedagogical tricks. What matters for an understanding of Pestalozzi's contribution to the definition of the child—and his teaching can be traced almost without interruption through Froebel and Montessori and Dewey to a faltering confederation of contemporary American educators—is a recognition of his emphasis on the home as the model of all education and on the principle that learning is based on the activity of the child. His notion of *Anschauung* remains difficult to understand; it is related to Locke's common sense and represents the process of observing-while-relating-observations that Pestalozzi thought critical for cognitive development. In the next selection, the translator shows his own unease with his English forms of *Anschauung* by noting each time it appears in Pestalozzi's text.

*   *   *

Johann Heinrich Pestalozzi (1746–1827)

Observation and Education

Friend! When I now look back and ask myself: What have I specially done for the very being of education? I find I have fixed

J. H. Pestalozzi. *How Gertrude Teaches Her Children.* Translated by Lucy E. Holland and F. C. Turner. Syracuse, N.Y.: Bardeen, 1894 (Fifth edition, 1915). The first publication in German was in 1801. Letters IX and X.

the highest, supreme principle of instruction in the recognition of *sense-impression as the absolute foundation of all knowledge.* Apart from all *special teaching* I have sought to discover the *nature of teaching itself;* and the *prototype,* by which Nature herself has determined the instruction of our race. I find I have reduced all instruction to 3 elementary means [form, number, and language]; and have sought for special methods which should render the results of all instruction in these three branches absolutely certain.

Lastly, I have brought these 3 elementary means into harmony with each other, and made instruction, in all three branches, not only harmonious with itself in many ways, but also with human nature, and have brought it nearer to the course of Nature in the development of the human race.

But while I did this I found, in necessity, that the instruction of our country, as it is *publicly and generally* conducted *for the people,* wholly and entirely ignores sense-impression as the supreme principle of instruction, that throughout it does not take sufficient notice of the prototype, within which the instruction of our race is determined by the necessary laws of our nature itself; that it rather sacrifices the *essentials of all teaching* to the hurly burly of *isolated teaching of special things* and kills the spirit of truth by dishing up all kinds of *broken truths,* and extinguishes the power of self-activity which rests upon it, in the human race. I found, and it was clear as day, that this kind of instruction reduces its particular methods neither to elementary principles nor to elementary forms; that by the neglect of sense-impression, as the absolute foundation of all knowledge, it is unable by any of its unconnected methods to attain the end of all instruction, clear ideas, and even to make those limited results, at which it solely aims, absolutely certain.

— — —

It could not be otherwise. Since we have contrived with deeply founded art, and still more deeply founded measures for supporting error, to rob our knowledge and our methods of instruction of all sense-impression, and ourselves of all power of gaining sense-impressions, the gilded, giddy pate of our culture could not possibly stand on any feet but those on which it does actually stand. Nothing else was possible. The drifting haphazard methods of our culture could in no subject attain the final end of public instruction, *clear ideas,* and *perfect facility* in what is essentially necessary for the people to know and to learn of all these subjects. Even the best of these methods, the abundant aids for teaching arithmetic, mathematics, and grammar must, under these circumstances, lose power, because, without finding any other foundation for all instruction, they have neglected sense-impression. So these means of instruction, word, number, and form, not being sufficiently subordinated to the one only foundation of all knowledge, sense-impression, must necessarily mislead our generation to elaborate these means of instruction unequally, superficially, and aimlessly, in the midst of error and deception; and by this elaboration, weaken our inmost powers, rather than strengthen and cultivate them. We become necessarily degraded to *lies and folly,* and branded as miserable, weak, unobservant, wordy babblers, by the very same powers and the very same mechanism with which the Art, holding the hand of Nature, might raise us up to *truth and wisdom.*

Even the knowledge gained by observation (*Anschauung*), forced upon us by our circumstances and our business, in spite of our folly (because it is impossible for any error in the Art to snatch this wholly from mankind)—even this kind of knowledge, being isolated, becomes one-sided, illusory, egotistic and illiberal. There is no help for it. Under such guidance we are forced to rebel against whatever is opposed to this one-sided, illiberal kind of observation (*Anschauung*), and to become insensible to all truth that may be beyond the limited range of our untrained senses. There is no help for it. We are forced under these circumstances, to sink ever deeper from generation to generation into the unnatural conventionality, the narrow-hearted selfishness, the lawless ambitious violence resulting from it, in which we now are.

Dear Gessner! thus, and in no other way, can we explain how, in the past century, during the latter part of which this delusion rose to its greatest height, we were plunged into a dreamy, or rather raving condition of baseless, frantic presumption. This perverted all our ideas of truth and justice. Yielding to the violent agitation of our wild and blind natural feelings, we sank down and a general overturning spirit of sansculottism took possession of us all in one way or another and resulted, as it must needs result, in the inner disorganization of all pure natural feelings, and of all those means of helping humanity, which rest upon those feelings. This led to the disappearance of all *humanity* from political systems; this again to the dissolution of a few political systems which had ceased to be human. But unfortunately this did not work to the advantage of humanity.

This, dear friend, is a sketch of my views on the latest events. Thus I explain the measures both of Robespierre and Pitt, the behaviour of the senators and of the people. And every time I reconsider it I come back to the assertion, that the deficiencies of European instruction, or rather, the artificial inversion of all natural principles of instruction, has brought this part of the world *where it is now;* and that there is no remedy for our present and future overturn in society, morality and religion, except to turn back from the superficiality, incompleteness, and giddy-headedness of our popular instruction, and to recognise that *sense-impression is absolutely the foundation of all knowledge;* in other words, *all knowledge grows out of sense-impression and may be traced back to it.*

Friend! sense-impression, considered as the point at which all instruction begins, must be differentiated from the *art of sense-impressions* or *Anschauung* which teaches us the relations of all forms. Sense-impression, as the common foundation of all 3 elementary means of instruction, must come as long before the art of sense-impression as it comes before the arts of reckoning and speaking. If we consider sense-impression as opposed to the art of sense-impression or *Anschauung,* separately and by itself, it is nothing but the presence of *the external object before the senses* which rouses a consciousness of the impression made by it. With it Nature begins all instruction. The infant enjoys it, the mother gives it him. But the Art has done nothing here to keep equal pace with Nature. In vain that most beautiful spectacle, the mother showing the world to her infant, was presentéd to its eyes, *the Art has done nothing, has verily done nothing for the people,* in connection with this spectacle.

Dear Gessner, I will here quote for you the passage that expressed this feeling about our Art more than a year ago.

"From the moment that a mother takes a child upon her lap, she teaches him. She brings nearer to his senses what nature has scattered afar off over large areas and in confusion, and makes the action of receiving sense-impressions and the knowledge derived from them, easy, pleasant, and delightful to him.

"The mother, weak and untrained, follows Nature without help or guidance, and knows not what she is doing. She does not intend to teach, she intends only to quiet the child, to occupy him. But, nevertheless, in her pure simplicity she follows the high course of Nature without knowing what *Nature* does through *her;* and Nature does very much through her. In this way she opens the world to the child. She makes him ready to use his senses, and prepares for the early development of his attention and power of observation.

"Now if this high course of Nature were used, if that were connected with it which might be connected with it; if the helping Art could make it possible to the mother's heart to go on with what she does instinctively for the infant, wisely and freely with the growing child; if, too, the heart and disposition of the father were also used for this purpose; and the helping Art made it possible for him to link, with the disposition and circumstances of the child, all the activities he needs, in order by good management of his most important affairs, to attain inner content with himself throughout his life, how easy would it be to assist in raising our race and every individual man in any position whatever, even amid the difficulties of unfavourable circumstances, and amid all the evils of unhappy times, and secure him a still, calm, peaceful life. O God! what would be gained for men. But we are not yet so far advanced as the Appenzell woman, who in the first weeks of her child's life, hangs a large, many-coloured, paper bird over his cradle, and in this way clearly shows the point at which the Art should begin to bring the objects of Nature firmly to the child's clear consciousness."

Dear friend! Whoever has seen how the two and three-weeks old child stretches hands and feet towards this bird, and considers how easy it would be for the Art to lay a foundation for actual sense-impressions of all objects of Art and Nature in the child by a series of such visible representations, which may then be gradually made more distinct and extended—Whoever considers all this and then does not feel how we have wasted our time on Gothic monkish educational rubbish, until it has become hateful to us,—truly cakes and ale are wasted on him.

To me the Appenzell bird, like the ox to the Egyptians, is a holy thing, and I have done everything to begin my instruction at the same point as the Appenzell woman. I go further. Neither at the first point, nor in the whole series of means of teaching, do I leave to chance what Nature, circumstance, or mother-love may present to the sense of the child before he can speak. I have done all I could to make it possible, by omitting accidental characteristics, to bring the essentials of knowledge gained by sense-impression to the child's senses before that age, and to make the conscious impressions he receives, unforgettable.

The first *course in the Mother's Book* is merely an attempt to raise sense-impression itself to an art, and to lead children by all 3 elementary divisions of knowledge, *form, number* and *words,* to a comprehensive consciousness of all sense-impressions, the more definite concepts of which will constitute the foundation of their later knowledge.

This book will not only contain representations of those objects most necessary for us to know, but also material for a continuous series of such objects as are fit, at the first sense-impression, to rouse a feeling in the children of their manifold relationships and similarities.

In this respect the Spelling Book does the same thing as the Mother's Book. Simply bringing sounds *to the ear* and rousing a consciousness of the impression made *through the hearing,* is as much *sense-impression* for the child as putting objects *before his eye,* and rousing a consciousness of the impression made *through the sense of sight.* Founded on this, I have so arranged the Spelling Book that its first course is nothing but *simple sense-impression,* that is, it rests simply on the effort to bring the whole series of sounds, that must afterwards serve as the foundation of language, *to the child's sense of hearing,* and to make the impression made by them permanent, *at exactly the same age* at which in the

Mother's Book I bring before his sense of sight the visible objects of the world, the clear perception of which must be the foundation of his future knowledge.

This principle, of raising sense-impression to an art, has a place, too, in our 3rd elementary means of knowledge. Number in itself, without a foundation of sense-impression, is a delusive phantom of an idea, that our imagination certainly holds in a dreamy fashion, but which our reason cannot grasp firmly as a truth. The child must learn to know rightly the inner nature of every form in which the relations of number may appear, before he is in a position to comprehend one of these forms, as the foundation of a clear consciousness of few or many. Therefore in the Mother's Book I have impressed the first ten numbers on the child's senses (*Anschauung*) even at this age in many ways, by fingers, claws, leaves, dots, and also as triangle, square, octagon, etc.

After I have done this in all three branches, and have made sense-impression the absolute foundation of all actual knowledge, I again raise sense-impression in all three subjects to the art of sense-impression (*Anschauung*), that is a power of considering all objects of sense-impression as *objects for the exercise of my judgment and my skill*.

In this way I lead the child, with the 1st elementary means of knowledge, *form*. Having made him acquainted, in the Mother's Book, with manifold sense-impressions of the objects and their names, I lead him to the A B C of the art of sense-impression (*Anschauung*). By this he is put in a position to give an account of the form of objects, which he *distinguished* in the Mother's Book, but did not *clearly* know. This book will enable the child to form clear ideas on the forms of all things by their relation to the square, and in this way to find a whole series of means within the compass of subjects of instruction, by which he may rise from vague sense-impressions to clear ideas.

As to the 2nd primary means of knowledge, *Number*, I go on in the same way. After I have tried by the Mother's Book to make the child clearly conscious, before he can speak, of the ideas of *the first ten numbers*, I try to teach him these expressions for few or many things, by gradually adding *one unit to another*, and making him know the nature of *two*, and then of *three*, and so on. And thus I bring the beginning of all reckoning to the clearest sense-impression of the child, and at the same time make him unforgetably familiar with the expressions which stand for them. Thus I bring the beginnings of arithmetic in general into sequences which are nothing but a psychological, certain, and unbroken march onwards from deeply impressed judgments, resting on sense-impression, to a little additional new sense-impression, but mounting only from 1 to 2 and from 2 to 3. The result of this course, ascertained by experience, is that when the children have wholly understood the beginning of any kind of calculation, they are able to go on without further help.

It is generally to be noticed with respect to this manner of teaching, that it tends to make the principles of each subject so evident to the children, that they can complete every step of their learning, so that in every case they may be absolutely considered as teachers of their younger brothers and sisters, as far as they have gone themselves.

The most important thing that I have done to simplify and illustrate number teaching is this: I not only bring the consciousness of the truth within all relations of numbers to the child, by means of sense-impression, but I unite this truth of sense-impression with the truth of the science of magnitudes, and have set up the square as the common foundation of the art of sense-impression and of arithmetic.

The third primary means of knowledge, *speech,* considered as an application of my principles, is capable of the greatest extension.

If knowledge of form and number should precede speech (and this last must partly arise from the first two), it follows that the progress of grammar is quicker than that of the art of sense-impression (*Anschauung*) and arithmetic. The impression made on the senses (*Anschauung*) by form and number *precedes* the art of *speech,* but the art of sense-impression and arithmetic *come after* the *art of speech* (*grammar*). The great peculiarity and highest characteristic of our nature, *Language,* begins in the power of making sounds. It becomes gradually developed by improving *sounds* to *articulate words;* and from *articulate words* to *language.* Nature needed ages to raise our race to perfect power of speech, yet we learn this art, for which Nature needed ages, in a few months. In teaching our children to speak we must follow exactly the same course Nature followed herein with the human race. We dare not do otherwise. And she unquestionably began with sense-impression. Even the simplest sound, by which man strove to express the impression that an object made on him, was an expression of a sense-impression. The speech of my race was long only a *power of mimicry and of making sounds* that imitated the tones of living and lifeless nature. From *mimicry* and *sound-making they came to hieroglyphics* and *separate words,* and for long they gave *special* objects *special* names. This condition of language is sublimely described in the first book of Moses, chap. ii., verses 19, 20: "The Lord God brought to Adam all the beasts of the earth, and all the birds under heaven, that he might *look upon them* and *name* them. And Adam gave every beast his name."

From this point speech gradually went further. Men first *observed* the striking differences in the objects that they *named.* Then they came to name properties; and then to name the differences in the *actions* and *forces* of objects. Much later the art developed of *making single words mean much,* unity, plurality, size, many or few, form and number, and at last to express clearly all variations and properties of an object, which were produced by changes of time and place, by modifying the form and by joining words together.

In all these stages, speech was to the race a *means* produced by art, not only of *representing* the actual process of making manifold ideas (*Intuitionen*) clear by the power of sound, but also of *making impressions unforgettable.*

Language-teaching is, then, in its nature, nothing but a collection of psychological means of expressing impressions (feelings and thoughts) and of making all their modifications that would be else *fleeting* and *incommunicable, lasting* and *communicable* by uniting them to words.

[Pestalozzi writes of language-learning.]

Yes, friend. I know that for a long, long time there will be but few who do not misunderstand me, and who recognise that dreams, sound and noise are absolutely worthless foundations for mental culture. The causes for this are many and deep seated. The love of babble is so closely connected with respect for what is called *good society*, and its pretension to wide general culture, and still more with the livelihood of many thousands among us, that it must be long, very long, before the men of our time can take that truth with love into their hearts, against which they have hardened themselves so long. But I go on my way and say again: All science-teaching that is dictated, explained, analysed, by men, who have not learnt to think and to *speak in accordance with the laws of Nature*, all science-teaching of which the definitions are forced as if by magic into the minds of children like a *Deus ex Machinâ*, or rather are blown into their ears as by a stage-prompter, so far as it does this must necessarily sink into a miserable burlesque of education. For where the primary powers of the human mind are left asleep, and when words are crammed upon the sleeping powers, we make dreamers, who dream unnaturally and inconstantly, in proportion as the words, crammed into these miserable gaping creatures, are big and pretentious. Such pupils dream of anything in the world except that they are asleep and dreaming; but the wakeful people round them feel all their presumption; and those who see most consider them night wanderers, in the fullest and clearest sense of the word.

The course of Nature in the development of our race is unchangeable. There are and can be no *two good* methods of instruction in this respect. There is but *one*—and this is the one that rests entirely upon the eternal laws of Nature. But of *bad* methods there are *infinitely many;* and the badness of every one *increases,* in proportion as it *deviates from* the *laws of Nature,* and *decreases* in proportion as it *approaches* to following these laws. I well know that this one good method is neither in my hands nor in any other man's, that we can only approach it. But its completion, its perfection must be the aim of him who would found human instruction upon truth, and thereby content human nature, and satisfy its natural claims. From this point of view, I declare, I pursue this method of instruction with all the powers that are in my hands. I have one rule for judging my own action, as well as the actions of all those who strive for this end—*by their fruits ye shall know them.* Human power, mother-wit, and common sense are to me the only evidence of the inner worth of any kind of instruction. Any method, that brands the brow of the learner with the stamp of completely stifled natural powers, and the want of common sense and mother-wit, is condemned by me, whatever other advantages it may have. I do not deny that even *such* methods may produce good tailors, shoemakers, tradesmen, and soldiers; but I do deny that they can produce a tailor or a tradesman who is *a man* in the highest sense of the word. Oh! if men would only comprehend that the aim of all instruction is, and can be, nothing but the development of human nature, by the harmonious cultivation of its powers and talents, and the promotion of manliness of life. Oh, if they would only ask themselves, at every step in their methods of education and instruction,—"Does it further this end?"

I will now again consider the influence of clear ideas upon the essential development of humanity. *Clear* ideas to the child are only *those to which his experience can bring no more clearness.* This principle settles, firstly, the order of the powers and faculties to be developed, by which the *clearness* of all ideas can gradually be arrived at; secondly, the *order* of *objects* by which exercises in definitions can be begun and carried on with the children; lastly, the *exact time* at which definitions of *any kind* contain real truth for the child.

It is evident that *clear ideas* must be worked out, or cultivated in the child by teaching, before we can take for granted that he is *able* to understand the result of such training—the clear idea, or rather its statement in words.

The way to *clear ideas* depends on making all objects clear to the reason in their proper order. This order again rests on the *harmony* of all the arts, by which a child is enabled to express himself clearly about the properties of all things, particularly about the measure, number, and form of any object. In this way, and no other, can the child be led to a comprehensive knowledge of the whole nature of any object, and become capable of defining it, that is, of stating its whole nature, with the utmost precision and brevity, in words. All definitions, that is, all such clear statements in words, of the nature of any object contain essential truth for the child, only so far as he has a clear, vivid background of sense-impression of the object. Where thorough clearness, in the sense-impression of the object to be defined, is wanting, he only learns to play with words, to deceive himself and blindly believe in words.

— — —

The most important means of preventing confusion, inconsequence, and superficiality in human education, rests principally on care in making the first sense-impression of *things most essential* for us to know, as clear, correct, and comprehensive as possible, when they are first brought before our senses, for contemplation (*Anschauung*). Even at the infant's cradle we must begin to take the training of our race out of the hands of blind, sportive Nature, and put it into the hands of that better power, which the experience of ages has taught us to abstract from the eternal laws of our nature.

You must generally distinguish between the laws of Nature and her course, that is, her single workings, and statements about those workings. In her law she is eternal truth, and for us, the eternal standard of all truth; but in her modification, in which her laws apply to every individual and to every case, her truth does not satisfy and content our race. The positive truth of the condition and circumstances of any individual case claims the same equal right of necessity, by virtue of eternal laws, as the common law of human nature itself. Consequently, the claim of necessity of both laws must be brought into harmony, if they are to work satisfactorily on men. Care for this union is essential for our race. The accidental is, by its existence and its consequences, as necessary as the eternal and unchangeable; but the accidental must, from its very existence and its inevitable consequences, be brought into harmony with the eternal and unchangable in human nature by means of the freedom of the human will.

Nature, on whom the inevitable laws of the existence and consequences of the accidental are based, seems only devoted to the whole, and is careless of the individual that she is affecting externally. On this side she is blind; and being blind, she is not the Nature that comes, or can come into harmony with the seeing, spiritual, moral nature of men. On the contrary, it is only spiritual and moral nature that is able to bring itself into harmony with the physical—and that can, and ought to do so. The laws of our senses, by virtue of the essential claims of our nature, must be subordinated to the laws of our moral and spiritual life. Without this subordination it is impossible that the physical part of our nature can ever influence the actual final result of our education, the production of manliness. Man will only become man through his inner and spiritual life. He becomes through it independent, free, and contented. Mere physical Nature leads him not hither. She is in her very nature blind; her ways are ways of darkness and death. Therefore the education and training of our race must be taken out of the hands of blind sensuous Nature, and the influence of her darkness and death, and put into the hands of our moral and spiritual being, and its divine, eternal, inner light and truth.

All, all that you carelessly leave to outer blind Nature sinks. That is true of lifeless nature as of living. Wherever you carelessly leave the earth to Nature, it bears weeds and thistles. Wherever you leave the education of your race to her, she goes no further than a confused impression on the senses, that is not adapted to your power of comprehension, nor to that of your child, in the way that is needed for the best instruction. In order to lead a child, in the most certain way, to correct and perfect knowledge of a tree or plant, it is not the best way, by any means, to turn him, without care, into a wood or meadow, where trees and plants of all kinds grow together. Neither trees nor plants here come before his eyes in such a manner as is calculated to make him observe their nature and relationships, and to prepare for a general knowledge of their subject by the first impression. In order to lead your child by the shortest way to the end of instruction, clear ideas, you must with great care, first put those objects before his eyes (in every branch of learning), which bear the most essential characteristics of the branch to which this object belongs, visibly and distinctly, and which are therefore fitted to strike the eye with the essential nature rather than the variable qualities. If you neglect this, you lead the child, at the very first glance, to look upon the accidental qualities as essential, and in this at least to delay the knowledge of truth, and miss the shortest road of rising from misty sense-impressions to clear ideas.

But if this error in your method of instruction is avoided, if the sequences of subjects in all branches of your instruction are brought to the child's sense-impression so arranged from the very beginning, that at the very first observation (*Anschauung*) the impression of the essential nature of an object begins to overpower the impression of its qualities, the child learns, from the very first, to subordinate the accidental properties of an object to its essential nature. He is, undoubtedly, moving on the safe path, in which his power develops daily of connecting, in the simplest manner, all accidental qualities with his full consciousness of the essential nature of all objects and their inner truth, and so to read all Nature as an open book. As a child, left to itself, peeping into the world without understanding, sinks daily from error to error, through the confusion of separate scraps of knowledge which he has found while so groping; so, on the contrary, a child who is led on this road from his cradle, rises daily from truth to truth. All that exists, or at least all that comes within the range of his experience, unites itself clearly and comprehensively with the power already existing in him, and there is no error behind his views. No bias to any kind of error has been artificially and methodically organized in him, and the *nihil admirari*, which has hitherto been considered the privilege of old age, becomes, thanks to this training, the portion of innocence and youth. Having arrived at this, if he possesses fair average abilities, the child will necessarily reach the final goal of instruction, clear ideas,—it matters little for the time being whether these lead him to the conclusion that we know nothing, or that we understand everything. In order to reach this high end, to organize the means and secure them, and especially to give the first sense-impressions of objects that breadth and accuracy which they demand, in order to avoid deficiencies and error at the foundation, and to build our sequences of methods of gaining knowledge on truth, I have kept all these objects fully in view in the Mother's Book. Friend, I have succeeded; I have so far confirmed my powers of gaining knowledge through my senses by this book, that I foresee that children trained by it, may throw away the book, and in Nature and all that surrounds them, find a better guide to my goal than that which I have given them.

Friend, the book as yet is not; yet I already see it superseded by its own action. . . .

* * *

The empiricist philosophy of Locke made the child interesting as an object of epistemological study and the educational innovations of Rousseau and Pestalozzi made him as interesting as he had been for the ancients as an object of pedagogical study. Moreover, there was contained in the doctrines of philosophers and teachers a species of child psychology. With varying precision and varying explicitness, the postulates of a theory of man developing could be found in many seventeenth- and eighteenth-century treatises on metaphysics and pedagogy. But the theories were bound to be somewhat diffuse and contradictory until the child became a fit object for scientific study. The necessary transformation—the transformation of the problem of development from speculation to empirical analysis—was to come with Darwin.

4

Darwin and the Beginnings
of Child Psychology

There is enough cruelty, enough poverty, and enough theology left in the world for us to imagine the life of a child bereft of the medical and social reforms of the last century or two. It is far harder to imagine what scholars thought of children before the publication and slow assimilation of *The Origin of Species* (1859). Our notion of the child—in fact, of all psychology—was changed so dramatically by Darwin's work that the remainder of this history will become an account of extended variations on the naturalist's basic themes.

There are several ways in which Darwin's speculations directed the history of child psychology. In the first place, the notion of species evolution gave a mechanism in full scientific dress for the notions of perfectibility that the ideologues of the eighteenth century had proposed on grounds less certain. To be sure, the struggle for survival was a grim affair that did not fit well with the conception of man as rational and free, but clearly the result of the ugly contest was the development of a truly superior being. Perhaps the loss of biological uniqueness was painful but in return Darwin provided a rationale for boundless expectations for man. Just as animal life had grown in a natural way from protozoan to rational being, so society had grown from its primitive savagery to Victorian sensibility and might yet grow more. In the hands of the practical social Darwinians, chief among them the members of the Establishment who had thus far survived the struggle, this doctrine did not always lead to greater interest in the protection of the child, but it became an article of faith in the Western community that evolution, developing and developed by science and industry, would bring society to its natural fulfillment.

But Darwin's proposals had more direct effects on the study of man. The notion that the phylogenetic progression had its homologues in the development of man in society (an idea of Rousseau's, too) found expression in the sociology of Sumner and his students. It took the study of primitive cultures from the hands of literate tourists and made it into anthropology. The Darwinian proposals did more than build a base for the comparative study of societies; Darwin looked the other way, toward the signs of man in animal life, and it was this innovation that assured him the enmity of theologians and influenced so strongly the formation of empirical psychology. With the chapter comparing "the mental powers of man and the lower animals" in *Descent of Man*,* Darwin invented the discipline of comparative psychology, and the course of its development is clear and unbroken through Romanes and Lloyd Morgan to Thorndike and Watson to contemporary investigators of animal behavior. There are ironies in the genealogical record; Darwin put psychology into the animal and made the comparative study of mind a wholesome and permitted occupation but, by modifications of greater or less scope, the study of animal behavior shifted until, in mid-twentieth century, the questions about mind that intrigued Darwin were abandoned but the systematic study of the animal was kept.

The contribution of the evolutionary revolution to psychology did not end with the creation of comparative psychology. In at least three other ways, widely varying in their later historical development, the Darwinian principles influenced psychology and the study of the child. At the most general level, so well assimilated into the definition of psychological problems that we forget its origins, lies the model of a struggle for existence among com-

---

* C. Darwin, *The Descent of Man and Selection in Relation to Sex.* (New ed.), New York: Appleton, 1897. The first edition was published in two volumes in 1871.

peting responses of the organism. Learning is an expression of the war among conflicting tendencies of the animal or person and the strongest of them survive. Taine saw this point clearly.

. . . So, in the struggle for life, in which all our images are constantly engaged, the one furnished at the outset with most force, retains in each conflict, by the very law of repetition which gives it being, the capacity of treading down its adversaries; this is why it revives, incessantly at first, then frequently, until at last the laws of progressive decay, and the continual accession of new impressions, take away its preponderance, and its competitors, finding a clear field, are able to develop in their turn.*

And, in a footnote to the passage, Taine writes, "The theory of the great English naturalist is nowhere more precisely applicable than in psychology." Henceforth, it will be difficult to see association as the passionless building of connections.

The irreducible contribution of Darwin to the study of children was, however, in his assignment of scientific value to childhood. Species develop, societies develop, man develops. From the publication of *The Origin of Species* to the end of the nineteenth century, there was a riot of parallel-drawing between animal and child, between primitive man and child, between early human history and child. The developing human being was seen as a natural museum of human phylogeny and history; by careful observation of the infant and child, one could see the descent of man. Enthusiasts found parallels of remarkable scope and the child-as-prototype movement reached its peak with the publication in 1901 of *The Child: A Study in the Evolution of Man* by Alexander Francis Chamberlain. Chamberlain discusses, with more restraint than some of his contemporaries showed, the place of the child in evolutionary theory and summarizes part of his conclusions in these words.

The "ages of man," the epochs noticeable in the origin and growth in the individual of somatic characteristics, anatomical and physiological peculiarities; "critical periods," physical and intellectual; epochal de-

* H. Taine, *On Intelligence* (Translated by T. D. Haye), 2 vol., New York: Holt, 1889. Vol. I, p. 81. The first French edition was published in 1869.

velopment of the senses, of language, etc.; periodicity and epochism in the growth of the sense of self, of character, of emotiveness, of psychic activities in general and in particular, of sociality, of religiosity, or morality, of the various artistic activities, etc., furnish a multitude of facts, many of which, seemingly, cannot receive their interpretation except upon the theory that they represent things once important, useful, necessary to, or characteristic of, the race-ancestry of the individual, in whom they are repeated more or less completely.*

Nothing much is left of this radical notion now. The functionalist revisions in biology and psychology cleared away almost all the defenders of what was held to be a teleological view of man and his workings; the late nineteenth-century notion of parallels between animal and man remains in the academic literature only as a half joking reference to the phrase "Ontogeny recapitulates phylogeny." But, as we shall see later, the idea of animal-child parallels has been subtly transmuted to remain one of the central postulates of child study.

Putting aside later refinements of the doctrine of developmental recapitulation, however, there is good reason for noting the enthusiasm of turn-of-the-century commentators for the assignment of remarkable animal and cultural analogues to the behavior of children. It was a fact in the history of child study, a fact as secure and as highly respected by contemporary true believers as was Hall's questionnaire method and today's Rorschach. But, more than that, the search for phylogenetic and societal shades in the child marked the beginning of a science of child behavior. Man was not to be understood by the analysis of his adult functions, an analysis that was rational in conception and closely linked to logic; rather, man was to be understood by a study of his origins—in nature and in the child. When did consciousness dawn? What were the beginnings of morality? How could we know the world of the infant? Questions like these which, in form of more or less sophistication, were to dominate child psychology for many years, derive their sense from a genetic view of man. The Rousseauan child is put on a firm biological pedestal. He is neither made at birth nor understandable in his adult guise

* A. F. Chamberlain, *The Child: A Study in the Evolution of Man*, London: Walter Scott, 1901, p. 446.

alone; man develops, grows, and becomes through the course of his first years, and it is the particular and special function of the child psychologist to record the visible changes. Darwin gave us the child as a legitimate source of scientific information about the nature of man. He also legitimized the baby journal.

As several commentators have noted, Rousseau was never more in error than when he predicted no imitators of his *Confessions*. In Brett's words, "The sentimental romance became the medium of self-expression, and the example set by Rousseau gradually became the basis of a new literature."* And a new psychology! The introspective analysis of sensation and emotion by eighteenth- and early nineteenth-century gentlemen prepared the ground for Fechner's quantification and for Wundt's systematization. That development is not part of our story, but diaries and notebooks also led to an innovation of great significance to child study—the baby biography. First used at length by Dieterich Tiedemann† the procedure of keeping a day-book of infant behavior (almost invariably, the behavior of the investigator's first child) became usual in the nineteenth century. Taine used his observations of children in his book *On Intelligence* (1869), and it was the publication of some notes on language acquisition by Taine that led Darwin to the preparation of the paper which follows here. Drawing on observations of his first-born, William Erasmus (Doddy), in 1840 and 1841, Darwin shows in brief compass the attraction and the problems of the baby biographer. No one can know as well as the attentive parent the subtle and cumulative changes that take place in the world of the child and in his behavior but, on the other hand, no one can distort as convincingly as a loving parent. Darwin, like almost every baby biographer after him, not only saw children, he also saw a living expression

---

* G. S. Brett, *A History of Psychology*, 3 vol., London: George Allen, 1912–1921, Vol. II, p. 321.

† Apparently, no full English translation of Tiedemann's *Record of an Infant's Life* (1787) exists, for all its popularity as a citation in secondary sources. Soldan's translation of Perez' commentary on Michelant's French translation of the original German [F. L. Soldan, *Tiedemann's Record of Infant-Life. An English version of the French translation and commentary by Bernard Perez.* Syracuse: Bardeen, 1890] does not permit any general statement about Tiedemann's techniques or principles.

of his theoretical position. The evolutionist is clearly at work in this charming little account, and there are two details that are particularly illuminating of Darwin's attitude and his psychology. One is the ascription to the child of specific affect (the "violent passion" of anger, for example), an ascription which we will find imitated for many years. The other is Darwin's perplexed and obviously parental proposition that the tendency to throw objects is inherited—in boys.

* * *

Charles Robert Darwin (1809–1882)

A Biographical Sketch of an Infant

M. Taine's very interesting account of the mental development of an infant, translated in the last number of MIND, has led me to look over a diary which I kept thirty-seven years ago with respect to one of my own infants. I had excellent opportunities for close observation, and wrote down at once whatever was observed. My chief object was expression, and my notes were used in my book on this subject; but as I attended to some other points, my observations may possibly possess some little interest in comparison with those by M. Taine, and with others which hereafter no doubt will be made. I feel sure, from what I have seen with my own infants, that the period of development of the several faculties will be found to differ considerably in different infants.

During the first seven days various reflex actions, namely sneezing, hickuping, yawning, stretching, and of course sucking and screaming, were well performed by my infant. On the seventh day, I touched the naked sole of his foot with a bit of paper, and he jerked it away, curling at the same time his toes, like a

C. Darwin, A biographical sketch of an infant, Mind, II, 1877, 286–294.

much older child when tickled. The perfection of these reflex movements shows that the extreme imperfection of the voluntary ones is not due to the state of the muscles or of the coordinating centres, but to that of the seat of the will. At this time, though so early, it seemed clear to me that a warm soft hand applied to his face excited a wish to suck. This must be considered as a reflex or an instinctive action, for it is impossible to believe that experience and association with the touch of his mother's breast could so soon have come into play. During the first fortnight he often started on hearing any sudden sound, and blinked his eyes. The same fact was observed with some of my other infants within the first fortnight. Once, when he was 66 days old, I happened to sneeze, and he started violently, frowned, looked frightened, and cried rather badly: for an hour afterwards he was in a state which would be called nervous in an older person, for every slight noise made him start. A few days before this same date, he first started at an object suddenly seen; but for a long time afterwards sounds made him start and wink his eyes much more frequently than did sight; thus when 114 days old, I shook a paste-board box with comfits in it near his face and he started, whilst the same box when empty or any other object shaken as near or much nearer to his face produced no effect. We may infer from these several facts that the winking of the eyes, which manifestly serves to protect them, had not been acquired through experience. Although so sensitive to sound in a general way, he was not able even when 124 days old easily to recognise whence a sound proceeded, so as to direct his eyes to the source.

With respect to vision,—his eyes were fixed on a candle as early as the 9th day, and up to the 45th day nothing else seemed thus to fix them; but on the 49th day his attention was attracted by a bright-coloured tassel, as was shown by his eyes becoming fixed and the movements of his arms ceasing. It was surprising how slowly he acquired the power of following with his eyes an object if swinging at all rapidly; for he could not do this well when seven and a half months old. At the age of 32 days he perceived his mother's bosom when three or four inches from it, as was shown by the protrusion of his lips and his eyes becoming fixed; but I much doubt whether this had any connection with vision; he certainly had not touched the bosom. Whether he was guided through smell or the sensation of warmth or through association with the position in which he was held, I do not at all know.

The movements of his limbs and body were for a long time vague and purposeless, and usually performed in a jerking manner; but there was one exception to this rule, namely that from a very early period, certainly long before he was 40 days old, he could move his hands to his own mouth. When 77 days old, he took the sucking bottle (with which he was partly fed) in his right hand, whether he was held on the left or right arm of his nurse, and he would not take it in his left hand until a week later although I tried to make him do so; so that the right hand was a week in advance of the left. Yet this infant afterwards proved to be left-handed, the tendency being no doubt inherited—his grandfather, mother, and a brother having been or being left-handed. When between 80 and 90 days old, he drew all sorts of objects into his mouth, and in two or three weeks' time could do this with some skill; but he often first touched his nose with the object and then dragged it down into his mouth. After grasping my finger and drawing it to his mouth, his own hand prevented him from sucking it; but on the 114th day, after acting in this manner, he slipped his own hand down so that he could get the end of my finger into his mouth. This action was repeated several times, and evidently was not a chance but a rational one. The intentional movements of the hands and arms were thus much in advance of those of the body and legs; though the purposeless movements of the latter were from a very early period usually alternate as in the act of walking. When four months old, he often looked intently at his own hands and other objects close to him, and in doing so the eyes were turned much inwards, so that he often squinted frightfully. In a fortnight after this time (i.e. 132 days old) I observed that if an object was brought as near to his face as his own hands were, he tried to seize it, but often failed; and he did not try to do so in regard to more distant objects. I think there can be little doubt that the convergence of his eyes gave him the clue and excited him to move his arms. Although this infant thus began to use his hands at an early period, he showed no special aptitude in this respect, for when he was 2 years and 4 months old, he held pencils, pens, and other objects far less neatly and efficiently than did his sister who was then only 14 months old, and who showed great inherent aptitude in handling anything.

Anger.   It was difficult to decide at how early an age anger was felt; on his eighth day he frowned and wrinkled the skin round his eyes before a crying fit, but this may have been due to pain or distress, and not to anger. When about ten weeks old, he was given some rather cold milk and he kept a slight frown on his forehead all the time that he was sucking, so that he looked like a grown-up person made cross from being compelled to do something which he did not like. When nearly four months old, and perhaps much earlier, there could be no doubt, from the manner in which the blood gushed into his whole face and scalp, that he easily got into a violent passion. A small cause sufficed; thus, when a little over seven months old, he screamed with rage because a lemon slipped away and he could not seize it with his hands. When eleven months old, if a wrong plaything was given him, he would push it away and beat it; I presume that the beating was an instinctive sign of anger, like the snapping of the jaws by a young crocodile just out of the egg, and not that he imagined he could hurt the plaything. When two years and three months old, he became a great adept at throwing books or sticks, &c., at anyone who offended him; and so it was with some of my other sons. On the other hand, I could never see a trace of such aptitude in my infant daughters; and this makes me think that a tendency to throw objects is inherited by boys.

Fear.   This feeling probably is one of the earliest which is experienced by infants, as shown by their starting at any sudden sound when only a few weeks old, followed by crying. Before the present one was 4½ months old I had been accustomed to make close to him many strange and loud noises, which were all taken as excellent jokes, but at this period I one day made a loud snoring noise which I had never done before; he instantly looked grave and then burst out crying. Two or three days afterwards, I made through forgetfulness the same noise with the same result. About the same time (*viz.* on the 137th day) I approached with my back towards him and then stood motionless: he looked very grave and much surprised, and would soon have cried, had I not turned round; then his face instantly relaxed into a smile. It is well known how intensely older children suffer from vague and undefined fears, as from the dark, or in passing an obscure corner in a large hall, &c. I may give as an instance that I took the child in question, when 2¼ years old, to the Zoological Gardens, and he enjoyed looking at all the animals which were like those that he knew, such as deer, antelopes &c., and all the birds, even the ostriches, but was much alarmed at the various larger animals in cages. He often said afterwards that he wished to go again, but not to see "beasts in houses"; and we could in no manner account for this fear. May we not suspect that the vague but very real fears of children, which are quite independent of experience, are the inherited effects of real dangers and abject superstitions during ancient savage times? It is quite conformable with what we know of the transmission of formerly well-developed characters, that they should appear at an early period of life, and afterwards disappear.

Pleasurable Sensations.   It may be presumed that infants feel pleasure while sucking, and the expression of their swimming eyes seems to show that this is the case. This infant smiled when 45 days, a second infant when 46 days old; and these were true smiles, indicative of pleasure, for their eyes brightened and eyelids slightly closed. The smiles arose chiefly when looking at their mother, and were therefore probably of mental origin; but this infant often smiled then, and for some time afterwards, from some inward pleasurable feeling, for nothing was happening which could have in any way excited or amused him. When 110 days old he was exceedingly amused by a pinafore being thrown over his face and then suddenly withdrawn; and so he was when I suddenly uncovered my own face and approached his. He then uttered a little noise which was an incipient laugh. Here surprise was the chief cause of the amusement, as is the case to a large extent with the wit of grown-up persons. I believe that for three or four weeks before the time when he was amused by a face being suddenly uncovered, he received a little pinch on his nose and cheeks as a good joke. I was at first surprised at humour being appreciated by an infant only a little above three months old, but we should remember how very early puppies and kittens begin to play. When four months old, he showed in an unmistakable manner that he liked to hear the pianoforte played; so that here apparently was the earliest sign of an aesthetic feeling, unless the attraction of bright colours, which was exhibited much earlier, may be so considered.

Affection.   This probably arose very early in life, if we may judge by his smiling at those who had charge of him when under two months old; though I had no distinct evidence of his distinguishing and recognising anyone, until he was nearly four months old. When nearly five months old, he plainly showed his wish to go to his nurse. But he did not spontaneously exhibit affection by overt acts until a little above a year old, namely, by kissing several times his nurse who had been absent for a short time. With respect to the allied feeling of sympathy, this was clearly shown at 6 months and 11 days by his melancholy face, with the corners of his mouth well depressed, when his nurse pretended to cry. Jealousy was plainly exhibited when I fondled a large doll, and when I weighed his infant sister, he being then 15½ months old. Seeing how strong a feeling jealousy is in dogs, it would probably be exhibited by infants at an earlier age than that just specified, if they were tried in a fitting manner.

Association of Ideas, Reason, &c.   The first action which exhibited, as far as I observed, a kind of practical reasoning, has already been noticed, namely, the slipping his hand down my finger so as to get the end of it into his mouth; and this happened on the 114th day. When four and a half months old, he repeatedly smiled at my image and his own in a mirror, and no doubt mistook them for real objects; but he showed sense in being evidently surprised at my voice coming from behind him. Like all infants he much enjoyed thus looking at himself, and in less than two months perfectly understood that it was an image; for if I made quite silently any odd grimace, he would suddenly turn round to look at me. He was, however, puzzled at the age of seven months, when being out of doors he saw me on the inside of a large plate-glass window, and seemed in doubt whether or not it was an image. Another of my infants, a little girl, when exactly a year old, was not nearly so acute, and seemed quite perplexed at the image of a person in a mirror approaching her from behind. The higher apes which I tried with a small looking-glass behaved differently; they placed their hands behind the glass, and in doing so showed their sense, but far from taking pleasure in looking at themselves they got angry and would look no more.

When five months old, associated ideas arising independently of any instruction became fixed in his mind; thus as soon as his hat and cloak were put on, he was very cross if he was not immediately taken out of doors. When exactly seven months old, he made the great step of associating his nurse with her name, so that if I called it out he would look round for her. Another infant used to amuse himself by shaking his head laterally: we praised and imitated him, saying "Shake your head"; and when he was seven months old, he would sometimes do so on being told without any other guide. During the next four months the former infant associated many things and actions with words; thus when asked for a kiss he would protrude his lips and keep still,—would shake his head and say in a scolding voice "Ah" to the coal-box or a little spilt water, &c., which he had been taught to consider as dirty. I may add that when a few days under nine months old he associated his own name with his image in the looking-glass, and when called by name would turn towards the glass even when at some distance from it. When a few days over nine months, he learnt spontaneously that a hand or other object causing a shadow to fall on the wall in front of him was to be looked for behind. Whilst under a year old, it was sufficient to repeat two or three times at intervals any short sentence to fix firmly in his mind some associated idea. In the infant described by M. Taine, the age at which ideas readily became associated seems to have been considerably later, unless indeed the earlier cases were overlooked. The facility with which associated ideas due to instruction and others spontaneously arising were acquired, seemed to me by far the most strongly marked of all the distinctions between the mind of an infant and that of the cleverest full-grown dog that I have ever known. What a contrast does the mind of an infant present to that of the pike, described by Professor Möbius, who during three whole months dashed and stunned himself against a glass partition which separated him from some minnows; and when, after at last learning that he could not attack them with impunity, he was placed in the aquarium with these same minnows, then in a persistent and senseless manner he would not attack them!

Curiosity, as M. Taine remarks, is displayed at an early age by infants, and is highly important in the development of their minds; but I made no special observation on this head. Imitation likewise comes into play. When our infant was only four months old I thought that he tried to imitate sounds; but I may have deceived myself, for I was not thoroughly convinced that he did so until he was ten months old. At the age of 11½ months he could readily imitate all sorts of actions, such as shaking his head and saying "Ah" to any dirty object, or by carefully and slowly putting his forefinger in the middle of the palm of his other hand, to the childish rhyme of "Pat it and pat it and mark it with T." It was amusing to behold his pleased expression after successfully performing any such accomplishment.

I do not know whether it is worth mentioning, as showing something about the strength of memory in a young child, that this one when 3 years and 23 days old on being shown an engraving of his grandfather, whom he had not seen for exactly 6 months, instantly recognised him and mentioned a whole string of events which had occurred whilst visiting him, and which certainly had never been mentioned in the interval.

Moral Sense.   The first sign of moral sense was noticed at the age of nearly 13 months: I said "Doddy (his nickname) won't give poor papa a kiss,—naughty Doddy." These words, without doubt, made him feel slightly uncomfortable; and at last when I had returned to my chair, he protruded his lips as a sign that he was ready to kiss me; and he then shook his hand in an angry manner until I came and received his kiss. Nearly the same little scene recurred in a few days, and the reconciliation seemed to give him so much satisfaction, that several times afterwards he pretended to be angry and slapped me, and then insisted on giving me a kiss. So that here we have a touch of the dramatic art, which is so strongly pronounced in most young children. About this time it became easy to work on his feelings and make him do whatever was wanted. When 2 years and 3 months old, he gave his last bit of gingerbread to his little sister, and then cried out with high self-approbation "Oh kind Doddy, kind Doddy." Two months later, he became extremely sensitive to ridicule, and was so suspicious that he often thought people who were laughing and talking together were laughing at him. A little later (2 years and 7½ months old) I met him coming out of the dining room with his eyes unnaturally bright, and an odd unnatural or affected manner, so that I went into the room to see who was there, and found that he had been taking pounded sugar, which he had been told not to do. As he had never been in any way punished, his odd manner certainly was not due to fear, and I suppose it was pleasurable excitement struggling with conscience. A fortnight afterwards, I met him coming out of the same room, and he was eyeing his pinafore which he had carefully rolled up; and again his manner was so odd that I determined to see what was within his pinafore, notwithstanding that he said there was nothing and repeatedly commanded me to "go away," and I found it stained with pickle-juice; so that here was carefully planned deceit. As this child was educated soley by working on his good feelings, he soon became as truthful, open, and tender, as anyone could desire.

Unconsciousness, Shyness.   No one can have attended to very young children without being struck at the unabashed manner in which they fixedly stare without blinking their eyes at a new face; an old person can look in this manner only at an animal or inanimate object. This, I believe, is the result of young children not thinking in the least about themselves, and therefore not being in the least shy, though they are sometimes afraid of strangers. I saw the first symptom of shyness in my child when nearly two years and three months old: this was shown towards myself, after an absence of ten days from home, chiefly by his eyes being kept slightly averted from mine; but he soon came and sat on my knee and kissed me, and all trace of shyness disappeared.

Means of Communication.   The noise of crying or rather of squalling, as no tears are shed for a long time, is of course uttered in an instinctive manner, but serves to show that there is suffering. After a time the sound differs according to the cause, such as hunger or pain. This was noticed when this infant was eleven weeks old, and I believe at an earlier age in another infant. Moreover, he appeared soon to learn to begin crying voluntarily, or to wrinkle his face in the manner proper to the occasion, so as to show that he wanted something. When 46 days old, he first made little noises without any meaning to please himself, and these soon became varied. An incipient laugh was observed on the 113th day, but much earlier in another infant. At this date I thought, as already remarked, that he began to try to imitate sounds, as he certainly did at a considerably later period. When five and a half months old, he uttered an articulate sound "da" but without any meaning attached to it. When a little over a year old, he used gestures to explain his wishes; to give a simple instance, he picked up a bit of paper and giving it to me pointed to the fire, as he had often seen and liked to see paper burnt. At exactly the age of a year, he made the great step of inventing a word for food, namely, *mum*, but what led him to it I did not discover. And now instead of beginning to cry when he was hungry, he used this word in a demonstrative manner or as a verb, implying "Give me food." This word therefore corresponds with *ham* as used by M. Taine's infant at the later age of 14 months. But he also used *mum* as a substantive of wide signification; thus he called sugar *shu-mum*, and a little later after he had learned the word "black," he called liquorice *black-shu-mum*,—black-sugar food.

I was particularly struck with the fact that when asking for food by the word *mum* he gave to it (I will copy the words written down at the time) "a most strongly marked interrogatory sound at the end." He also gave to "Ah," which he chiefly used at first when recognising any person or his own image in a mirror, an exclamatory sound, such as we employ when surprised. I remark in my notes that the use of these intonations seemed to have arisen instinctively, and I regret that more observations were not made on this subject. I record, however, in my notes that at a rather later period, when between 18 and 21 months old, he modulated his voice in refusing peremptorily to do anything by a defiant whine, so as to express "That I won't"; and again his humph of assent expressed "Yes, to be sure." M. Taine also insists strongly on the highly expressive tones of the sounds made by his infant before she had learnt to speak. The interrogatory sound which my child gave to the word *mum* when asking for food is especially curious; for if anyone will use a single word or a short sentence in this manner, he will find that the musical pitch of his voice rises considerably at the close. I did not then see that this fact bears on the view which I have elsewhere maintained that before man used articulate language, he uttered notes in a true musical scale as does the anthropoid ape Hylobates.

Finally, the wants of an infant are at first made intelligible by instinctive cries, which after a time are modified in part unconsciously, and in part, as I believe, voluntarily as a means of communication,—by the unconscious expression of the features,—by gestures and in a marked manner by different intonations,—lastly by words of a general nature invented by himself, then of a more precise nature imitated from those which he hears; and these latter are acquired at a wonderfully quick rate. An infant understands to a certain extent, and as I believe at a very early period, the meaning or feelings of those who tend him, by the expression of their features. There can hardly be a doubt about this with respect to smiling; and it seemed to me that the infant whose biography I have here given understood a compassionate expression at a little over five months old. When 6 months and 11 days old he certainly showed sympathy with his nurse on her pretending to cry. When pleased after performing some new accomplishment, being then almost a year old, he evidently studied the expression of those around him. It was probably due to differences of expression and not merely of the form of the features that certain faces clearly pleased him much more than others, even at so early an age as a little over six months. Before he was a year old, he understood intonations and gestures, as well as several words and short sentences. He understood one word, namely, his nurse's name, exactly five months before he invented his first word *mum;* and this is what might have been expected, as we know that the lower animals easily learn to understand spoken words.

* * *

The linkage through Darwin of child and animal psychology is not without its historical implication; animal psychologists of great eminence—Hunter, Hull, Skinner, and Miller among them— have studied the child. They did so, in part, because they had children of their own and could not resist exploring the incoherence of the young. But the relation between the study of animals and the study of children is more intimate than that. A psychology devoted to the construction of adult and complex forms of behavior from the minimal bits of associative bonds must look to beginnings. The animal and the child are imperfect adults for the associationist and imperfect in a critically important way. They can be assumed to have fewer, or more simple, units of behavior than does the full man, and their apparent simplicity may permit finding the beginning of the thread that is woven into the inexplicably complicated pattern of adult human behavior. Both animal and child psychology have, in part, freed themselves from their historical origins, but even now child psychology becomes more easily comprehensible to the observer if it is recognized that one great branch of the discipline—almost all of the American school—derives, in intellectual and human descent, from the comparative studies of Charles Darwin and stands in close relation with the students of animal behavior.

Moreover, the animal psychologists, for all of their desire to read human characteristics into their subjects, were steadily forced to rely on observations of behavior. Romanes tells of talking dogs ("How are you, grandmama") and maintains that the absence of speech in animals is an anatomical rather than a physiological barrier,* but most of the comparative psychology

---

* G. J. Romanes, *Mental Evolution in Man. Origin of Human Faculty*, New York: Appleton, 1889. The dog and the anatomical conclusion appear in a footnote on p. 128.

of our time has been based on observation rather than introspection. So it had to be with infants; their inability to talk to the observer has placed child psychology in an alliance of method with animal psychology from Darwin to the present. Conversely, the child was of little interest to Wundt and his American successors.

During the earlier periods of the child's life experimental methods are hardly applicable at all. The results of experiments which have been tried on very young children must be regarded as purely chance results, wholly untrustworthy on account of the great number of sources of error. For this reason it is an error to hold, as is sometimes held, that the mental life of adults can never be fully understood except through the analysis of the child's mind. The exact opposite is the true position to take. Since in the investigation of children and of savages [Wundt might have added, " *a fortiori* of animals"], only objective symptoms are in general available, any psychological interpretation of these symptoms is possible only on the basis of mature adult introspection which has been carried out under experimental conditions. For the same reasons, it is only the results of observations of children and savages which have been subjected to a similar psychological analysis, which furnish any proper basis for conclusions in regard to the nature of mental development in general.*

Rarely in the history of psychological controversy has an issue been so dichotomously put. Wundt staked the future of psychology and the definition of the experimental procedure itself on introspective mental analysis. There was no place for child or animal in such a scheme; the structuralists had no place in the development of child psychology and, when the Wundtian school collapsed, it was under the assault of the Darwinians, animal and child.

But there were others in the tradition of German philosophy and physiology who saw the meaning of Darwin for behavioral research. Chief among these in the late nineteenth century was Wilhelm Preyer, Professor of Physiology in Jena. His encomium on Darwin catches some of the excitement that must have shaken the biologists of Europe.

---

* W. Wundt, *Outlines of Psychology* (Translated by C. H. Judd), New York: Stechert, 1907, p. 336. The first German edition appeared in 1897.

If a new sun had appeared in the sky, the astonishment of educated men from San Francisco to Moscow, from Melbourne to Bergen, could hardly have been greater than it was then. The effect of *The Origin of Species* can be compared with that of a great fire that burns up the old parchments of natural history, the scholastic herbaria which had been stored up by the centuries, the dry systems into which living nature was squeezed—a fire that permitted new ideas to grow from its ashes, drawing new sparks from dead stones, opening new ways into the open.°

Preyer had his reservations about what he called "pseudo-Darwinism" and its materialistic metaphysics, but he understood that intellectual history had taken an unprecedented turn with Darwin.

Most of Preyer's work was either physiological or philosophical in character, but with one book he entered and changed the history of child psychology. *Die Seele des Kindes* was published in 1881, was quickly and widely translated, and became a birthmark of child study. Organized in the then-current scheme of psychological classification (Senses, Will, and Intellect), *Mind of the Child* is based in large measure on a diary Preyer kept for the first three years of his son's life. But, as a sign of his interest in the comparison of species, he included data on animal behavior at many places in his account. There are several ways in which Preyer's work became directive of the development of child study. His organizational scheme, so far in advance of the parent's diaries of Darwin and Taine, remained the model for later biographers of the child; although several of his essential categories—notably Will—became unpopular in the writings of later child psychologists, the treatment of early infantile development under the headings Sensation, Motor Activity, Expression (or Emotion), and Intelligence is with us still and can be seen with great clarity in the organization of Carmichael's *Manual of Child Psychology*.†
Preyer did not invent the classificatory scheme; rather, he loosely joined the organization of developmental embryology to that of

° W. Preyer, *Aus Natur- und Menschenleben*, Berlin: Allgemeiner Verein für Deutsche Literatur, X, 1885. The article on Darwin is between pp. 257 and 269; the quotation is from p. 266.
† L. Carmichael, *Manual of Child Psychology* (2nd Ed.), New York: Wiley, 1954. The first edition was published in 1946.

midcentury German psychology and infused the mixture with the spirit of the Darwinian revolution.

However little we count Preyer as original, he set a pattern for child study that has vigorous successors even today. There are some surprising errors in the book ("All children immediately after birth are deaf"), but the selections from *Mind of the Child* which are presented in the next pages illustrate a more subtle and confusing tendency in Preyer's reports. They contain an interweaving of observation, interpretation, and commentary that cannot always be dissected, and the reader must make a complicated decision, often without adequate evidence, about the likelihood of Preyer's being deceived by his parental affection or, far more often, his theoretical presuppositions. For today's student of children, *Mind of the Child* continues to be a source of provoking observations (for example, Preyer's remarkably perceptive remarks on fear of the strange) and of disconcerting arguments about the nature of children.

Preyer's theory of the child, as often implicit as stated, is of far greater interest than is his method. His lack of enthusiasm for empirical epistemology and his conviction that the child will grow and that many of his functions mature with little help from the environment is stated pointedly in the preface to his book.

The mind of the new-born child, then, does not resemble a *tabula rasa*, upon which the senses first write their impressions, so that out of these the sum-total of our mental life arises through manifold reciprocal action, but the tablet is already written upon before birth, with many illegible, nay, unrecognizable and invisible, marks, the traces of the imprint of countless sensuous impressions of long-gone generations. . . . [By careful observation of the child], we perceive what a capital each individual has inherited from his ancestors—how much there is that is not produced by sense-impressions, and how false is the supposition that man learns to feel, to will, and to think, only through his senses.

Preyer's adherence to the *tabula referta* view of the child is clear in his compounds of observation and interpretation, but he goes further. He apparently believed that, by refraining "as far as possible" from training his son in the usual ways of parents, he might see the nearly pure unfolding of the child's inborn functions. This peculiar postulate did not end with Preyer; we shall meet it in full flower with Gesell. In Preyer, we see a fine early statement of the Fallacy of Specific Training, Naturalist's Form: If a response of the child is not specifically trained by action of the parents, then the appearance of that response may be considered evidence for the maturation of a congenital (perhaps even inherited) function. It is essential to remember that Preyer is bringing the attitude of the natural historian to the study of the child as well as his method.

Preyer's limitations as an observer are as clear as his strengths, his prejudices about heredity as clear as his attempts to be objective. What is more difficult to see are the restrictions placed on his contribution by the notion of emergence of functions. There is in *Mind of the Child* an air of expectation; adults see color, when will the child; adults speak, when will the child; adults show directed movement, when will the child? Preyer keeps score on the appearance of adult functions in the development of the child; as Claparède had pointed out, the great biographer of a baby never understood Rousseau's proposal that the behavior of the child be considered a legitimate area of study in its own right, with its own rules, without *necessary* relation to adult behavior and its rules. In Preyer's defense, it must be noted that, with the possible exception of Rousseau himself, no child psychologist before Piaget seriously assumed the task of understanding the child's behavior without frequent reference to its adult forms. Even so, Rousseau escaped the implications of his proposal by remaining programmatic and moralistic in tone and Piaget has not been wholly successful. Preyer did not try; for him, as for most of his ancestors and descendents in child study— see, for example, Mrs. Hall's account of the appearance of compassion*—the child is a reduced adult, showing on schedule the signs of his fulfillment.

* W[inifred] S. Hall, The first 500 days of a child's life, *Child Study Monthly*, 2, 1896–1897, 330–342, 394–407, 458–473, 522–537, and 586–608.

*   *   *

Wilhelm Preyer (1841–1897)

Expression and the Feeling of Self

Expressions of countenance and gestures arise chiefly, as is well known, from imitation. Not only persons born blind, but also those who become blind at an advanced age, are distinguished from those who have sight by their lack of the play of feature. Their expression of countenance shows only slight changes; their physiognomy appears fixed, uniform; the muscles of the face move but little when they are not eating or speaking. Little children also lack a characteristic play of feature, hence the difficulty of making portraits of them, or even of describing them. Different as is the contented face from the discontented, even on the first day, different as is the intelligent face from the stupid, the attentive from the inattentive, the difference can not be completely described. In the second half of the first year children act after the example of the members of the family. Speak gravely to a gay child of a year old, and it becomes grave; if it is sober, and you show a friendly face, the child in many cases brightens up in an instant. Yet it would be premature to conclude from this that all the means of expression by the countenance are acquired solely through imitation. Some mimetic movements, of which we have already spoken, are of reflex origin. The same is true of gestures. Others may be instinctive.

As every gesture is wont to appear in association with the expression of countenance appropriate to it, when it has a language value, it seems advisable to treat together expressions and gestures which together form pantomime, and to separate the purely

W. Preyer. *Mind of the Child.* Translated by H. W. Brown. New York: Appleton, 1888–1889. The first publication in German was in 1881. Vol. 1, pp. 293–301; Vol. 2, pp. 189–207.

expressive muscular movements of the infant from its other movements, in our attempt to trace their origin.

So long as the child can not yet speak words and sentences,
it effects an understanding with other children and with adults
by the same means that are employed by the higher animals for
mutual understanding, by demonstrative movements and attitudes, by sounds expressive of emotion or feeling, of complaining,
exultation, alluring, repelling, or desiring, and by dumb looks.
These very means of expression are employed by the child when
it entertains itself in play with inanimate objects.

— — —

The first smiling is the movement most often misunderstood.
Every opening of the mouth whatever, capable of being interpreted as a smile, is wont to be gladly called a smile even in the
youngest child. But it is no more the case with the child than
with the adult that a mere contortion of the mouth fulfills the
idea of a smile. There is required for this either a feeling of
satisfaction or an idea of an agreeable sort. Both must be strong
enough to occasion an excitement of the facial nerves. A smile
can not be produced by a mere sensation, but only by the state
of feeling that springs from it, or by the agreeable idea developed
from it, however vague it may yet be.

Now, as has been shown already, the number of sensations
associated with a pleasurable feeling in the first days of life is
very small, and an idea, in the proper sense of the word, the
new-born child unquestionably can not have as yet, because he
does not yet perceive. The child that is satisfied with nursing at
its mother's breast, or with the warmth of the bath, does not
smile in the first days of life, but only shows an expression of
satisfaction, because for the moment all unpleasant feelings are
absent. But how easily such a condition of comfort manifests
itself by a very slight lifting of the corner of the mouth, is well
known. If we choose to call this a smile, then even sleeping babies
smile very early. On the tenth day of his life I saw my child,
while he was asleep, after having just nursed his fill, put his mouth
exactly into the form of smiling. The dimples in the cheeks became distinct, and the expression of countenance was, in spite of

the closed eyes, strikingly lovely. The phenomenon occurred several times. On the twelfth day appeared, along with the animated movements of the facial muscles, a play of features in the waking condition, also, that one might take for a smile. But this play of the muscles of the mouth lacked the consciousness that is required to complete the smile, as does the smile of the sleeping child. On the twenty-sixth day, first, when the child could better discriminate between his sensations and the feelings generated by them, did the smile become a mimetic expression. The babe had taken his milk in abundant quantity, and was lying with his eyes now open and now half-closed, and with an indescribable expression of contentment on his countenance. Then he smiled, opening his eyes, and directed his look to the friendly face of his mother, and made some sounds not before heard, which were appropriate to his happy mood. But the idea had not yet arisen of the connection of the mother's face with the mother's breast, the source of enjoyment. Nor can we at this period assume an imitation, by the child, of the smile of the mother, because at first inanimate objects (tassels) are smiled at, and before the fourth month no imitative movements at all were attempted.

Not only the first-mentioned very early movements of smiling, but also this perfect smile is connected with a condition of contentment, and there is no reason to regard it as less hereditary in character than is screaming with pain, which no one would refer to imitation.

Later the child smiles when he is smiled at, but not always by any means. Strangers may smile at him in ever so friendly a manner, yet the wondering little face, usually merry, now sober, remains immobile. The first imitations of the smile in children are not so free from deliberation as the smiles of many adults, which through training and the conventional forms of greeting have degenerated into mere formality.

The original smile of satisfaction at new, agreeable feelings, a smile which may continue even in sleep, and which appears only in a cheerful frame of mind, remains in force still later. By an unusual expression of intensity in the more brightly gleaming eye, as well as by lively movements of the arms and legs, most plainly by laughing and smiling, the infant manifests his satisfaction—e. g., in music (in the eighth week)—without any one's giving him in any other way the least occasion for it.

The date of the first smile varies very much, therefore, according as we take for a smile a spontaneous expression of pleasure, or the communication of an agreeable condition, or the satisfaction at a pleasing idea; here belongs the first imitated smile, and the statements that the first smile appears in well-developed children about the fourth week, as the expression of pleasure (Heyfelder), in the sixth to the eighth week (Champneys), in the seventh and ninth week (Darwin), or that in the seventh to the tenth week (Sigismund) the babe smiles for the first time, are as indefinite as the statement that, at the end of the second week, his mouth takes on a lovely expression like a smile. It depends essentially on the nature of the occasion of the smile at what date the first smile shall be fixed.

One child first smiles at its image in the glass in the twenty-seventh week; another, in the tenth (see below); the one observed by myself, in regard to this point, in the seventeenth week, and not at all till that time. It was rather a laugh than a smile that surprised me on the one hundred and sixteenth day, whereas even on the one hundred and thirteenth the image in the mirror was regarded with a fixed and attentive look, to be sure, but without any sign of satisfaction. In these cases it is simply the joy at the distinct, new perception—an idea, therefore, that occasions the smile; in other cases it is pleasure in impressions of agreeable tastes, of softness or warmth, or joy in pleasing sound, or simply the feeling of satiety (fourteenth week), and then it is usually accompanied by a peculiar sound, which is always much softer in the first months than the expressions of displeasure. But, when the quite young child does not feel well, or is hungry, it can not smile any more. The surest sign of convalescence is the reappearance of this significant movement of the mouth.

From the smile to the laugh is but a step, and the laugh is often only a strengthened and audible smile. The first laugh upon a joyous sense-impression is, however, essentially different from that which springs from the heightened self-consciousness at the perception of the ludicrous; and the limit of time given for that, of six to seventeen weeks, is surprisingly late. Pliny thinks no child laughs before the fortieth day. I observed an audible and visible laugh, accompanied by a brighter gleam of the eye, in my child, for the first time, on the twenty-third day. He was pleased with a bright, rose-colored curtain that was hanging above him, and he made peculiar sounds of satisfaction, so that I was first led by these to pay attention to him. The corners of his mouth were drawn somewhat upward. At this period no laugh yet appeared when the child was in the bath, but there also the expression of the little face with the widely-opened eyes was that of great satisfaction. Laughing appears at first simply as an augmentation of this expression of pleasure. It is often repeated in the same way in the fifth and sixth weeks—in the eighth especially—at the sight of slowly-swinging, well-lighted colored objects, and on hearing the piano.

The child's laugh appeared for the first time, in the period from the sixth to the ninth week, as a sign of joy at a familiar, pleasing impression, his eyes being fixed on his mother's face. But the laugh at the friendly nodding to him, and singing, of the members of the family, was then already much more marked, and was later accompanied by rapid raisings and droppings of the arms as sign of the utmost pleasure (sixth month). This last childish movement continued for years as an accompanying phenomenon of laughing for joy. But it is to be noticed that this laugh first began to be persistently loud in the eighth month (in play with the mother); every one could then at once recognize it as a laugh without looking in that direction. In this the child made a peculiar impression of gayety upon every one who saw him.

Loud laughing at new objects that please, and are long looked at, is still frequent in the ninth month; so also at new sounds in the fifteenth month; then follows laughing at the efforts to stand with support. In the last three months of the first year, however, the character of the laugh appears to become different, as it becomes more conscious. The child laughs with more understanding than before. But he with a laugh grasps at his own image in the glass, and makes a loud jubilant noise, in the eleventh month, when he is allowed to walk, although he must be held firmly when doing so. At the end of the first year, to these independent utterances of pleasure had been added the purely imitative laughing when others laughed. Yet self-consciousness manifested itself also in this, through vigorous crowing with employment of abdominal pressure. Roguish laughing I first noticed toward the end of the second year. Scornful laughing and lachrymal secretion during continuous laughter I have never observed in children under four years of age.

From the sum total of my observations in regard to the smiling and laughing of infants, it results unquestionably that both are original expressive movements, which may be distinctly perceived in the first month, which by no means take place the first time through imitation, and which, without exception, from the beginning express feelings of pleasure; in fact, my child laughed in his sleep at the end of his first year of life, probably having a pleasant dream, and did not wake on account of it.

The reasons are not yet known why feelings of pleasure are expressed just in this manner—i. e., by uncovering the teeth, and even before the teeth are present, by lengthening the opening of the mouth, along with lifting the corners of the mouth, by peculiar sounds and a brighter gleam of the eye (secretion of lachrymal fluid, without its going so far as the formation of tears), and lively accompanying movements of the arms. The causes must be hereditary. But Darwin rightly urges that they do not operate so early as the causes of crying and weeping, because crying is more useful to the child than laughing. And if he saw two children distinctly smile for the first time in the seventh week, we ought to infer from that not so much a failure to notice earlier attempts as the existence of individual differences. That he perceived the first decided laugh in the seventeenth week shows how unlike individual infants are in this respect. Probably much depends on the surroundings and on the behavior of the family. But in all children the expression of pleasure begins with a scarcely perceptible smile, which passes very gradually, in the course of the first three months, into conscious laughing, after the cerebral cortex has so far developed that ideas more distinct can arise. In the second month is perceived also the reflex laughing that follows tickling which I could besides (in the third year) distinguish almost invariably from expressive laughing by the sound alone, without knowing what was going on, although I

was in a neighboring room when I heard it. This "thoughtless"
laugh sounds, on the contrary, exactly like the child's laugh often
heard continously at this time, which occurred when he heard
and saw adults laugh at jests unintelligible to him, and which
was long continued without any meaning in it. Laughing incites
still more to imitation and is more contagious than crying. The
laughter of man seems even to have an enlivening effect on intelligent animals (dogs), which draw the corners of the mouth
far back, and spring, with an animated gleam of the eye, into the
air. I had a large Siberian dog that laughed in this manner. It is
known that monkeys also laugh. These facts favor the hereditary
character of the movement of laughing—all the more as tickling
of the skin of the arm-pit excites laughing in children and monkeys
in the same way, when they are gay, as Darwin informs us. But
if a crying child is tickled in the same manner, it does not laugh.

— — —

Before the child is in a condition to recognize as belonging to
him the parts of his body that he can feel and see, he must have
had a great number of experiences, which are for the most part
associated with *painful feelings*. How little is gained for the development of the notion of the "I" by means of the first movements of the hands, which the infant early carries to the mouth,
and which must give him, when he sucks them, a different feeling
from that given by sucking the finger of another person, or other
suitable objects, appears from the fact that, e. g., my child for
months tugged at his fingers as if he wanted to pull them off, and
struck his own head with his hand by way of experiment. At
the close of the first year he had a fancy for striking hard substances against his teeth, and made a regular play of gnashing
the teeth. When on the four hundred and ninth day he stood up
straight in bed, holding on to the railng of it with his hands,
he bit himself on his bare arm, and that the upper arm, so that
he immediately cried out with pain. The marks of the incisors
were to be seen long afterward. The child did not a second time
bite himself in the arm, but only bit his fingers, and inadvertently
his tongue.

The same child, who likes to hold a biscuit to the mouth of any member of the family to whom he is favorably disposed, offered the biscuit in the same way, entirely of his own accord, to his own foot—sitting on the floor, holding the biscuit in a waiting attitude to his toes—and this strange freak was repeated many times in the twenty-third month. The child amused himself with it.

Thus, at a time when the attention to what is around is already very far developed, one's own person may not be distinguished from the environment. Vierordt thinks that a discrimination between the general feelings (i. e., those caused by bodily states) and the sensations that pertain to the external world exists in the third month. From my observation I can not agree with him; for, although the division may begin thus early, yet it does not become complete until much later. In the ninth month the feet are still eagerly felt of by the little hands, though not so eagerly as before, and the toes are carried to the mouth like a new plaything. Nay, even in the nineteenth month it is not yet clear how much belongs to one's own body. The child had lost a shoe. I said, "Give the shoe." He stooped, seized it, and gave it to me. Then, when I said to the child, as he was standing upright on the floor, "Give the foot," in the expectation that he would hold it out, stretch it toward me, he grasped at it with both hands, and labored hard to get it and hand it to me.

How little he understands, even after the first year of his life has passed, the difference between the parts of his own body and foreign objects is shown also in some strange experiments that the child conducted quite independently. He sits by me at the table and strikes very often and rapidly with his hands successive blows upon the table, at first gently, then hard; then, with the right hand alone, hard; next, suddenly strikes himself with the same hand on the mouth; then he holds his hand to his mouth for a while, strikes the table again with the right hand, and then on a sudden strikes his own head (above the ear). The whole performance gave exactly the impression of his having for the first time noticed that it is one thing to strike oneself, one's own hard head, and another thing to strike a foreign hard object (forty-first week). Even in the thirteenth month the child often raps his head with his hand to try the effect, and seems surprised at the hardness of the head. In the sixteenth month he used not unfrequently to set the left thumb against the left side of the head, and at the same time the right thumb against the right side of the head, above the ears, with the fingers spread, and to push at the same time, putting on a strange, wondering expression of face, with wide-open eyes. This movement is not imitated and not inherited, but invented. The child is doubtless making experiments by means of it upon the holding of the head, head-shaking, resistance of his own body, perhaps also upon the management of the head, as at every thump of the thumbs against the temporal bones a dull sound was heard. The objectivity of the fingers was found out not much before this time by involuntary, painful biting of them, for as late as the fifteenth month the child bit his finger so that he cried out with pain. Pain is the most efficient teacher in the learning of the difference between subjective and objective.

Another important factor is the *perception of a change produced by one's own activity* in all sorts of familiar objects that can be taken hold of in the neighborhood; and the most remarkable day, from a psychogenetic point of view, in any case an extremely significant day in the life of·the infant, is the one in which he first experiences the *connection of a movement executed by himself with a sense-impression following upon it*. The noise that comes from the tearing and crumpling of paper is as yet unknown to the child. He discovers (in the fifth month) the fact that he himself in tearing paper into smaller and smaller pieces has again and again the new sound-sensation, and he repeats the experiment day by day and with a strain of exertion until this connection has lost the charm of novelty. At present there is not, indeed, as yet any clear insight into the nexus of cause; but the child has now had the experience that he can himself be the cause of a combined perception of sight and sound regularly, to the extent that when he tears paper there appears, on the one hand, the lessening in size; on the other hand, the noise. The patience with which this occupation—from the forty-fifth to the fifty-fifth week especially—is continued with pleasure is explained by the gratification at being a cause, at the perception that so striking a transformation as that of the newspaper into fragments has been effected by means of his own activity. Other occupations of this sort, which are taken up again and again with a persistency incomprehensible to an adult, are the shaking of a bunch of keys, the opening and closing of a box or purse (thirteenth month); the pulling out and emptying, and then the filling and pushing in, of a table-drawer; the heaping up and the strewing about of garden-mold or gravel; the turning of the leaves of a book (thirteenth to nineteenth month); digging and scraping in the sand; the carrying of footstools hither and thither; the placing of shells, stones, or buttons in rows (twenty-first month); pouring water into and out of bottles, cups, watering-pots (thirty-first to thirty-third months); and, in the case of my boy, the throwing of stones into the water. A little girl in the eleventh month found her chief pleasure in "rummaging" with trifles in drawers and little boxes. Her sister "played" with all sorts of things, taking an interest in dolls and pictures in the tenth month (Frau von Strümpell). Here, too, the eagerness and seriousness with which such apparently aimless movements are performed is remarkable. The satisfaction they afford must be very great, and it probably has its basis in the feeling of his own power generated by the movements originated by the child himself (changes of place, of position, of form) and in the proud feeling of being a cause.

This is not mere playing, although it is so called; it is *experimenting*. The child that at first merely played like a cat, being amused with color, form, and movement, has become a *causative being*. Herewith the development of the *"I"-feeling* enters upon a new phase; but it is not yet perfected. Vanity and ambition come in for the further development of it. Above all, it is *attention* to the *parts of his own body* and the *articles of his dress*, the nearest of all objects to the child's eye, that helps along the separation in thought of the child's body from all other objects.

I therefore made special observation of the directing of his look toward his own body and toward the mirror. In regard to the first I took note, among other facts, of the following:

17th Week.   In the seizing movements, as yet imperfect, the gaze is fixed partly on the object, partly on *his own hand,* especially if the hand has once seized successfully.

18th Week.   The very attentive regarding of the fingers in seizing is surprising, and is to be observed daily.

23rd Week.   When the infant, who often throws his hands about at random in the air, accidentally gets hold of one hand with the other, he regards attentively both his hands, which are often by chance folded.

24th Week.   In the same way the child fixes his gaze for several minutes alternately upon a glove held by himself in his hands and upon his own fingers that hold it.

32nd Week.   The child, lying on his back, *looks* very frequently *at* his *legs* stretched up vertically, especially at his *feet,* as if they were something foreign to him.

35th Week.   In every situation in which he can do so, the child tries to grasp a foot with both hands and carry it to his mouth, often with success. This monkey-like movement seems to afford him special pleasure.

36th Week.   His own hands and feet are no more so frequently observed by him without special occasion. Other new objects attract his gaze and are seized.

39th Week.   The same as before. In the bath, however, the child sometimes looks at and feels of *his own skin* in various places, evidently taking pleasure in doing so. Sometimes he directs his gaze to his legs, which are bent and extended in a very lively manner in the most manifold variety of positions.

55th Week.   The child looks for a long time attentively at a person eating, and follows with his gaze every movement; grasps at the person's face, and then, after *striking himself on the head,* fixes his gaze on his own hands. He is fond of playing with the fingers of the persons in the family, and delights in the bendings and extensions, evidently comparing them with those of his own fingers.

62nd Week.   Playing with his own fingers (at which he looks with a protracted gaze) as if he would pull them off. Again, one hand is pressed down by the other flat upon the table until it hurts, as if the hand were a wholly foreign plaything, and it is still looked at wonderingly sometimes.

From this time forth the gazing at the parts of his own body was perceptibly lessened. The child *knew* them as to their form, and gradually learned to distinguish them from foreign objects as parts belonging to him; but in this he by no means arrives at the point of considering, "The hand is mine, the thing seized is not," or "The leg belongs to me," and the like; but because all the visible parts of the child's body, on account of very frequently repeated observation, no longer excite the optic center so strongly and therefore appear no longer interesting—because the experiences of touch combined with visual perceptions always recur in the same manner—the child has gradually become accustomed to them and *overlooks* them when making use of his hands and feet. He no longer represents them to himself separately, as he did before, whereas every new object felt, seen, or heard, is very interesting to him and is separately represented in idea. Thus arises the definite separation of object and subject in the child's intellect. In the beginning the child is new to himself, namely, to the representational apparatus that gets its development only after birth; later, after he has become acquainted with himself, after he, namely, his body, has lost the charm of novelty for him, i. e., for the representational apparatus in his brain, a dim feeling of the "I" exists, and by means of further abstraction the concept of the "I" is formed.

[Preyer describes behavior in front of a mirror, early language of self-reference, and the "self" of acephalic infants.]

Only by means of very frequent coincidences of unlike sense-impressions, in tasting-and-touching, seeing-and-feeling, seeing-and-hearing, seeing-and-smelling, tasting-and-smelling, hearing-and-touching, are the inter-central connecting fibers developed, and then first can the various representational centers, these "I"-makers, as it were, contribute, as in the case of the ordinary formation of concepts, to the formation of the corporate "I," which is quite abstract.

This abstract "I"-concept, that belongs only to the adult, thinking human being, comes into existence in exactly the same way that other concepts do, viz., by means of the individual ideas from which it results, as e. g., the forest exists only when the trees exist. The subordinate "I's," that preside over the separate sense-departments, are in the little child not yet blended together, because in him the organic connections are still lacking; which, being translated into the language of psychology, means that he lacks the necessary power of abstraction. The co-excitations of the sensory centers, that are as yet impressed with too few memory-images, can not yet take place on occasion of a single excitation, the cerebral connecting fibers being as yet too scanty.

These co-excitations of parts of the brain functionally different, on occasion of excitation of a part of the brain that has previously often been excited together with those, form the physiological foundation of the psychical phenomenon of the formation of concepts in general, and so of the formation of the "I"-concept. For the special ideas of all departments of sense have in all beings possessed of all the senses—or of four senses, or of three—the common quality of coming into existence only under conditions of time, space, and causality. This common property presupposes similar processes in every separate sense-center of the highest rank. Excitation of one of these centers easily effect similar co-excitations of centers that have often been excited together with them through objective impressions, and it is this similar co-excitement extending itself over the cerebral centers of all the nerves of sense that evokes the composite idea of the "I."

According to this view, therefore, the "I" can not exist as a unit, as undivided, as uninterrupted; it exists only when the separate departments of sense are active with their *egos*, out of which the "I" is abstracted; e. g., it disappears in dreamless sleep. In the waking condition it has continued existence only where the centro-sensory excitations are most strongly in force; i. e., where the attention is on the strain.

Still less, however, is the "I" an aggregate. For this presupposes the exchangeability of the component parts. The seeing *ego*, however, can just as little have its place made good by a substitute as can the hearing one, the tasting one, etc. The sum-total of the separate leaves, blossoms, stalks, roots, of the plant does not, by a great deal, constitute the plant. The parts must be joined together in a special manner. So, likewise, it is not enough to add together the characteristics common to the separate sense-representations in order to obtain from these the regulating and controlling "I." Rather there results from the increasing number and manifoldness of the sense-impressions a continually increasing growth of the gray substance of the child's cerebrum, a rapid increase of the inter-central connecting fibers, and through this a readier co-excitement—association, so called—which units feeling with willing and thinking in the child.

This union is the "I," the sentient and emotive, the desiring and willing, the perceiving and thinking "I."

* * *

Buying the Darwinian ethos did not commit everyone to a hereditarian view of man. Seguin, in an angry report to an international meeting of educators, made this clear in 1873. Quite apart from the comic relief his remarks provide, the comparison of his flowery excess with Preyer's usual good sense puts the embryologist's work in better perspective.

. . . experienced physicians will testify that, when their hands receive a new-comer, they plainly read upon his features the dominant feelings and emotions of its mother during that intra-uterine education whose imprints trace the channel of future sympathies and abilities. . . . [If it is noble to educate and cure the abnormal person] how much higher is the work of preventing these degeneracies in the incipient being, by averting those commotions which storm him in the holy region intended for a terrestial paradise during the period of evolution.*

Preyer's reputation probably outruns his contribution to child psychology; there can be no doubt that Granville Stanley Hall's contribution far outruns his present reputation. A man who can lay defensible claim to being a founder of American psychology, Madison to James' Washington, and without qualification the

---

* E. Seguin, Prenatal and infantile culture, *Popular Science Monthly*, **10**, 1876, 38–43. The quotation given is on p. 39.

founder of child psychology in the United States, Hall has shrunk from title page to short footnote in less than fifty years. Founder of the *American Journal of Psychology*, teacher of Dewey, Jastrow, Gesell, and Terman, author of over 400 books and papers in psychology and education, chief of one of the first psychological laboratories in America, host of Freud's only visit to the United States—Hall's influence in American psychology was great and, by the usual rules of eminence, should have been lasting. It was not. In part, Hall's reputation went into eclipse with the disaster that overtook Clark University on his retirement as president; in part, Hall was a victim, like so many others, of the Watsonian purge; in part, his refusal to stand on one intellectual position long enough to acquire a label in a time when the lines between schools of psychology were being drawn black prevented the placement of Hall in any convenient pigeonhole.

Hall's place as scholar of psychology will remain in shadow—the paper that appears later on in this chapter will certainly not retrieve his reputation—but his place in the history of psychology is fixed by his success as entrepreneur and evangelist of child study. From the Boston kindergarten studies of 1880 until his death in 1924, Hall was committed to the notion that the study of development was at the heart of the problem of understanding man. He introduced Preyer to American readers, he created adolescence as an area of psychological investigation in a two-volume monument of diligence and enthusiasm, he championed the cause of psychoanalysis in a hostile community, he developed questionnaire procedures for the study of children to a fine point, and, as may be guessed from the listing, he scattered his talents and his energy from horizon to horizon. He wrote on psychological interpretations of Jesus Christ and the American flapper; sex, senescence, war, physical education, the nature of universities, morality, Hegel, spiritism, and music. As he notes somewhat sadly, he is rare in having fallen under both the *odium sexicum* and the *odium theologicum*. His mind was open to every aspect of human experience except, perhaps, mathematics and metaphysics. Gesell wrote of Hall's intellectual extravagance but added, "he nevertheless was a naturalist Darwin of the mind, whose outlook embraced the total phylum, and [he] lifted psychology above the sterilities of excessive analysis and pedantry."* On the evidence, one is inclined to believe that his colleagues never forgave him for that. They certainly never forgave his interest in sex and psychoanalysis. In the words of one, "[Hall] has not the slightest conception of what an exact scientific method consists in—what, in fact, one could predict of any one who swallows whole the Freudian mythology."†

There was more to Hall's failure than dilletantism; his life contained competing tendencies that were divided among men and movements. It is hardly surprising that Hall could not keep them all within himself and remain whole. When Hall wrote his first paper about children, *The Contents of Children's Minds*,‡ he was creating a new intellectual discipline and shaping it to his conception of man. When he died, child psychology was sorted into at least half a dozen insulated lines of development, none of which could claim him as founder or seer.

Hall's antipathies were as zealously held as were his sympathies and they indicate how badly he predicted the course of American psychology. Speaking on the unity of mental science at the St. Louis World's Fair in 1904, Hall marked out the enemies of psychology—mathematics, metaphysics, and epistemology. On the first and, for Hall, primary opponent of proper psychology, he let loose his grandest rhetoric.

. . . indeed, I think, [that] every attempted application of mathematics to psychology, save only for the simple algebraic or other treatment of statistical data, have later proved an illusion, if not a mere affectation; and we owe today no more to any concept susceptible of mathematical

* A. Gesell [Autobiography], in E. G. Boring et al. *A History of Psychology in Autobiography*, Vol. IV. Worcester, Mass.: Clark University Press, 1952, p. 127. The first three volumes in this series (1930, 1932, and 1936) were edited by C. Murchison.
† Lorine Pruette, *G. Stanley Hall: A Biography of a Mind*, New York: Appleton, 1926, p. 195. For a somewhat more sober account of Hall's life and work, see the memorial issue of *Publications of the Clark University Library*, 7, No. 6, 1925, largely the work of L. N. Wilson. Hall spoke for himself in *Life and Confessions of a Psychologist*, New York: Appleton, 1923.
‡ G. S. Hall, The contents of children's minds, *Princeton Review*, 59, 1883, 249–272.

formulation than modern physiology does to the old iatric school that so elaborately treated the bones as levers.*

Hall's rage against the scientifically irrelevant problems of metaphysics—mind and body, freedom and necessity, parallelism and interaction—was both more restrained and more progressive in spirit than his remarks on mathematics but, when he came to a dissection of epistemology, he again cut himself off from the future of the science he helped to create.

The human soul inherits the result of a vast experience acquired by the race, but innate in the individual, but the latter cannot validate much of it in his own restricted life. . . . What we inherit is so much better organized than what we acquire, it is so dominate and, perhaps, so unmodifiable and unaccountable, that the world and self seem shadowy. . . .

Hall taught that psychologists should not spend time in fruitless speculation about matters beyond observation; psychology should be, like the rest of American life, practical and inductive. " . . . the first and, perhaps, chief danger to psychology as a science today seems to me to be its tendency, as by an iron law, to gravitate to methods that are too abstract, deductive, speculative, and effectively exact." There is no record of the response of John Watson, present in the audience, to these remarks.

One of Hall's most revealing papers, *The Story of a Sand Pile*,† tells of the creative behavior of children confronted with the possibilities of a load of sand. They worked with the spirit and zest of Robinson Crusoe, digging, exploring, constructing, destroying. So it was with Hall—not a Darwin of the mind but a Robinson Crusoe of the mind for whom the study of human experience was as formless and as much fun as a sand pile. He ranged across all human behavior, daring to look at religion and sex with the same enthusiastic incompetence that he brought to the study of curricula and questionnaires. One may suspect that he handled the

* H. J. Rogers (Ed.), *International Congress of Arts and Sciences*, Universal Exposition, St. Louis, 1904, 8 vol., Boston: Houghton Mifflin, 1906–1907, Vol. V, pp. 582, 583.

† G. S. Hall, The story of a sand pile, in G. S. Hall and some of his pupils, *Aspects of Child Life and Education*, New York: Appleton, 1907, pp. 142–156.

ambiguity of diversity by rarely committing himself to a school, a method, or a theory. He was truly committed to the questionnaire as a technique of studying development, he was truly committed to the study of the evolving child, and he was truly committed to Clark University; beyond these, the world was Stanley Hall's sand pile and he played there with a joy that has not been rivaled among psychologists. He guaranteed the presence of child study as a legitimate field of study, and he forced psychoanalysis on the attention of American scientists; his other contributions to the history of child psychology must be found in the work of his students and in the work of his colleagues who, moved either by the contagion of his enthusiasm or the arousal of hostility to his ideas, advanced the study of the child along lines not altogether congenial to Hall.

Hall's first study of children contains the germ of his later refinements of the questionnaire. It is less interesting, however, even as a historical document than some of the later syllabi sent out from Clark. There were more than one hundred questionnaire studies carried out during Hall's years at Clark on themes as diverse as his interests. From the large number of printed studies, there is presented here an abridgment of an abridgment of his study of dolls. The naiveté or lack of concern about reliability, the apparent willingness to accept unsupported testimony, the sometimes exciting flights of speculation (Hall's strictures against speculation did not apply when there were data in hand), the attempt to bridge from child to animal to culture, the flamboyance of the style—all are characteristic of the works of this remarkable man. There have been diggers in the sand pile of child study since him, but in a sense, Hall has had no descendents—only heirs.

* * *

Granville Stanley Hall (1844–1924)

A Study of Dolls

Dolls have so long been one of the chief toys of children, and
are now so nearly universal among both savage and civilized
peoples, that it is singular that no serious attempt has ever been
made to study them. The topic of this paper is not only relatively
new, but the field it opens is one of vast complexity, many-sided
interest, and of the greatest significance both for psychology and
pedagogy. When a thoughtful mother asks what is the best form,
size, material, amount of elaborateness or mechanical devices,
dress, paraphernalia, degree of abandon in doll play, proper and
improper imitations of human life, whether doll play is instinctive with and good for boys as well as girls, or for any generalizations concerning dolls' names, doll families, dolls' diseases, the
age at which the doll instinct is strongest, when it legitimately
declines, whether paper dolls precede, follow, or coexist with
dolls of three dimensions, doll anatomy, doll psychology, the real
source of the many instincts that are expressed in doll play, its
form among savage races, whether it is related to idolatry, and if
so, how,—for answer to nearly all these problems one would search
the meager and fragmentary doll literature in vain. Indeed, this
paper, imperfect as it is, is the first to call attention to the importance of a strongly neglected, new, but exceedingly rich
psychogenetic field.

It was considerations like these that led one of us [Hall] after
a careful preliminary survey based on informal examinations of

A. C. Ellis and G. S. Hall, A study of dolls. *Pedagogical Seminary,* **4,** 1896, 129–175.
Abridged and reprinted in G. S. Hall and some of his pupils, *Aspects of Child Life and
Education,* New York: Appleton, 1907, pp. 157–204. The present selection was
abridged from *Aspects of Child Life and Education.*

many children of different ages, . . . to print and circulate among about eight hundred teachers and parents a questionnaire which brought [648] returns. . . . These returns were of very varied degrees of merit. Some were long letters of reminiscence by adults, some were observations by mothers, and others were of the doll history of individual children. There were also school compositions by pupils of high and normal schools; 94 boys were reported on, the rest were girls; 96 were reminiscences, and the majority were written by females between fourteen and twenty-four. Altogether this constituted a stack of thousands of pages of manuscript. After a considerable time spent by both of us in a preliminary survey of this material, it was decided that, intractable, and lacking in uniformity as it was, it merited as careful a statistical treatment as could be given it, and this laborious task was finally undertaken by [Ellis], who also conducted quite a voluminous correspondence, gathered the literary references with careful epitomes thereof, selected and condensed typical cases from the returns, preserving every salient phrase and incident, and issued a supplementary syllabus to get better statistical results.

These latter returns were given to [Hall] under whose supervision they were tabulated, and to whom [Ellis's] tables, correspondence, digests, conclusions, suggestions, and everything else were turned over, and who must therefore bear the responsibility of the attempt herewith made to present such account of all these varied data as he is able to do under limitations of both time and space, which are such as leave much to be desired. He has also freely added inferences, data, etc.

Material of Which Dolls Are Made, Substitutes, and Proxies

Of 845 children, with 989 preferences, between the ages of three and twelve, 191 preferred wax dolls; 163, paper dolls; 153, china dolls; 144, rag dolls; 116, bisque dolls; 83, china and cloth dolls; 69, rubber dolls; 12, china and kid dolls; 11, pasteboard dolls; 7, plaster of Paris dolls; 6, wood dolls; 3, knit dolls; while a few each preferred papier-maché, clay, glass, cotton, tin, celluloid,

French, Japanese, brownie, Chinese, sailor, negro, Eskimo dolls, etc. Many children gave several as equally desirable, or their preferences changed and many preferred the substitute to the real doll.

We have grouped as substitutes objects used and treated by children as if they were dolls. Such treatment always involves ascribing more or less psychic qualities to the object, and treating it as if it were an animate or sentient thing. Nothing illustrates the strength of the doll instinct and the vigor of the animistic fancy like the following list of doll substitutes. In answers to the first syllabus, pillows were treated as dolls by 39 children, who often tied strings around the middle of the pillow, using a shawl for the skirt; sticks, sometimes dressed in flowers, leaves, and twisted grass were used by 29; bottles, filled with different-colored water and called different people, some with doll-head corks, by 24; cob or ear of corn (red ears favored, corn silk for the hair, a daisy perhaps serving for a hat) by 19; dogs by 18; cats and kittens by 15; shawls by 14; flowers by 12; clothespins (one a sailor, one a woman, sometimes both, used as servants) by 11; blocks by 9; children by 7; pieces of cloth by 7; daisies (taking off all but two petals, marking eyes, and making grass mothers) by 6; newspapers by 6; stuffed elephants (seemed like a real baby) by 6; clothes pegs by 5; peanuts by 5; sticks of wood by 5; apples by 4; clay pipes by 4; kindergarten material by 4; handkerchiefs by 4; mud and clay by 4; chairs and stools by 3; buttons by 3; potatoes (one end the head, with eyes, matches used for arms and legs) by 3; wishbones by 3; nine-pins by 3; squashes by 3; toothpicks by 3; vegetables by 3; yarn strings by 3. The following are each mentioned twice as having been used as dolls: acorns, aprons, bootjacks, feathers, doughnuts, cucumbers, spools, shells, pumpkins (dressed in own clothes), towels (knotted in the middle), rubber balls, brooms (dressed in bolster case), nails, bedposts, sticks of candy (dressed), button hooks, keys and umbrellas.

The following are each mentioned once as doll substitutes: box, jug, coat, orange peel, cribbage peg, chicken, whisk broom, board with face painted on it, croquet ball, dish top, finger of a person dressed as doll, hand dressed as doll, with thumb and finger wrapped up for arms, water bottle, celery, one corner of a blanket (the other was mother), log, shoe, curtain tassel, roll of batting, bundle from the store, turkey wing named Dinah, washboard (two legs, so much like a man), wooden spoon, weed, piece of lath, salt bag stuffed, fish, piece of Porterhouse steak, sweet potato, stuffed stocking, stuffed cat, hitching post (so dressed up as to scare horses), stick of stove wood, tongs, toy monkey, radish, scissors in a spool, sheet, shoulder blanket, stone block, spoon, petunia (stem pushed through for head and neck), pin, pronged stick (looked like arms and legs), linen book rolled up and marked, knife, fork and spoon (called servants), knitting needles, lead pencils, half-burned matches (black for hair), marbles, oranges, penholder, beets, grapes (pulps for heads, splints for arms and legs, set sailing in cucumber boats), geraniums, green peaches (with pins for arms and legs), gateposts (by a party of children), gourds, hickory nuts, hollyhocks, horse-chestnuts (pin for arms and legs), cuffs rolled up, dress folded, fuchsia, feather, forks, glass, corn husks, beans, berries, cradle quilt, carrot, crochet hook, hairbrush, cane, cricket, clamp, carpenter's plane, axle of toy cart, a bench, books, balls, and bric-a-brac.

In reply to the supplementary question, out of 579 children 57 had used a cat as a doll; 41, clothespins; 26, sticks; 21, vegetables; 20, a pillow. Only 26 of all these were boys. As an instance of flower dolls one correspondent writes:

I often took pansies for dolls because of their human faces; the rose I revered too much to play with, it was like my best wax doll, dressed in her prettiest, but always sitting in state in a big chair in some secluded corner where little visitors would not spy her out. I loved these nature dolls far better than the prettiest store dolls and ascribed special psychic qualities to them. The hepaticas seemed delicate children to be tenderly cared for but which soon drooped and faded. Violets were sturdy little ones which enjoyed a frolic and could be played with. The pansy was a willing, quick, bright flower child, the rose her grown-up sister, pretty, always charmingly dressed, but a quiet and sedate spectator. Violets were shy, good-natured children, but their pansy cousins were often naughty and would not play. The hepaticas were invalids and cripples who watched their livelier brothers and sisters and were entertained by stiff maiden aunts, marigolds, with long curls. The dahlias were colored servants and mammies; yellow violets were mischievous, fun-loving boys; sweet peas were the nurses with cap and kerchief on; the morning-glories were governesses and teachers. I often made little boats to give my flower dolls rides on the river. We built harbors, but in rough weather so many lives were lost that our pleasure was marred.

— — —

Children are often under a long-continued delusion concerning the material of which dolls are made. Even long after it is *known* that they are wood, wax, etc., it is *felt* that they are of skin, flesh, etc. To find a doll's head hollow or that it is sawdust, while it suggests to very young children the same as contents of their own body, is with older children a frequent source of disenchantment and sometimes marks the sudden end of the doll period. In some cases allowances for the doll's moral or physical disabilities are made on account of the material of which they are found to consist. Wooden dolls will not bend; so are obstinate. Babies are differentiated as "meat dolls," but the differences of temperature are noted with strange rarity. It is singular how slow and late children learn what the "hard things" under their own skin (bones) are, and how easily, after a trifling injury, they think the body a bag of blood, or somehow get the impression that they are blown up and grow by inflation, or are themselves full of sawdust or of stomach, which fills even arms and legs. Discussions with skeptical brothers, who assert that the doll is nothing but wood, rubber, wax, etc., are often met with a resentment as keen as that vented upon missionaries who declare that idols are but sticks and stones, or, to come near home, upon those who assert cerebral, automatic, or necessitarian theories of the soul.

In our returns curly hair is preferred to straight; red cheeks are a special point of beauty, as are red knees in fewer cases. Boy dolls are only about one twelfth of all, and it is remarkable how few dolls are babies rather than little adults. Children are very prone to focus their interest upon peculiar slippers, shoes, the upward or downward look of the eyes, some peculiar turn and carriage of the head, some cute expression, "like a clown," "funny as if it was going to cry or shout," "stuck up," "smiling," "sweet," "tanned," etc. Some particular dress, name, complexion, or even defect is often focused on. Aversions follow the same rule.

Of 579 answers to questions 13, 14, and 15 of the supplementary paper, 463 reported for the age below five as follows: 266 preferred babies; 126, children; 71, adults. From five to ten, 314 reported, of whom 105 preferred babies; 159, children; 50, adult dolls. From ten to fifteen years of age, 45 reported a preference for babies; 64, for children; 32, for adults. On the whole, babies were thus preferred 416 times and children and adults 502 times. Children lead babies after the age of five, the ratio of adult dolls increasing with age. Boys' dolls are least often infants. Among 45 feeble-minded girls the ratio of dolls as babies is highest.

Out of 579 answers to the second questionnaire, 88 mentioned preference for blue eyes; 27, for brown eyes; and 8, for black eyes. As to hair preferences 118 mention light hair; 62, curly hair; 27, dark hair; 8, real hair; and 5, red hair; while 15 mention love for red cheeks; 7, nice teeth; 8, pretty hands or feet; 3, red lips.

Some children have a strong preference for old dolls, however ugly, and are indifferent to new ones, however fine; some love and some hate heirloom dolls. Some have sudden changes of affection; an old doll that has been long loved is perhaps suddenly repelled, thrown or given away, or even burned, and a new favorite chosen. Some never like lady or Japanese dolls, but their affection has a very limited range. Children with many dolls often have one for Sunday or one is queen, mother, or teacher; some profess to be absolutely impartial, loving all their dolls exactly alike. Often a sudden craze for doll dressmaking, hair combing, fantastic buttons, very small or very large dolls, shoes, hats, movable eyes, is reported, suggesting something akin to Kraft-Ebing's fetichism on the one hand, and the strange focusing on single features of face or dress seen in children's drawings on the other, and indicating how psychic growth tends to focalize, now in this, now in that direction. This we consider a point of great importance and suggestiveness for school work when fully wrought out. Mind may have its nascent periods like the body. Now interest centers on hair, which must be in long braids or otherwise done up, or be worn short, parted sideways, banged. Now it is a fat, round, baby face, plump red cheeks, teeth, pretty neck, joints, that are doted on. So it is with articles of dress, etc.

[There follow sections on dolls' psychic qualities, feeding, sleep, sickness, death, names, discipline, hygiene, families, and accessories.]

The number and vast variety of objects more or less dollified well illustrate the remark of Victor Hugo—that as birds may take almost every material for a nest, so nothing resists the childish instinct to find or make dolls out of everything, and stones, books, balls, buttons, stove hooks, nails, bricks, washboards, flowers, pins, articles of food, objects with no trace of anything that can be called face, limbs, or head, are made dolls. Hugo's Cossette dressed, hugged, and put to sleep a naked sword. Occasionally immovable things like posts, stumps, and even trees are more or less dollified. The quick imagination of childhood makes an eye out of a speck or dot, and perhaps imagines the other features. This instinct cannot be entirely explained as nascent parenthood, but must include some elements of the widespread animism, if not fetichism, of children and savages. The valuable study of Dr. Fewkes, the Roman games, the Doll Feast of Japan, and some of the etymologies point this way, as do, perhaps, the rare cases of children who make God dolls, whipping them for watching, etc. The fear of the spirits of burned dolls, of black dolls, of evil eye, and some forms of special aversion point the same way. As the optic nerve, whether heated, chilled, touched with chemicals or electricity, can only respond by giving the sensation of light, so primitive humanity sees personality in everything. This again is abundantly proved in returns to another syllabus already worked up, illustrating children's feeling for inanimate as well as animate nature. However disconnected the words *doll* and *idol*, some psychic connection cannot be doubted.

. . . As object lessons setting forth invisible beings in concrete form, idolatry is perhaps as much more persistent than dolls, as memory of abstract is more persistent than that of concrete words in progressive aphasia, and for analogous reasons. Idols may, perhaps, be valuable object lessons in religion for children at the low pagan stage and may yet have a role to play in elementary religious training, but their danger is analogous in kind to that sometimes feared for excessive and too prolonged doll cult, viz., that it may arrest the higher development of parental instincts, check interest in free play with children, and place puppets and dummies where real personalities ought to be. If deities were certain to appear later in concrete form and break the charm of idols, so that the danger of forever putting an unworthy symbol in place of that which it symbolizes could be as effectually obviated as interest in "meat babies" and live children is sure to supplant dolls, idolatry would lose its dangers. Both the psychological significance and the educational value of the image worship of the Catholic church and of religious pictures, figures, and of spiritual beings are topics upon which carefully made home experiments and observations, which would be of great value, are needed and could be made.

The relatively small proportion of dolls which represents infants, and the large proportion representing adults, shows again that the parental instinct is far less prominent in doll play than is commonly supposed.

— — —

Our returns do not show any law of relationship between the size of the doll and the size or age of the child, save that the extremes of large and small develop their chief charm well on in the doll period. Things large, like things far off, fail of exciting interest and of being comprehended by children, and are almost as effectively out of their range as things microscopic are for adult eyes. As the microscope and telescope bring minute and distant objects within our purview, so a doll microcosm opens up a world of relationship so large, and simplifies things so complex, as to be otherwise closed to the infant mind. If we take a

large view of the doll problem, it thus comprises most of the
most important questions of education.

That boys are naturally fond of and should play with dolls
as well as girls, there is abundant indication. One boy in a
family of girls, or boys who are only children, often play with
dolls up to seven or eight years of age. It is unfortunate that
this is considered so predominantly a girl's play. Most boys
abandon it early or never play, partly because it is thought girlish
by adults as well as by children. Of course boy life is naturally
rougher and demands a wider range of activities. The danger,
too, of making boy milliners is of course obvious, but we are
convinced that, on the whole, more play with girl dolls by boys
would tend to make them more sympathetic with girls as children,
if not more tender with their wives and with women later. Again,
boys as well as girls might be encouraged to play with boy dolls
more than at present, with great advantage to both. Boys, too,
seem to prefer exceptional dolls,—clowns, brownies, colored,
Eskimo, Japanese, etc. Boys, too, seem fonder than girls of monkey
and animal dolls, and are often very tender of these, when they
maltreat dolls in human shape. Again, dolls representing heroes
of every kind and non-existent beings, dragons, and hobgoblins
find their chief admirers among boys. A boy of six I know was
fascinated with a rude Jack-o'-lantern, would lie on the floor
and talk to it by the hour, ask it questions and get what he deemed
real answers, and was charmed by its horrid features. Boys are
little prone to doll luxury or elaborate paraphernalia and are
content with ruder dolls than girls, and the doll function is
naturally far less developed than with girls.

In discussing the degree and kind of reality of the doll world,
we approach one of the most difficult of psychological problems.
Children seem to delight in giving way to illusions, and even
delusions here, which it is extremely difficult for the adult mind
to understand. Often in the midst of the most absorbing play,
the slightest criticism, a word of appeal to reason, the most
trivial fact of real life, annihilates in an instant the entire doll
cosmos. The wedding, school, or funeral is left unfinished, the
half-dressed doll dropped in the most painful attitude and left
in the cold for perhaps an indefinite period. Sometimes we see

traces of a struggle almost painful between faith and doubt, either of which may triumph. The doll may have a definite personality, be a real member of the family and not a toy, or a "hybrid between a baby and fetich," be a real part of the child's self, be fanned, its bruises rubbed and wept over; or, again, as in one case, may be the hero of a vividly fancied romance, lose money, work its way out West, become rich, travel east, be shipwrecked on a desert island, etc; real personalities may lose interest in comparison with it, and all this may be kept up with some consistency for years,—one normal woman of twenty-seven and another of forty still play with dolls,—absorption in the play blotting out the grossest incongruities, the doll being a real companion and crony sharing every secret and confidence in solitude *a deux,* on journeys, and elsewhere, so that the child's psychic life seems entirely bound up with it. The subjective and objective, will, feeling, and knowledge are strangely mixed. One child had tried all her life to keep her doll from knowing she was not alive. Dolls are buried without dying, fed without eating, bathed without water, are now good, now bad, now happy, now tearful, without the slightest change, the child furnishing the motive power and all its moods being mirrored in another self. It seems to be at about the age of six, three years before the culmination of the doll passion, that the conflict between fancy and reality becomes clearly manifest. Abandonment to the doll illusion and the length of the doll period seems less in the western than in the eastern children, and decreases as dolls and their accessories become elaborate. With every increase of knowledge of anatomy or of the difference between living tissue and dead matter, between life and mechanism, this element of doll play must wane.

Perhaps nothing so fully opens up the juvenile soul to the student of childhood as well-developed doll play. Here we see fully revealed things which the childish instinct often tends to keep secret. It shows out the real nature which Plato thought so important that he advised drunkenness as a revealer of character. The doll often fears ghosts or lightning, and becomes conscious of sex as the child does. Flogging the doll for not being in the right place, being untidy, etc., often marks the rise of the child's consciousness of order and cleanliness. Whispered confidences with the doll are often more intimate and sacred than with any human being. The doll is taught those things learned best or in which the child has most interest. The little mother's real ideas of morality are best seen in her punishments and rewards of her doll. Her favorite foods are those of her doll. The features of funerals, weddings, schools, and parties which are reënacted with the doll are those which have most deeply impressed the child. The child's moods, ideals of life, dress, etc., come to utterance in free and spontaneous doll play. Deaf girls teach their dolls the finger alphabet, blind ones sometimes want bandages or glasses for their dolls. I know a mother of a sickly child who says she can anticipate the symptoms of all the illnesses of her daughter because they are first projected upon the doll before the child has become fully conscious of them in herself. Children often express their own desire for goodies euphemistically by saying, "Dolly wants it." Thus the individuality of children sometimes is more clearly revealed in the characters they give their dolls than in their own traits. Long-kept dolls thus often grow up, as it were, with the child, their infantile qualities expanding into those of childhood and then youth. Paper dolls, often with picture food, which seem more ideal and more often associated with fairy stories, betray the evanescent stages of the doll psychosis as it fades into adult life.

Is doll play an early cropping out of mother love as Schneider and Victor Hugo and others think? And are dolls representatives of future children? This appears to be true only in a limited and partial sense, and we must readjust our views upon this point. Some mothers, very fond of their children now, never cared much for dolls, while many of our returns show that unmarried women and childless wives have been most enthusiastic devotees of dolls, and in such cases the doll cult seems often to be most prolonged. It also seems natural for small boys. Certainly other functions are more pronounced. There seems to be a premonition of the parental instinct in early childhood, which fades as the dawn of adolescence approaches, as the fetal hair falls off to make place for a ranker growth much later. The saying that the first child is the last doll is, I believe, not true of normal women. The treatment of and feeling toward a doll and a child are more unlike than the teeth of first and second dentition. That the first may hypertrophy and dwarf the second is undoubted. Indeed it is just possible that the ideal mother never plays dolls with great abandon. Despite the increased extent of doll play, its intensity seems a little on the wane among the best people, and too many accessories lessen the educational value of this play in teaching children to put themselves in the parent's place, in deepening love of children, and of motherhood.

The educational value of dolls is enormous, and the protest of this paper is against longer neglect of it. It educates the heart and will, even more than the intellect, and to learn how to control and apply doll play will be to discover a new instrument in education of the very highest potency.

[Hall presents anthropological data on dolls.]

During the two years that have intervened since the first syllabus was issued this subject has steadily grown in both interest and importance to the editors' minds, until this paper seems but the faintest and feeblest beginning of the many more special investigations that ought to be made in its field. Where could the philologist, for example, find a richer field for the study of the principle of analogy, the law of diminutives and of conferring names generally, and I know not what else, than in a far more extended and systematic investigation of dolls' names? The whole subject of idolatry, the use and psychology of images and pictures of God, Christ, angels, saints, etc., suggests, but only begins to reveal its richness here. When we reflect on the rôle that tutelary and ancestral images, puppets, heroic and mythological dolls have played in the past, the question must force itself upon our minds whether some well-devised form not only of image worship but even of fetichism might not be made as helpful in early religions as object lessons have been in secular education since Comenius. We do use pictures and statuettes of classical mythology to great advantage. Are we now advanced and strong enough to utilize the powerful instinct of idolatry still further, so as to get its stimulus and avoid its great and obvious dangers? Children's ideas of life, death, soul, virtue and vice, disease, sickness, all the minor morals of dress, toilet, eating, etc., of family, state, church, theology, etc., are all as open as day, here, to the observer, and although unconscious to themselves, almost anything within these large topics can be explored by the observing, tactful adult, without danger of injuring that naïveté of childhood which is both its best trait and its chief charm. What topic yet proposed for child study is not, at least in part, illustrated here?

Imperfect as this study is, however, alas for the tact and intuitive power of the parent and kindergartner that does not find in the children's and mothers' records a wealth of helpful and immediately practical suggestions for their daily task of unfolding childhood from within. We have carefully refrained from psychologic or pedagogic generalizations, which have been often very tempting, because the time has not yet come for conclusions or specific rules of application. Prematureness and rashness here would involve danger of great harm; but, as further researches are needed on the scientific side, special studies on the practical side are no less desiderated.

*   *   *

William James was appalled by the "raw philistinism" of Hall's group and so was his friend and warm admirer, James Mark Baldwin. Baldwin came, like Hall, from philosophy through Darwin to genetic psychology and, like Hall, was a prolific writer and an enthusiast. There the resemblance narrows; Baldwin remained a philosopher in attitude and a systematizer in intention, his aim the architectonic reconstruction of the psychology of thought. Baldwin established laboratories at Toronto, Johns Hopkins (where he brought Watson in 1908), and Princeton, but his interest in psychological method and in the disheartening accumulation of graphs and tables waned steadily over the years. His slight contributions to the "new experimental psychology" were completed by the turn of the century.

Two interconnected areas of interest occupied Baldwin during his relatively short career in American psychology—the evolution of behavior in the race and in the child, an interest that linked him to the major intellectual development of the time, and the construction of a genetic theory of thought. Although at first glance his work on mental development, based in part on observations of his two children (a clear gain on Preyer but as nothing to Piaget's three!), is of greater relevance to the history of child study, it is rather in his epistemological writings that Baldwin's message for contemporary views of the child lies. *Thought and Things,*＊ brilliant and one of the few truly original documents in psychology, crowded with invented words and all the apparatus of a philosophical system, caused a slight flurry among philosophers and was steadfastly and monotonously ignored by psychologists. Signs of Baldwin appear in the work of G. H. Mead; and, through him, in some parts of contemporary social thought.

As will be seen, Baldwin found his true intellectual successor in Jean Piaget, but among his colleagues in psychology, Baldwin's treatise on thought caused no perceptible stir. The reasons are not hard to find. Baldwin allied himself with no school; he found Hall "narrow-minded," psychoanalysis "based on sometimes unreal and always extravagant presuppositions," behaviorism "not psychology." He wanted to stand between the idealism of the German philosophers and the pragmatism of the Americans, and he wanted to manage this affiliation by means of an empirical theory of thought based on genetic principles. More than that, his distaste for the laboratory and his conviction that the ultimate ground on which an understanding of man would arise was an esthetic one made Baldwin's position utterly unassimilable to American psychology in its brawling infancy. Baldwin left the arena of contention geographically in 1909 and spent the remaining twenty-five years of his life in Mexico and France. His emigration left him without students and without a platform for the teaching of his psychophilosophy. His obituary notices in American journals had the strange tone of describing a man who had been dead in fact for many years.

＊ J. M. Baldwin, *Thought and Things. A Study of the Development and Meaning of Thought or Genetic Logic*, New York: Macmillan. Vol. I: Functional logic, or genetic theory of knowledge (1906); Vol. II: Experimental logic, or genetic theory of thought (1908); Vol. III: Interest and art, or genetic epistemology (1911). Baldwin saw this work as completed with *Genetic Theory of Reality*, New York: Putnam, 1915.

In his most influential book, from which the selection given below is taken, Baldwin inhibited his interest in the construction of psychological theory long enough to report some interesting observations about color sensitivity, handedness, and imitation in his children. Baldwin's role in child psychology, however, is not that of a particularly keen observer; he was the chief theoretician and philosopher of the Darwinian changes. He had strong feelings about the role of theory in science, to be sure, and was not reluctant to sing them out.

The most vicious and Philistine attempt in some quarters [there can be no doubt that he is speaking toward Hall] to put science in the strait-jacket of barren observation, to draw the life-blood of all science—speculative advance into the meanings of things—this ultra-positivistic cry has come here as everywhere else, and put a ban upon theory. On the contrary, give us theories, theories! Let every man who has a theory pronounce his theory! That is just the difference between the average mother and the good psychologist—she has no theories, he has; he has no interests, she has. She may bring up a family of a dozen and not be able to make a single trustworthy observation; he may be able, from one sound of one yearling, to confirm theories . . . momentous for the future training and welfare of the child.*

Baldwin's theories were wide-ranging. He saw the child as vital in the process of selection; under his principle of orthoplasy, variations in the child were protected long enough for the environment to select the most successful forms of behavior. "The fact of variation [in the behavior and temperament of children] . . . is the only means to human progress—the only supply of material for the selection of the fittest under the action of a progressive social environment." This comment also contains Baldwin's great interest other than the child—his noteworthy understanding of the role of social forces in the development of the child and the species. He recognized, as some of the other social Darwinians did not, that the procedures of selection in human beings were almost

* J. M. Baldwin, *Mental Development in the Child and the Race*, New York: Macmillan, 1895. The quotations given here are from p. 31 and pp. 37ff. See also J. M. Baldwin, *Development and Evolution including Psychophysical Evolution, Evolution by Orthoplasy, and the Theory of Genetic Modes*, New York: Macmillan, 1902.

exclusively those of the social order and that analogies with activities like animal food-getting were limited at best.

The heart of Baldwin's theories combined his interest in the child and in society; he attempted to construct a theory of knowledge based on genetic principles and the action of the social environment. For him, his position was a "radical modification of the current Spencer-Bain theory of the action of pleasure and pain" in psychological economy. Baldwin was unsatisfied with mechanisms for psychological change which were *merely selective;* he insisted that a principle of invention was needed. "*Actually new things—novelties—are daily achieved in life, mind and society;* results which we cannot interpret in terms of the mere composition of the elements involved."* He wrote his highly technical *Thought and Things* in demonstration of his thesis, with particular regard to the development of logic. But, as early as 1895, the major postulates of his system had been invented and were in use. It will be seen that the child enters Baldwin's speculations only as a reminder of certain observations, but the theory is truly developmental; it shows an understanding of the problems involved in explaining the thought of the child, which contemporary psychology is just beginning to recognize.

Baldwin accepted the importance of the formation of habits in explaining behavior, and he goes beyond the limitations of the Spencer-Bain notion of "habit" to assert a position far more modern. As psychologist, he was a motor-theorist like Munsterberg and Holt, and he hoped that association could be reduced to the compounding ("assimilation") of motor discharges.

In what has been said of the principle of association, we find ground for the reduction of its particular forms to the one law of *assimilation.* . . . In assimilation—and in the "apperception" of the Herbartians—we have the general statement of all the forms, nets, modes of grouping, which old elements of mental content bring to impose upon the new. In the light of their motor effects, we are able to construe all these elements of content under the general principle of habit, and say that the assimilation of any one element to another, or the assimilation of

* J. M. Baldwin, *Darwin and the Humanities*, Baltimore: Review Publishing, 1909, p. 87.

any two or more such elements to a third, is due to the unifying of their motor discharges in the single larger discharge which stands for the apperceived result. . . . Put generally . . . we may say that assimilation is due to the tendency of a new sensory process to be drawn off into preformed [not necessarily congenital; they may be the result of earlier habits] motor reactions; these preformed reactions in their turn tending to reinstate, by the principle of imitation, the old stimulations or memories which led to their preformation, with all the associations of these memories. These memories, therefore, tend to take the place of, or stand for, or include the new stimulations which are being thus assimilated.*

This is heady wine for readers of current theories of child development, but there is stronger spirit to come. Baldwin offered, as a supplement to the habitual use of assimilation, a new mental principle which would account for novelty and invention in behavior—the principle of *accommodation*. He comes very close indeed to the idea of reinforcement in these pages—even with "organic centralization" close to secondary reinforcement. But, before we make Baldwin into a learning theorist, it is wise to remember his later epistemological work, in which the child as active exploring "theorist" of reality makes his appearance.

*   *   *

James Mark Baldwin (1861–1934)

Habit and Accommodation in Development

After the foregoing detailed statements of facts and theories, and the solution of certain particular genetic problems, we may come to a general synthesis. What is the least that we can say about

J. M. Baldwin, *Mental Development in the Child and the Race* (3rd Ed. Revised), New York: Macmillan, 1906, pp. 452–467.

* J. M. Baldwin, *Mental Development in the Child and the Race*, (3rd Ed. Revised), New York: Macmillan, 1906, pp. 293ff.

an organism's development? Everybody admits that two things must be said: first, it develops by getting *habits* formed; and second, it develops by getting new adaptations which involve the breaking up or modification of habits—these latter being called *accommodations.*

The law of habit may now be stated generally in some such way as this: *Habit is the tendency of an organism to continue more and more readily processes which are vitally beneficial.*

This principle we have found an axiom in biology and psychology. In psychology great instances of it are readily cited— instinct, emotional expression, the performance of movements pictured in the attention, even attention itself. In order to [have] habit, it has become evident, the organism must have *contractility* —ability to make a response in movement to a stimulus—and then it must have *some incentive to make and keep making the right kind of movement.* The essential thing about habit, then, is this: *the maintenance of advantageous stimulations by the organism's own movements.* Now what is the incentive to the right kind of movement? The answer to this question carried us farther.

Three answers are possible. The only incentive may be the actual stimulus, altogether outside the organism, and the right movement may be only a chance selection from many random movements. This is the ordinary biological theory. The stimulus is supposed to "come along" very often, and, moreover, to be very varied in its kind, locality, etc.; so that by repeating happy chance movements, habits are formed, and by compounding the habits, these habits become complex and varied. So the creature develops. On this view development is entirely an expression of the one principle of nervous Habit.

The second answer says: the incentive is in part, as before, outside the organism, that is, the external stimulus must remain constant; but the organism, after the first reaction to the stimulus, tends to repeat its *lucky reactions* again. This is the psychological theory. It finds in this tendency to repeat lucky movements the nervous analogue of pleasure, and makes it with the principle of *excess discharge,* following upon pleasure, the additional thing. There is thus an internal organic "incentive." By this the ceature 'goes out,' and secures its own repetitions or avoidances, but only in the lines of lucky chance accommodations. This we have designated—in the principal form in which it has been held—the Spencer-Bain theory.

But this latter theory, superior as it is to the more mechanical or "repetition" view of the biologists, has had in its statement a radical defect, the intimations of Darwin—who nowhere, to my knowledge, fully expresses an opinion—possibly excepted. It has held, in Spencer and Bain, that the pleasure or pain is from the first secured by *lucky adaptive movement*. This, I have argued above in detail, cannot be the case; for movements themselves reflect pleasure or pain only as they serve as stimuli, reproduce stimuli, or are associated with stimuli. On the contrary, the *stimuli as such* are the agents of good or ill, pleasure or pain; and this pleasure or pain process—index, as it is, of the fundamental vital processes—dictates the *very first adaptive movement toward or away from certain kinds of stimulations*. This is the third answer and the correct one. Otherwise the principle of excess—as in the form of the "heightened nervous wave" of Spencer—only serves to confirm in habits the lucky adaptations already hit upon.

How shall we further conceive the process whereby, from many movements thus generally adapted, some are *selected* as special adaptations, or particular motor functions? This, it is clear, is the question of *Accommodation*. It occurs by means of excess reactions. It is opposed to habit in two ways: first, it has reference to *new* movements,—a prospective reference,—while habit has reference always to movements more or less old, a retrospective reference,—and so it runs ahead of habit; and second, it tends, by the selection of new movements, to come into direct conflict with old habitual movements, and so to disintegrate habits. Let us look, then, at accommodation also more closely, gathering up what has gone before in earlier chapters.

In general formula: *Accommodation is the principle by which an organism comes to adapt itself to more complex conditions of stimulation by performing more complex functions.*

Various functions have been shown in what precedes to illustrate this principle; all functions which the individual has *learned*. Learning to act is just accommodation, nothing more nor less. Speech, tracery, handwriting, piano-playing, all motor acquisitions, are what accommodation is, *i.e.* adaptations to more complex conditions. The common thing about them all is evident from the foregoing statement of the requirements of development: *the maintenance of stimulus by selection from excessive motor discharges.* This is *Imitation.* In brief, any reaction whatever, no matter how produced,—by accident, by suggestion, by obedience, by volition, by effort, under stress of pain or excitement of pleasure,—any reaction by which a useful stimulus is hailed back and enjoyed, or a damaging one fled from and escaped,—any such is a case of accommodation, and falls under the principle of "circular reactions" or "Imitation" now expounded.

But continued accommodation is possible only because the other principle, *habit,* all the time conserves the past and gives *points d'appui* in solidified structure for new accommodations. Inasmuch, further, as the copy becomes, by transference from the world to the mind, capable of internal revival, in memory, accommodation takes on a new character—a conscious, subjective character—in *Volition.* Volition arises as a phenomenon of "persistent imitative suggestion," as we have argued. That is, volition arises when a copy remembered vibrates with other copies remembered or presented, and when all the connections, in thought and action, of all of them, are together set in motion incipiently. The "set" of motives together with a certain excess function is what we call attention; and the final co-ordination of all the motor elements involved is volition. The physical basis of memory, association, thought, is, therefore, that of will also,—the cerebrum, —and pathological cases show clearly that aboulia is fundamentally a defect of synthesis in perception and memory, arising from one or more breaks in the copy system whose rise has been sketched in what precedes.

We have seen—to proceed farther on our way—that there is one type of reaction, and only one, in which these two principles have a common application: *reactions whose issue tends to reinstate, in whole or part, the very stimulation that started the reaction.* Accommodation is there, in such a reaction, since the advantageous stimulation stands a better chance of repetition if the organism tends thus to get it; but since this repeated stimulus again stimulates to action, and action again follows—there also is habit. So accommodation, *by the very reaction which accommodates,* hands over its gains immediately to the rule of habit. And this is the universal rule.

How true, as a fact, this form of adaptation is! A fact often noticed, always admired, never explained—that organisms move toward the source of light and heat and colour! How can an organism get such a splendid property—that of being so modified by what is good for it, that it itself responds in a way to get it again, and then, by thus getting it again, makes its future enjoyments of it sure and easy? This the theories given attempt to explain: by the law of "Excess" with functional selection the stimulus is maintained, and by the law of "Sensori-motor association" the process is fixed in easy habit.

The interaction of these two principles, Accommodation and Habit,—Excess and Association,—gives rise to a two-fold factor in every organic activity of whatever kind. In organisms of any development—where a nervous system, say, is present,—the environment being a changing one, every structure, with its function, represents a habit which is being constantly modified by the law of accommodation. But these modifications themselves, as we have seen, provide again for their own habituation; so there is a constant erosion, and a constant accretion, to the net attainments of the organism. And each function can be understood only in the light of both the influences which have contributed to it. Impulse, for example, is twofold; instinct is twofold; attention is twofold; emotion is twofold: each illustrates habit, but each has grown by changes due to accommodation. Is not this a reconciliation *in principle* of the opposed theories of these functions, one saying that these great organic functions came only by composition, and the other that they came only by selection, intelligent or biological?

We have now seen how great habits are formed. "Natural" and "organic" selection fix them, and at the same time render them more prominent, *i.e.* as instincts, by erasing the evidences of their origin, and abbreviating the phylogenetic process in the growth of the individual. I use the phrase "organic centralization" to denote this great outcome of development,—the differentiation of functions in lines of adaptation which run apart, so far as their particular offices and structural products are concerned, but which are yet centralized. For they are centralized when considered together, as constituting, in unity and plan, the common life of the organism. When considered each for itself also, as a well-knit whole of many coordinated units, the same centralization is shown about a smaller centre; such as the movements involved in a particular instinct, or the series of movements of the facial muscles in an "expression." There would possibly be no need for further exposition of these points, since they are corollaries from the general theory already sketched, were it not that there are certain further applications.

There are two such applications which are new, I think, and which serve to gather into one point of view conflicting opinions regarding two of the most refractory facts in current psychology. I refer to the question of the existence of special nerves for pleasure and pain, or either; and to the attention.

The question arises: If accommodation is secured by a special form of reaction called "excess," what relation does this reaction itself sustain to the principle of habit? Does the excess function itself also become centralized? Does it tend to become a separate co-ordinated function, as other motor discharges do?

It is to be expected that, in so far as the environment in which an organism lives is constant, any accommodation reaction would, *taken for itself*, tend to become a habit. So far as the presumption goes, we should expect to find two great kinds of reaction implicated with pleasure and pain. The pain reaction would tend to withdraw the organism from the stimulus which gives pain; and the pleasure reaction would tend to bring the organism into closer relation with the stimulus which gives pleasure. These two kinds of reaction would be possible for any muscular group whatever. All that would then be required would be some sense organ which would distinguish between the conditions of stimulation which *regularly* give pleasure,—reacting to them with the forward moving reaction,—and those which regularly give pain—reacting to them with the withdrawing movement. This is probably the case. . . . It then becomes a matter of scientific discovery whether actual pain nerves exist or not, in connection with any particular function. That depends upon what the race conditions of stimulation have actually been. If the pain stimulus has been regular and peculiar enough, possibly it has got itself a special apparatus; research must decide. But if not, then not. This latter, the negative, is probably the case with pleasure. The stimulus to pleasant function is so general and normal, that pleasure has not become well "specialized" either in the organism, or, as is very plain, in consciousness. Yet in the special cases in which functions have been perpetual, important, and uniform, there we do find pleasure as acute and definitely localized as pain is, *e.g.* in the sexual function, as physiologists have noted; it is not at all improbable that this function has a pleasure nerve apparatus. So it is possible and probable that pain is both a sensation, and a *quale* or "tone" of other sensations, emotions, etc.; a sensation,—if it has developed its own apparatus of reacting to definite, well-localized pain-giving stimulations constantly present; a *quale*,—because the organism is never completely balanced in its environment, the stimulations representing misadjustment and pain are not all constant, and there are demands for the more general function, as in the intellectual life. So the accommodation function of pain, in connection with all possible stimulations, must go on just the same whether there be a sensation pain or not; especially in the sphere of thought, sentiment, and the attentive life, since this is the latest, most complex, and least uniform kind of accommodation.

On the physical side, too, the matter seems clear. The excess process at the basis of pleasure and pain finds channels of outflow which serve over and over again for the reaction required to repeat the pleasure, or stop the pain. The same connection thus serving for many instances, becomes well-worn and habitual; and so a connection is formed—a circuit—for pleasure or pain, like the ordinary sensori-motor circuits. If light, for example, considered as constant stimulation, serves to develop, for its different intensities, an organ—the eye—and certain nerves, which react only to it, *as luminous;* why can it not also develop, in connection with certain of its intensities, a further organ and nerve which react only to it as *painful?* It is, indeed, inevitable that, under favourable conditions, such a pain-apparatus should be developed and fixed by natural selection.

This recognizes the distinction between "pleasure and pain" on one side, and "agreeableness and disagreeableness," on the other, as developed in recent work. Pain as sensation-content is distinct from pain as *quale* of other contents. On my view, this is a distinction due to development. Pain, as sensation, is pain become *habitual* enough, under constancy of stimulation, to have its own apparatus, *i.e.* it is pain as *peripheral* function. Pain, on the other hand, as *quale* of mental content generally, is pain of irregular stimulation, or pain of *accommodation, i.e.* pain as *central* function. I do not agree, therefore, with Münsterberg, in finding in the movements of flexion and extension, which my theory requires in common with his, the *genetic* sources of "agreeable" or "disagreeable" tone. The whole theory of development, as I have shown above, if it is to move at all, requires that this accommodation pain or pleasure be due, in the first instance, to stimulus, and that the flexion and extension movements be the organic mode of accommodation to the pleasure or pain-giving stimulus.

Nevertheless, so great is organic complexity, when we come to take the principle of association into account, that, after all, in developed organisms, Münsterberg may be right in making the flexion and extension movements themselves the direct basis of the agreeable and disagreeable *quale*. For we have seen in the case of emotion that movements at first purely purposive, serving utility or accommodation to stimulus, themselves get, by association, to represent the degree of success or failure in accommodation, and so come themselves to give body to the emotion. In like manner, these flexion and extension movements may have passed, from being expressive or utility movements, to be the forerunners of the condition which they at first served only to express. And it may well be that they are thus an intermediate link between *quale* pleasure-pain, and sensation pleasure-pain. This is supported by the evidence—so far as it goes—which locates the nerve apparatus of sensation pleasure-pain in the muscles. On this view, it is for reporting flexion and extension movements that this nervous apparatus has developed; these flexion and extension movements standing in place of the pleasure- and pain-giving stimuli to which the organism has become accommodated.

Possibly the most important question which remains over, and upon which the distinction now made between original and derived pain reactions seems to throw some light, is that which concerns the relations of so-called "systematic" to "single-organ" pains. Theories divide on the question whether pains relate to the welfare of the system as a whole or to the welfare—nourishment, vitality, etc.—of particular organs. And on account of the conflicting evidence some throw over the "welfare" theory of pleasure and pain altogether. The principles which we have seen to be operative in development, show us, however, that we are able to reconcile the contradiction, at least in some degree. If sensational pain be a specialized function with its own motor reaction, then in it we have the single-organ position confirmed, and are able to account for the conflicts which sometimes arise—as so many writers, from Mill to the present, have pointed out—between the welfare of the organism as a whole and that of the particular organ or part. On the other hand, the existence of the non-sensational or *quale* pain still remains as an index of central and deep-seated vital conditions, and makes its own claim to being the original derivation-form of the pain consciousness. Genetically, we cannot begin life history with single-organ pains; for apart from the impossible assumption, then, of differentiated organs, such separate and special pain reactions would not take the place of the general form of hedonic reaction which we have found in organic development. On the other hand, the existence of special sensation pains in connection with functions of particular organs, and the probable existence of pain nerves, testify to the difference, in highly developed organisms, of the two sorts of pain. Moreover, the fact that pleasure is not so evidently dualistic,—not clearly sensational at all,—this is an additional evidence that the distinction between systemic and single-organ function is, with respect to its hedonic aspect, as it is also, of course, in respect to its very existence at all, a matter of evolution.

And another application may be made of the principle of specialization. One of the objections most current to the view that the original pain reaction took the form of diminished vitality, suppressions of movement, contractions, and flexions, is that the facts show that often pain reactions are very violent. The struggle of an animal to escape painful conditions, to rid itself of its annoyance, to defeat its enemy by aggressive and offensive action, all this is notorious. How, it is asked, can this be if the function of pain, in its relation to movement, is essentially inhibitory? The facts again are indisputable on both sides. We have seen some of the facts in the foregoing pages. In considering special emotional reactions and attitudes, we saw the variety and intensity of those accompanying fear, anger, etc., emotions of a painful character. But, on the other hand, we have also seen that the child and the little animal learn movements by withdrawing and suppressing those actions which issue in pain. How can this contradiction be reconciled? There are two influences at work, I think,—both already spoken of,—to which the seeming contradiction is due.

First, there is the principle of antagonism which Darwin used under the name "antithesis" and which we have seen in an earlier chapter to show itself in the special form of muscular antagonism with the corresponding series of antithetic motor attitudes. Much of the violent reaction under pain is the positive use of the muscular combinations antagonistic to those through which the actual pain stimulation would discharge. When in pain from a movement, or from a mere condition without movement, we do not violently stimulate the same movement which brought the pain, nor the movements appropriate to continue the unpleasant condition. These are suppressed by the law of inhibition and withdrawal. But we do throw into violent activity certain antagonistic or associated muscular combinations whose action brings relief. The real "excess" does not attach therefore to the pain reaction as such, but to the benefit-bringing actions which are the proved resources of the organism when in conditions of pain.

Second, there is no reason that the pain reactions themselves— the reactions of withdrawal, retraction, flexion—should not be at times intense. We have seen that by the principle of centralization, reactions of the imitative type, whether they be painful or pleasurable, become habits. This tendency to habit, we now also see, has in the case of pain taken on a positive form in pain as sensation, with probably a nerve apparatus of its own. When this has once happened the response to pain condition would, by the law of dynamogenesis, be intense when the stimulation is itself intense. This would mean that in the growth of the organism it has been advantageous to respond vigorously to stimulations which were damaging and so to get rid of them. That does not disprove the contention that the normal response to pain is a lessened one. It is as if a man put more money into a losing venture as the most effective way to turn it into a gaining venture; and it simply means that in business, as in development, it is only at a higher stage that certain complex conditions realize themselves at all.

Putting these explanations together there does not remain, I think, much evidence, apart from those convulsive semipathological chaotic writhings and twistings into which violent physical pain may throw the organism, that pain reactions as such are ever expansive and aggressive. They may be intense, they may be associated with all sorts of utility reactions, and they may represent nothing but sheer mechanical revolt, as Darwin long ago showed.

Now the same effect of "centralization" is seen in the attention, as may be gathered from the positions already taken. Attention has been defined as genetically the reverberation of the "excess" process as it has become fixed in habit. By the law of "sensorimotor association," this backward wave gets connected with all the sensory processes. Now just in as far as this wave is the same for different sensations, just in so far it tends to be "centralized," in a constant function—integrated into a habit—involving a regular set of motor phenomena, such as the wrinkling of the brows, setting of the glottis, etc., always found in acts of attention. The organism thus acquires a *habit of accommodation*, on a higher level. This is attention. When memory and imagination appear, this new form of response enables the organism to throw itself into attitudes favourable to the best reception and assimilation of material of all kinds.

Yet as with pain, so here. This attention-habit, this centralized function, is not all that the attention is. The original excess function must be kept in view. No preliminary setting of attention is an adequate accommodation to an intellectual stimulus, an idea still to be received; it is adequate only to hold stimuli by which it has been before excited. Each new accommodation to idea carries a motor excess discharge of its own, and this also enters into the sense of attention, making each act of attention, and each sense-type of attention, different, as was said above.

The terms of interaction of the two principles, finally, require that the reaction maintain its stimulus, and that this stimulus again repeat the reaction. The one type of reaction, therefore, which an organism must have, is a "circular" or stimulus-repeating one. We have found it best to name this type of reaction, for the purposes of psycho-physical definition, IMITATION, and to call it, as a typical neurological function, "circular reaction." This is the UNIT, therefore, the essential fact, of all motor-development; and this shows the simplicity of the whole theory.

The place of imitation has now been made out in a tentative way throughout the development of the active life. It seems to be everywhere. But it is, of course, a matter of natural history that this type of action is of such extraordinary and unlooked-for importance. If we grant a phylogenetic development of mind, reaction of the imitative type, as defined above, may be considered the mode and the only mode of the progressive adaptation of the organism to its environment. The further philosophical questions as to the nature of mind, its worth and its dignity, remain under adjudication. We have learned too much in modern philosophy to argue from the natural history of a thing to its ultimate constitution and meaning—and we commend this consideration to the biologists. As far as there is a more general lesson to be learned from the considerations advanced, it is that we should avoid just this danger, i.e. of interpreting one kind of existence for itself, in an isolated way, without due regard to the other kinds of existence with which its manifestations are mixed up.

The antithesis, for example, between the self and the world is not a finished antithesis psychologically considered. The self is realized by taking in "copies" from the world, and the world is enabled to set higher copies only through the constant reactions of the individual self upon it. Morally I am as much a part of society as physically I am a part of the world's fauna; and as my body gets its best explanation from the point of view of its place in a zoölogical scale, so morally I occupy a place in the social order; and an important factor in the understanding of me is the understanding of it.

The great question, which is writ above all natural history records, is—when put in the phraseology of imitation,—What is the final World-copy, and how did it get itself set?

* * *

When Baldwin turned his attention fully to the development of a genetic theory of thought, at that very time when psychology was waking from its Wundtian sleep to find Watson and Freud at the bedside, it became even harder for his colleagues to follow him. Watsonian and positivistic Philistinism drove Baldwin's work into oblivion in a way that Hall neither could nor would. Half a century later, Baldwin's propositions about the nature of human knowledge and the nature of the child have the ring of currency, but, for those intervening decades, this giant of American psychology was effectively silenced by the social forces in psychology, by his exile, and by the difficulty of his language.

Baldwin believed that logic was a social and developmental invention and that its origin and growth could be traced in the child and the culture. He spoke of the " 'community' of logical propositions" and he continued to emphasize the social context of knowledge, but he also saw the child as inventing logic (as he constructed the world) in his adaptation to the environment. Baldwin's notions of the *resisting environment* and the *insisting self* foretell Piaget. Formal logic, then, is not the beginning, but the end of a developmental sequence. Although Baldwin confined his detailed treatment to the growth of logic, his system clearly subsumes all categories of human knowledge; he dealt at least briefly with the formation of the notion of *object* in his *Development and Evolution*. With help from Piaget, it is possible to reach the Baldwin of genetic logic. Still too advanced or too exotic for modern taste, however, is Baldwin's central organizing idea—that human knowledge is best expressed as an ideal of Beauty and that the aesthetic definition of knowledge (indeed of life) is the one that man must seek.*

* J. M. Baldwin, *Genetic Theory of Reality*, New York: Putnam, 1915, p. 331.

Before we leave the nineteenth century for the diversity that succeeded it, it is fitting to hear just a word from Hippolyte Taine. His was a major part in the development of French psychology from Rousseau to Sartre and his work *On Intelligence* was important for Charcot and Binet and, through them, for Freud and Piaget. In the diary notes by Taine that prompted Darwin to publish his own, the French psychologist discusses the early development of language. After reporting a number of incisive observations, Taine wrote the following paragraph, a demonstration in miniature of the historical principle that Baldwin's work demonstrates in full size—that the psychology of cognitive development, just prior to the assaults of Watson and Freud, was moving into areas of productive interest that have only in the last years been reopened.

* * *

Hippolyte Adolphe Taine (1828–1893)

The Acquisition of Language

On summing up the facts I have just related we arrive at the following conclusions, which observers should test by observations made on other children.

At first a child cries and uses its vocal organ, in the same way as its limbs, spontaneously and by reflex action. Spontaneously and from mere pleasure of action it then uses its vocal organ in the same way as its limbs, and acquires the complete use of it by trial and error. From inarticulate it thus passes to articulate sounds. The variety of intonations that it acquires shows in it a superior delicacy of impression and expression. By this delicacy it

H. Taine, M. Taine on the acquisition of language in children. A note in *Mind,* **2,** 1877, 252-259. Originally published in *Revue Philosophique,* **1,** 1876, 5–23, in a note that included observations on primitive language as well.

is capable of general ideas. We only help it to catch them by the suggestion of our words. It attaches to them ideas that we do not expect and spontaneously generalizes outside and beyond our categories [*cadres*]. At times it invents not only the meaning of the word, but the word itself. Several vocabularies may succeed one another in its mind by the obliteration of old words, replaced by new ones. Many meanings may be given in succession to the same word which remains unchanged. Many of the words invented are natural vocal gestures. In short, it learns a ready-made language as a true musician learns counterpoint or a true poet prosody; it is an original genius adapting itself to a form constructed bit by bit by a succession of original geniuses; if language were wanting, the child would recover it little by little or would discover an equivalent.

5

Development and Diversity:

1900–1930

At the turn of the new century, child study appeared to be well established as an independent discipline. Societies for the communication of information about research with children were set up, a series of biographical studies appeared, Hall's students busily scattered their questionnaires to teachers and parents, and the journal of the field—Hall's *Pedagogical Seminary*—provided room for the expression of fact and speculation about child behavior. But, in hindsight, there is a curious thinness about child study in the first decade of the twentieth century; although the child's entire experience is probed, there is only superficial attention given to method, metric, and mechanism. The introspective method of general psychology was clearly unavailable to the student of children; and the questionnaire, although designed to correct this failure somewhat by retrospective accounts of childhood, was beginning to sag in its promise. The other substitute for introspection, for the investigator of animals as well as for the student of children, was careful observation of a botanical sort, but the continuing dependence of psychologists on the hardly edited description of emergent functions in animals and children became increasingly less satisfying. Baldwin's advocacy of theory had not taken child psychology off its stubbornly empirical standpoint; the excitement of Galton's first explorations into the study

of human variation had not been fulfilled; study of psychopathology in children threatened to become the new physiognomy.

The decade had not run its course before change was discernible in all aspects of child study. Binet and Simon developed procedures of observation that carried the study of individual variation to new levels of sophistication and precision; Freud presented, in a series of shattering papers, a genuinely novel conception of the child; Pavlov began to turn his attention to the research that was to give flagging associationism a mechanism and a model; Watson began the conversations with Knight Dunlap that were to result in a rewriting of psychology—all within the span of a few years. Neither psychology nor man would be the same again.

The twentieth century's first revolution in child study—the measurement of intelligence—was long prepared for and it broke upon psychology with little contention. Shortly after the publication of *The Origin of Species,* another grandson of Erasmus Darwin began the studies of human variability that were to result eventually in one of the most productive research fields of modern psychology. Francis Galton's interest ranged as widely as those of his more illustrious cousin—he made a sober statistical study of the objective efficacy of prayer, and his studies of audition were seminal—but the center of Galton's work remained throughout his lifetime on the precise assessment of human variability. Nor did Galton have any doubts about the sources of differences among men.

I have no patience with the hypothesis occasionally expressed and often implied, especially in tales written to teach children to be good, that babies are born pretty much alike, and that the sole agencies in creating differences between boy and boy, and man and man, are steady application and moral effort. It is in the most unqualified manner that I object to pretentions of natural equality. The experiences of the nursery, the school, the University, and of professional careers are a chain of proofs to the contrary.*

In full recognition of the contribution of education to the development of variation, Galton had no room in his view of man for

---

* F. Galton, *Hereditary Genius: An Inquiry into Its Laws and Consequences,* New York: Meridian Books, 1962 (a reprint of the second edition of 1892), p. 56. The first edition appeared in 1869.

"natural equality." His conviction, it should be noted, was essential to his method. In *Hereditary Genius*, he examined the genealogies of eminent jurists, statesmen, "commanders," literary personages, poets, scientific leaders, artists, "divines," oarsmen, and "wrestlers of the North Country" to demonstrate the remarkably high number of eminent relatives they possessed, usually in the same area of achievement. It would have been fatal to Galton's method and to his conclusion to assume that some mechanism other than heredity could operate to produce the familial pools of talent that he discovered. He was not unaware of the problems of separating nature and nurture, to use his favorite names for the contrast.

Man is so educable an animal that it is difficult to distinguish between that part of his character which has been acquired through education and circumstance, and that which was in the original grain of his constitution. . . . The interaction of nature and circumstance is very close, and it is impossible to separate them with precision. . . . We need not, however, be hypercritical about distinctions; we know that the bulk of the respective provinces of nature and nurture are totally different, although the frontier between them may be uncertain, and we are perfectly justified in attempting to appraise their relative importance.*

To this end, Galton made a number of innovations of thought and of method which remain part of science.

Perhaps the most momentous of Galton's innovations was his extensive use of statistics. Basing his developments on Quetelet's fundamental *Letters on Probability*, Galton assessed the likelihood of obtaining so many notables in so few families and he began to work out the techniques of correlation that were brought to elegance by Pearson. Galton corrected Darwin's view of twinning and was the first to point out the theoretical significance of the comparison between identical and fraternal twins. He exchange-transfused rabbits to demonstrate the fallacy of Darwin's assumptions about the inheritance of acquired characteristics through vascular changes. He presented sufficient data on individual

* F. Galton, *Inquiries into Human Faculty and Its Development*, New York: Macmillan, 1883, p. 177 and pp. 181ff.

differences in fingerprints to convince Scotland Yard that they should use them as a means of criminal identification.

The interest of Galton in physiognomic variation which lead to his work on fingerprints also guided his invention of the composite photograph as a technique of describing differences among groups. By overlaying carefully prepared photographs of scores of persons, Galton was able to build a portrait of representative consumptives, or criminals, or normal men. His interest in physiognomy foreshadowed a similar interest of Binet's and is not unrelated to the search for typological variation in autonomic functioning that is busily pursued nowadays, but it had some unfortunate short-term consequences. The physiognomists like Francis Warner became so secure in their ability to diagnose mental dullness and developmental lag by the tilt of a hand or the twitch of a cheek or the sag of a shoulder (Warner called these "nerve-signs") that the mental test movement met persisting opposition from the physiognomic diagnosticians.*

For all the variety and enthusiasm of his studies, Galton's primary and lasting contribution to child study was his emphatic statement of the importance of assessing individual variation and of assessing it in a precise way. His motivation was eugenic—he clearly wanted to preserve the racial purity of the elect—but he opened the way to a wider attack on problems in the measurement of man developing.

The first systematic study of mental variation with age in the school child was made by J. Allan Gilbert in early 1894 in the schools of New Haven.† In addition to the usual measurements of weight and height, Gilbert devised nine tests of physical and mental ability, among them reaction time, sensitiveness to color differences, and time-memory. For all measures, he showed the expected changes with age as well as some interesting sex differences, but his tests showed a disappointing relation to "general mental ability." Only differences in reaction time separated the children teachers called "dull" from their classmates and even this

* F. Warner, *The Study of Children and Their School Training*, New York: Macmillan, 1897.
† J. A. Gilbert, Researches on the mental and physical development of school-children, *Studies from the Yale Psychological Laboratory*, **2**, 1894, 40–100.

measure of Gilbert's was unstable and did not differentiate "bright" and "average" children. Nonetheless, the form of Gilbert's attack on the measurement of mental ability was sound; he was trapped, in a way that was to become familiar to American psychologists, by the tools in hand. Gilbert used the psychophysical procedures that were currently in good reputation; after the fact, it is not surprising that time-memory and muscle-sense are not closely related to the performance of children in school.

Over the next several years, other students of children joined the search for what was to become the "mental test," notably Blin in France. But the laurel was to go to Binet and Simon who seized on a practical problem of school administration posed for them by the Minister of Education to develop a series of tests that, under revision and translation, became the model of intelligence tests and, for some psychologists at least, the definition of intelligence.

Binet was concerned with problems of reasoning and intelligence throughout his life, from his early speculative attempts to dissect all cognitive process into associations to his last and incomplete work on a full system of psychology. His associationism came to pieces during his work at the Salpêtrière on hypnotism and hysteria, and by 1890 Binet had begun the empirical and theoretical studies that would carry him to the intelligence scale. Like so many students of children, his interest in a closer examination of the origins of intelligent behavior was awakened by the birth of his own children. They figure as subjects in a study of infantile movement and walking; also, of far greater significance, Marguerite and Armande were Binet's subjects in *L'Étude expérimentale de l'intelligence**. The results of this study confirmed several of Binet's earlier conclusions—that the thematic character of thought and the existence of imageless thought rule out a simple associationistic view of rational intelligence, that there are wide individual differences in style of thought, and that only a combination of introspection (both by the subject and the experimenter) and objective measures would provide a key to the measurement of intelligence. He brought these conclusions to the task the Minister set.

* A. Binet, *L'Etude expérimentale de l'intelligence*, Paris: Schleicher, 1903.

Alfred Binet (1857–1911) and Theophile Simon (1873–1961)

The Measurement of Intelligence

We here present the first rough sketch of a work which was directly inspired by the desire to serve the interesting cause of the education of subnormals.

In October, 1904, the Minister of Public Instruction named a commission which was charged with the study of measures to be taken for insuring the benefits of instruction to defective children. After a number of sittings, this commission regulated all that pertained to the type of establishment to be created, the conditions of admission into the school, the teaching force, and the pedagogical methods to be employed. They decided that no child suspected of retardation should be eliminated from the ordinary school and admitted into a special class, without first being subjected to a pedagogical and medical examination from which it could be certified that because of the state of his intelligence, he was unable to profit, in an average measure, from the instruction given in the ordinary schools.

But how the examination of each child should be made, what methods should be followed, what observations taken, what questions asked, what tests devised, how the child should be compared with normal children, the commission felt under no obligation to decide. It was formed to do a work of administration, not a work of science.

It has seemed to us extremely useful to furnish a guide for future Commissions' examination. Such Commissions should understand from the beginning how to get their bearings. It must be made

A. Binet and Th. Simon, *The Development of Intelligence in Children* (Translated by Elizabeth S. Kite), Copyright © 1916, The Williams and Wilkins Co., Baltimore, 2, Md., U. S. A. Reprinted with permission of the publisher. Originally published in *L'Année Psychologique*, **11**, 163–244, 1905.

impossible for those who belong to the Commission to fall into the habit of making haphazard decisions according to impressions which are subjective, and consequently uncontrolled. Such impressions are sometimes good, sometimes bad, and have at all times too much the nature of the arbitrary, of caprice, of indifference. Such a condition is quite unfortunate because the interests of the child demand a more careful method. To be a member of a special class can never be a mark of distinction, and such as do not merit it, must be spared the record. Some errors are excusable in the beginning, but if they become too frequent, they may ruin the reputation of these new institutions. Furthermore, in principle, we are convinced, and we shall not cease to repeat, that the precision and exactness of science should be introduced into our practice whenever possible, and in the great majority of cases it is possible.

The problem which we have to solve presents many difficulties both theoretical and practical. It is a hackneyed remark that the definitions, thus far proposed, for the different states of subnormal intelligence, lack precision. These inferior states are indefinite in number, being composed of a series of degrees which mount from the lowest depths of idiocy, to a condition easily confounded with normal intelligence. Alienists have frequently come to an agreement concerning the terminology to be employed for designating the difference of these degrees; at least, in spite of certain individual divergence of ideas to be found in all questions, there has been an agreement to accept *idiot* as applied to the lowest state, *imbecile* to the intermediate, and *moron* (débile) [Goddard invented the word "moron"] to the state nearest normality. Still among the numerous alienists, under this common and apparently precise terminology, different ideas are concealed, variable and at the same time confused. The distinction between idiot, imbecile, and moron is not understood in the same way by all practitioners. We have abundant proof of this in the strikingly divergent medical diagnoses made only a few days apart by different alienists upon the same patient.

— — —

We cannot sufficiently deplore the consequence of this state of uncertainty recognized today by all alienists. The simple fact, that specialists do not agree in the use of the technical terms of their science, throws suspicion upon their diagnoses, and prevents all work of comparison. We ourselves have made similar observations. In synthesizing the diagnoses made by M. Bourneville upon patients leaving the Bicêtre, we found that in the space of four years only two feeble-minded individuals have left his institution although during that time the Bureau of Admission has sent him more than thirty. Nothing could show more clearly than this change of label, the confusion of our nomenclature.

What importance can be attached to public statistics of different countries concerning the percentage of backward children if the definition for backward children is not the same in all countries? How will it be possible to keep a record of the intelligence of pupils who are treated and instructed in a school, if the terms applied to them, feeble-minded, retarded, imbecile, idiot, vary in meaning according to the doctor who examines them? The absence of a common measure prevents comparison of statistics, and makes one lose all interest in investigations which may have been very laborious. But a still more serious fact is that, because of lack of methods, it is impossible to solve those essential questions concerning the afficted, whose solution presents the greatest interest; for example, the real results gained by the treatment of inferior states of intelligence by doctor and educator; the educative value of one pedagogical method compared with another; the degree of curability of incomplete idiocy, etc. It is not by means of *a priori* reasonings, of vague considerations, of oratorical displays, that these questions can be solved; but by minute investigation, entering into the details of fact, and considering the effects of the treatment for each particular child. There is but one means of knowing if a child, who has passed six years in a hospital or in a special class, has profited from that stay, and to what degree he has profited; and that is to compare his certificate of entrance with his certificate of dismissal, and by that means ascertain if he shows a special amelioration of his condition beyond that which might be credited simply to the considerations of growth. But experience has shown how imprudent it would be to place confidence in this comparison, when the two certificates come from different doctors, who do not judge in exactly the same way, or who use different words to characterize the mental status of patients.

— — —

In looking closely one can see that the confusion comes principally from a fault in the method of examination. When an alienist finds himself in the presence of a child of inferior intelligence, he does not examine him by bringing out each one of the symptoms which the child manifests and by interpreting all symptoms and classifying them; he contents himself with taking a subjective impression, an impression as a whole, of his subject, and of making his diagnosis by instinct. We do not think that we are going too far in saying that at the present time very few physicians would be able to cite with absolute precision the objective and invariable sign, or signs, by which they distinguish the degrees of inferior mentality.

[Binet and Simon present "a few historical notes" describing the contributions of Pinel, Esquirol, Morel, Bourneville, Sollier, and in detail, Blin.]

Before explaining [our new] methods let us recall exactly the conditions of the problem which we are attempting to solve. Our purpose is to be able to measure the intellectual capacity of a child who is brought to us in order to know whether he is normal or retarded. We should therefore, study his condition at the time and that only. We have nothing to do either with his past history or with his future; consequently we shall neglect his etiology, and we shall make no attempt to distinguish between acquired and congenital idiocy; for a stronger reason we shall set aside all consideration of pathological anatomy which might explain his intellectual deficiency. So much for his past. As to that which concerns his future, we shall exercise the same abstinence; we do not attempt to establish or prepare a prognosis and we leave unanswered the question of whether this retardation is curable, or even improvable. We shall limit ourselves to ascertaining the truth in regard to his present mental state.

Furthermore, in the definition of this state, we should make some restrictions. Most subnormal children, especially those in the

schools, are habitually grouped in two categories, those of backward intelligence, and those who are unstable. This latter class,
which certain alienists call moral imbeciles, do not necessarily
manifest inferiority of intelligence; they are turbulent, vicious,
rebellious to all discipline; they lack sequence of ideas, and
probably power of attention. It is a matter of great delicacy
to make the distinction between children who are unstable, and
those who have rebellious dispositions. Elsewhere we have insisted upon the necessity of instructors not treating as unstable,
that is as pathological cases, those children whose character is not
sympathetic with their own. It would necessitate a long study,
and probably a very difficult one, to establish the distinctive signs
which separate the unstable from the undisciplined. For the
present we shall not take up this study. We shall set the unstable
aside, and shall consider only that which bears upon those who
are backward in intelligence.

This is not, however, to be the only limitation of our subject
because backward states of intelligence present several different
types. There is the insane type—or the type of intellectual decay
—which consists in a progressive loss of former acquired intelligence. Many epileptics, who suffer from frequent attacks, progress toward insanity. It would be possible and probably very
important, to be able to make the distinction between those with
decaying intelligence on the one hand, and those of inferior intelligence on the other. But as we have determined to limit on this
side also, the domain of our study, we shall rigorously exclude all
forms of insanity and decay. Moreover we believe that these are
rarely present in the schools, and need not be taken into consideration in the operation of new classes for subnormals.

Another distinction is made between those of inferior intelligence and degenerates. The latter are subjects in whom occur
clearly defined, episodical phenomena, such as impulsions, obses-
sions, deliriums. We shall eliminate the degenerates as well as
the insane.

Lastly, we should say a word upon our manner of studying
those whom most alienists call idiots but whom we here call of
inferior intelligence. The exact nature of this inferiority is not
known; and today without other proof, one very prudently re-

fuses to liken this state to that of an arrest of normal development. It certainly seems that the intelligence of these beings has undergone a certain arrest; but it does not follow that the disproportion between the degree of intelligence and the age is the only characteristic of their condition. There is also in many cases, most probably a deviation in the development, a perversion. The idiot of fifteen years, who, like a baby of three, is making his first verbal attempts, can not be completely likened to a three-year old child, because the latter is normal, but the idiot is not. There exists therefore between them, necessarily, differences either apparent or hidden. The careful study of idiots shows, among some of them at least, that whereas certain faculties are almost wanting, others are better developed. They have therefore certain aptitudes. Some have a good auditory or musical memory, and a whole repertoire of songs; others have mechanical ability. If all were carefully examined, many examples of these partial aptitudes would probably be found.

Our purpose is in no wise to study, analyze, or set forth the aptitudes of those of inferior intelligence. That will be the object of a later work. Here we shall limit ourselves to the measuring of their general intelligence. We shall determine their intellectual level, and, in order the better to appreciate this level, we shall compare it with that of normal children of the same age or of an analogous level. The reservations previously made as to the true conception of arrested development, will not prevent our finding great advantage in a methodical comparison between those of inferior and those of normal intelligence.

To what method should we have recourse in making our diagnosis of the intellectual level? No one method exists, but there are a number of different ones which should be used cumulatively, because the question is a very difficult one to solve, and demands rather a collaboration of methods. It is important that the practitioner be equipped in such a manner that he shall use, only as accessory, the information given by the parents of the child, so that he may always be able to verify this information, or, when necessary, dispense with it. In actual practice quite the opposite occurs. When the child is taken to the clinic the physician listens a great deal to the parents and questions the child very little, in fact scarcely looks at him, allowing himself to be influenced by a very strong presumption that the child is intellectually inferior. If, by a chance not likely to occur, but which would be most interesting some time to bring about, the physician were submitted to the test of selecting the subnormals from a mixed group of children, he would certainly find himself in the midst of grave difficulties, and would commit many errors especially in cases of slight defect.

The organization of methods is especially important because, as soon as the schools for subnormals are in operation, one must be on his guard against the attitude of the parents. Their sincerity will be worth very little when it is in conflict with their interests. If the parents wish the child to remain in the regular school, they will not be silent concerning his intelligence. "My child understands everything," they will say, and they will be very careful not to give any significant information in regard to him. If, on the contrary, they wish him to be admitted into an institution where gratuitous board and lodging are furnished, they will change completely. They will be capable even of teaching him how to simulate mental debility. One should, therefore, be on his guard against all possible frauds.

In order to recognize the inferior states of intelligence we believe that three different methods should be employed. We have arrived at this synthetic view only after many years of research, but we are now certain that each of these methods renders some service. These methods are:

1. *The medical method*, which aims to appreciate the anatomical, physiological, and pathological signs of inferior intelligence.

2. *The pedagogical method*, which aims to judge of the intelligence according to the sum of acquired knowledge.

3. *The psychological method*, which makes direct observations and measurements of the degree of intelligence.

From what has gone before it is easy to see the value of each of these methods. The medical method is indirect because it conjectures the mental from the physical. The pedagogical method is more direct; but the psychological is the most direct of all because it aims to measure the state of the intelligence as it is at the present moment. It does this by experiments which oblige the subject to make an effort which shows his capability in the way of comprehension, judgment, reasoning, and invention.

The Psychological Method

The fundamental idea of this method is the establishment of what we shall call a measuring scale of intelligence. This scale is composed of a series of tests of increasing difficulty, starting from the lowest intellectual level that can be observed, and ending with that of average normal intelligence. Each group in the series corresponds to a different mental level.

This scale properly speaking does not permit the measure of the intelligence, because intellectual qualities are not superposable, and therefore cannot be measured as linear surfaces are measured, but are on the contrary, a classification, a hierarchy among diverse intelligences; and for the necessities of practice this classification is equivalent to a measure. We shall therefore be able to know, after studying two individuals, if one rises above the other and to how many degrees, if one rises above the average level of other individuals considered as normal, or if he remains below. Understanding the normal progress of intellectual development among normals, we shall be able to determine how many years such an individual is advanced or retarded. In a word we shall be able to determine to what degrees of the scale idiocy, imbecility, and moronity correspond.

The scale that we shall describe is not a theoretical work; it is the result of long investigations, first at the Salpêtrière, and afterwards in the primary schools of Paris, with both normal and subnormal children. These short psychological questions have been given the name of tests. The use of tests is today very common, and there are even contemporary authors who have made a specialty of organizing new tests according to theoretical views, but who have made no effort to patiently try them out in the schools. Theirs is an amusing occupation, comparable to a person's making a colonizing expedition into Algeria, advancing always only upon the map, without taking off his dressing gown. We place but slight confidence in the tests invented by these authors and we

have borrowed nothing from them. All the tests which we propose have been repeatedly tried, and have been retained from
among many, which after trial have been discarded. We can cer-
tify that those which are here presented have proved themselves
valuable.

We have aimed to make all our tests simple, rapid, convenient,
precise, heterogeneous, holding the subject in continued contact
with the experimenter, and bearing principally upon the faculty
of judgment. Rapidity is necessary for this sort of examination.
It is impossible to prolong it beyond twenty minutes without
fatiguing the subject. During this maximum of twenty minutes,
it must be turned and turned about in every sense, and at least
ten tests must be executed, so that not more than about two
minutes can be given to each. In spite of their interest, we were
obliged to proscribe long exercises. For example, it would be
very instructive to know how a subject learns by heart a series of
sentences. We have often tested the advantage of leaving a person by himself with a lesson of prose or verse after having said to
him, "Try to learn as much as you can of this in five minutes."
Five minutes is too long for our test, because during that time the
subject escapes us; it may be that he becomes distracted or thinks
of other things; the test loses its clinical character and becomes too
scholastic. We have therefore reluctantly been obliged to re-
nounce testing the rapidity and extent of the memory by this
method. Several other equivalent examples of elimination could
be cited. In order to cover rapidly a wide field of observation, it
goes without saying that the tests should be heterogeneous.

Another consideration. Our purpose is to evaluate a level of
intelligence. It is understood that we here separate natural intelligence and instruction. It is the intelligence alone that we seek
to measure, by disregarding in so far as possible, the degree of
instruction which the subject possesses. He should, indeed, be
considered by the examiner as a complete ignoramus knowing
neither how to read nor write. This necessity forces us to forego
a great many exercises having a verbal, literary or scholastic character. These belong to a pedagogical examination. We believe
that we have succeeded in completely disregarding the acquired
information of the subject. We give him nothing to read, noth-

ing to write, and submit him to no test in which he might succeed by means of rote learning. In fact we do not even notice his inability to read if a case occurs. It is simply the level of his natural intelligence that is taken into account.

But here we must come to an understanding of what meaning to give to that word so vague and so comprehensive, "the intelligence." Nearly all the phenomena with which psychology concerns itself are phenomena of intelligence; sensation, perception, are intellectual manifestations as much as reasoning. Should we therefore bring into our examination the measure of sensation after the manner of the psycho-physicists? Should we put to the test all of his psychological processes? A slight reflection has shown us that this would indeed be wasted time.

It seems to us that in intelligence there is a fundamental faculty, the alteration or the lack of which, is of the utmost importance for practical life. This faculty is judgment, otherwise called good sense, practical sense, initiative, the faculty of adapting one's self to circumstances. To judge well, to comprehend well, to reason well, these are the essential activities of intelligence. A person may be a moron or an imbecile if he is lacking in judgment; but with good judgment he can never be either. Indeed the rest of the intellectual faculties seem of little importance in comparison with judgment. What does it matter, for example, whether the organs of sense function normally? Of what import that certain ones are hyperesthetic, or that others are anesthetic or are weakened? Laura Bridgman, Helen Keller and their fellow-unfortunates were blind as well as deaf, but this did not prevent them from being very intelligent. Certainly this is demonstative proof that the total or even partial integrity of the senses does not form a mental factor equal to judgment. We may measure the acuteness of the sensibility of subjects; nothing could be easier. But we should do this, not so much to find out the state of their sensibility as to learn the exactitude of their judgment.

The same remark holds good for the study of the memory. At first glance, memory being a psychological phenomenon of capital importance, one would be tempted to give it a very conspicuous part in an examination of intelligence. But memory is distinct from and independent of judgment. One may have good sense and lack memory. The reverse is also common. Just at the present time we are observing a backward girl who is developing before our astonished eyes a memory very much greater than our own. We have measured that memory and we are not deceived regarding it. Nevertheless that girl presents a most beautifully classic type of imbecility.

As a result of all this investigation, in the scale which we present we accord the first place to judgment; that which is of importance to us is not certain errors which the subject commits, but absurd errors, which prove that he lacks judgment. We have even made special provision to encourage people to make absurd replies. In spite of the accuracy of this directing idea, it will be easily understood that it has been impossible to permit of its regulating exclusively our examinations. For example, one can not make tests of judgment on children of less than two years when one begins to watch their first gleams of intelligence. Much is gained when one can discern in them traces of coördination, the first delineation of attention and memory. We shall therefore bring out in our lists some tests of memory; but so far as we are able, we shall give these tests such a turn as to invite the subject to make absurd replies, and thus under cover of a test of memory, we shall have an appreciation of their judgment.

Measuring Scale of Intelligence

GENERAL RECOMMENDATIONS. The examination should take place in a quiet room, quite isolated, and the child should be called in alone without other children. It is important that when a child sees the experimenter for the first time, he should be reassured by the presence of someone he knows, a relative, an attendant, or a school superintendent. The witness should be instructed to remain passive and mute, and not to intervene in the examination either by word or gesture.

The experimenter should receive each child with a friendly familiarity to dispel the timidity of early years. Greet him the moment he enters, shake hands with him and seat him comfortably. If he is intelligent enough to understand certain words, awaken his curiosity, his pride. If he refuses to reply to a test,

1. ABSENCE OF SOLUTION. This is either a case of mutism, or refraining from making an attempt, or an error so great that there is nothing satisfactory in the result. We indicate the absence of result by the algebraic sign minus (−).

2. PARTIAL SOLUTIONS. A part of the truth has been discovered. The reply is passable. This is indicated by a fraction; the fraction in use is ½. When the test permits several degrees one can have ¼, or ¾, etc.

3. COMPLETE SOLUTION. This does not admit of definition. It is indicated by the algebraic sign plus (+).

4. ABSURDITIES. We have cited a great number of examples and insist upon their importance; they are indicated by the exclamation sign (!).

The cause for certain defective replies can sometimes be grasped with sufficient clearness to admit of classification.

Besides the failure to comprehend the tests as a whole, we encounter:

1. Ignorance; the subject does not know the sense of a word or has never seen the object of which one speaks. Thus a child does not know a poppy. We write an I.

2. Resistance to the examination because of bad humor, unwillingness, state of nerves, etc. We write an R.

3. Accentuated timidity. We write a T.

4. The failure of attention, distraction. We write a D. The distraction may be of different kinds. There is an accidental distraction, produced by an exterior excitant or an occasional cause. For example, the case of a normal who spoils a memory test because he must use his handkerchief. There is constitutional distraction frequent among subnormals. We have ascertained among them the following types: Distraction from scattered perceptions. Distraction from preoccupation. Distraction from inability to fix the attention.

Pedagogical Method

The pedagogical method consists in making an inventory of the total knowledge of a subject, in comparing this total with that of a normal subject, in measuring the difference, and in finding if the difference in the knowledge of a subject is explained by the insufficiency of scholastic training.

The first idea of this method was suggested to us by reading the pamphlets in which Dr. Demoor and his colleagues explain the function of the special school at Brussels. To this school are admitted all children "pedagogically retarded." The pedagogically retarded are those whose instruction puts them two years behind normal children of the same age.

In France, our ministerial commission estimated that these pedagogically retarded, or to speak more accurately, these children lacking education, do not need to be sent to a special class; being normal they ought to remain in the ordinary schools, there to make up their instruction. We have thought that since it is of practical value to make a distinction between the normal who is lacking in school training and the subnormals, this distinction could be made in the type of scholastic knowledge beneficial to each of these classes.

The normal retarded child is one who is not at the level of his comrades of the same age, for causes that have no relation to his intelligence; he has missed school, or he has not attended regularly, or he has had mediocre teachers, who have made him lose time, etc. The subnormal ignoramus is one whose ignorance comes from a personal cause; he does not learn as quickly as his comrades, he comprehends less clearly, in a word, he is more or less impervious to the usual methods of instruction. We now have a method of recognizing subnormal ignoramuses; this consists in estimating at the same time their degree of instruction and their knowledge. Thus the idea of the pedagogical method originated.

Having acknowledged what we owe to Dr. Demoor and to his colleagues, we must nevertheless add that these authors do not seem to appreciate the need of precise methods of evaluating even among normals the amount of retardation in instruction. It is probable that in their practice the amount of this retardation is taken into account. Teachers do not hesitate, however, to make estimates of this nature. They will say without hesitation that such a child is two years or three years retarded. The value of these estimates is as yet undetermined.

We have found the following direction of great value to teachers who are attempting to designate the subnormals in their school. "Any child is subnormal who, in spite of regular or sufficient schooling, is two years behind children of the same age." This criterion fixes the ideas and evades some uncertainties. But even though it constitutes a great improvement over subjective appreciation, which has no guide, it has still the fault of lacking precision. It remains to be seen what is acquired from school instruction by normal children of different ages; one must to some extent make a barometer of instruction. On the other hand there remains to be organized rapid methods which permit one to tell with precision the degree of instruction which a candidate has attained. These two lines of research can scarcely be followed out except by persons belonging to the teaching profession.

— — —

To sum up, the pedagogical method is two fold. It consists in establishing as it were the balance sheet of the scholastic knowledge acquired by the child; on the other hand it consists in establishing the balance sheet of extra-scholastic knowledge. The general result will be found, not by a complete inventory—that would take too long—but by tests bearing upon a small number of questions judged to be representative of the whole.

The pedagogical method is somewhat indirect in its manner of arriving at the state and degree of the intelligence; it grasps the intelligence through the memory only. One who is rich in memory may be poor in judgment. One even finds imbeciles who have an amazing memory. It is right to add that in spite of this, these imbeciles are but little instructed, which proves to us that instruction, although it depends principally upon memory, demands also other intellectual faculties, especially judgment. One must not therefore exaggerate the bearing of this theoretic criticism which we here make upon the pedagogical method.

The disadvantages which our use of the method permits us already to suspect, are the following: in the first place it cannot be applied to very young children, of from 3 to 6 years, and it is especially important to point out mental debility at that age; in the second place it requires that one should know the scholastic attainments of each child. It is not always easy to see clearly into the past life of a child. Did he miss his class three years ago? If he followed the class, had he in his temperament, his state of health, his habits, special reasons for relaxation? Was his master a poor one, did he fail to understand the child? The quest may find itself face to face with facts, which from their remoteness and their nature, are very difficult to evaluate. These doubtful cases will not be in the majority, let us hope; but they will present themselves in abundance. M. Vaney has noted several in a statistical study, which is restricted, however. Dr. Demoor finds 50 doubtful in a total of 246 retarded and subnormal children; that is approximately one-fifth doubtful. These facts show that the pedagogical method has its imperfections. It should not be employed exclusively.

Medical Method

We speak here of the medical method considered in its narrowest sense; we make the improbable hypothesis of a physician who would judge an idiot simply from medical signs, and without attempting, even in the most empirical form, a psychological appreciation of the intelligence of the patient. We make the supposition in order to better understand the proper field for each method.

What are then the somatic symptoms which the physician can utilize for making a diagnosis of inferior mentality?

There is, we believe, a distinction to be made between two studies, that of the causes and that of the actual condition. When the actual state has been determined, after one has established in a summary manner or by a searching method that a subject has an inferior degree of intelligence, the physician plays an important rôle, owing to his special knowledge; it is he, who above everyone else can throw light upon the etiology of each case, can determine, for example, that the child suffers from *mal comitial* or is afflicted with myxoedema or that his respiration is disturbed by adenoids, that his nutrition is weakened, etc., and that a relation of cause and effect exists between these diverse maladies and his inferior intelligence. The etiology, once determined, serves to guide the prognosis and the treatment. It is not a matter of indifference to know the ill from which the child suffers; if his imbecility is due to epileptic causes, or rather consists in a state of decadence brought about by frequent attacks, the prognosis is less hopeful than if his intellectual weakness is the result of traumatism; in the latter case, one can hope that the lesion is made once for all and has not a progressive tendency. But these considerations upon the etiology, the prognosis and the treatment, remain subordinate to the study of the actual state of the intelligence; and as it is the actual state that we wish to study here we shall set aside every other question no matter how interesting it may be.

It is very evident that for a diagnosis of the actual state of the intelligence the physician who would rigorously ignore all psychology, would very much diminish his resources. Nevertheless he would still have some resources left. There are many somatic symptoms that can be considered as indirect and possible signs of inferior intelligence.

What are these signs? Here, we must first of all dissipate many illusions. The subnormal does not of necessity constantly announce itself by evident anatomical defects. The physical descriptions of the idiot and the imbecile that one finds in classic treatises are not always correct; and even if they were, they would not apply in the least to morons. But the morons constitute the majority. It is the morons that must be recognized in the schools, where they are confounded with normals; it is they who offer the greatest obstacle to the work of education. The diagnosis of moronity is at the same time the most important and the most difficult of all. Let us look therefore into the methods to be employed, to facilitate this diagnosis, from the simple examination of the body.

Medical literature contains actually a great number of observations which may be helpful if they are first submitted to organization. A great many anomalies of different orders have been noted among the subnormals; anatomical anomalies, physiological anomalies and the anomalies of heredity and of growth. In a recent book, Dr. Ley has made an excellent résumé of what is known of the diagnostic signs of abnormality, to which he has added personal observations of his own. We shall present to the reader in a rapid survey all that scientists have ever thought to look for, to examine, to analyze and to weigh among subnormals.

We shall take account only of clinical signs, that is to say of verifiable symptoms upon the living individual; and as we have already stated, we shall occupy ourselves mainly with the recognition of moronity.

A complete examination should cover the following points.

Hereditary antecedents.
Development.
Anatomical examination.
Psychological examination.

[A detailed treatment of these categories follows.]

*   *   *

With the publication of these papers, mental testing again crossed the ocean and, on its return to the United States, fell into the fertile soil that produced thousands of studies of intelligence testing during the next decades. Just as it was to be the American port for psychoanalysis, Clark University was the link between Europe and America in the development of testing research. While Binet and Simon were presenting detailed reports of their first work on the French scale, Lewis M. Terman and Arnold Gesell were finishing their dissertations at Worcester, both under Sanford.

Terman, having "had enough of the questionnaire method," set about the study of what "mental processes are involved in the thing we are accustomed to call intelligence" independently of both the French work and that of Spearman. Characteristically, the title of his dissertation was *Genius and Stupidity;* seven bright and seven stupid schoolboys (of different ages!) were intensively tested on eight tasks that promised to provide closer relation with "the thing we are accustomed to call intelligence" than did the

Gilbert items.* They did, but when Terman turned again to tests in 1910, he made the Binet scales the heart of his work. The explosive use and imitation of the Stanford revision of the Binet tests are a matter of record; the measurement of human ability became, if not the most fruitful, certainly the most enthusiastic, subsegment of American psychology. Yet, for all his contribution to an understanding of the technical and statistical problems of testing and to our knowledge of gifted children, Terman made no important theoretical statement about the nature of intelligence or about human development. The promulgation of general principles of ontogenesis and the use of tests as a polemical device became the duty of Terman's friend and colleague at Los Angeles State Normal School, Arnold Gesell.

Gesell had presented a dissertation on jealousy in animals and human beings for his degree in psychology at Clark and was already interested in studying the behavior of very young children.† During his medical training at Yale, he established the clinic of child development that was to be a center of research and rhetoric on the child for over thirty years. Gesell stands in the near distance of our history—far enough away to have attained the status of legend and symbol, too close to see with a scholarly indifferent eye. The ambiguity arises in part because Gesell's doctrinal heirs continue his work forcefully and with great influence, partly because Gesell became, for the behaviorists interested in children, the bugbear hereditarian. His refusals to be moved as psychology became more often defined by its studies of learning and his surprising indifference to the progress of psychoanalysis combined to make Gesell fair game for many hunters. The importance of his contribution can be seen only through the still-settling dust of contention, but there can be no doubt that Gesell continued, with remarkable equanimity, the traditions of Darwin, Galton, and Hall.

* L. M. Terman, Genius and stupidity. A study of some of the intellectual processes of seven "bright" and seven "stupid" boys, *Pedagogical Seminary*, 13, 1906, 307–373. For the sophistication of the later Terman, see his *The Measurement of Intelligence*, Boston: Houghton Mifflin, 1916.

† A. L. Gesell, Jealousy, *Amer. J. Psychol.*, 17, 1906, 437–496.

Gesell was not concerned merely with watching the unraveling of development with eye and camera, even with that first motion-picture camera from Pathé that had been used in the filming of *Birth of a Nation.* His monumental *Atlas* and the publication of standards for development mark only one part of his scientific commitment.* Description was always, for Gesell, in the service of two goals—one clinical and the other theoretical—but the detail and volume of his descriptive works (together with the avid reception given his books by mothers keen on quantifying the hitherto imprecise business of comparing babies) block an appreciation of his intentions.

The clinical goal toward which Gesell was directed throughout his career was the diagnosis of developmental pathology; his interest in the abnormal child is shown in a number of his papers, and notably in *Developmental Diagnosis.*† Although he overestimated a great deal the usefulness of his developmental schedules in the prediction of later pathology and intellectual functioning. Gesell turned the attention of his colleagues irrevocably toward the infant in developmental trouble. In this way, Gesell well represents the tradition of clinical pediatrics that we saw beginning with Cadogan and his contemporaries.

But it was as the most articulate spokesman for maturation as the central concept of developmental psychology that Gesell takes his place in the history of child study. In many places, he laid out the principles of his view of man and, although the elegance of his language sometimes fogs the message, Gesell's opinions cannot be doubted. They can be put in catechismal form. What is the principle of development? Maturation is the necessary condition of developmental change. What is the role of environment? Although the environment provides a setting for growth and may on occasion direct the particular shape of development, the contribution of environmental variation to variation in development is relatively slight. What determines growth? Within wide limits

* A. Gesell and others, *An Atlas of Infant Behavior. A Systematic Delineation of the Forms and Early Growth of Human Behavior Patterns,* 2 vols., New Haven, Conn.: Yale University Press, 1934.

† A. Gesell and Catherine S. Amatruda, *Developmental Diagnosis,* New York: Hoeber, 1941. The second edition appeared in 1947.

of variation in experience—typically, those limits which permit life to continue—the child will grow as his germ plasm directs.

For Gesell, these were not programmatic assumptions; they represented the facts as he saw them. The tendency to grow is the strongest force in life and it cannot be diverted or misguided by the kind of cultural variation that children normally encounter. Nor is the relation between age and developing behavior a superficial graphical function. Age is a convenient line along which to show the orderliness of development (on the metrical images of science, Gesell sounds like the radical behavorist, B. F. Skinner). Beyond the age-behavior relation lies a mechanism which has its rules, its higher order, and its roots in anatomy and physiology. Gesell was an ethologist of human behavior at a time uncongenial to the notion that the major dimensions of one's development were determined at the conceptional union. In the present climate of child psychology, sympathetic to behavioral cataloguing by the ethologists and willing once more to admit the claims of heredity, Gesell's theory of man seems far less extravagant than it did when it was written.

The next selection is interesting, not only because it reveals Gesell's convictions well, but because it shows better than most such documents the sober and reflective man, innocent of prejudice, being forced by the evidence to take the position from which he started. After a longish introduction on the artificiality of the distinction between Nature and Nurture (a position all child psychologists occupy, pointing the finger at their extremist opponents who are not as balanced as they), Gesell begins to bring together the data that will inevitably support his conclusion that "the inborn tendency toward optimum development is so inveterate that [the child] benefits liberally from what is good in our practice, and suffers less than he logically should from our unenlightenment."

* * *

Arnold Lucius Gesell (1880–1961)

Growth and Personality

There are two sharply contrasted doctrines of development. One emphasizes heredity and the powerlessness of environment. The other exalts environment and makes it the architect of the growing organism. The former doctrine traces the make-up of the individual to all determining unit characters of genes. Even complex psychological characteristics are attributed to these original packets of chromosomal material. The alternative doctrine suggests that even physical characteristics are molded by the conditions of development; and that mental characteristics, including capacity, talent and temperament are ultimately the result of training and conditioning.

Such contrasts in developmental doctrine are to be found not only in theoretical discussions but in the literature of education and reform. When Robert Owen founded the first nursery school in America just a century ago he was moved by an ardent faith in environment. At the National Capitol before the President, the Congress, and the Supreme Court, he stated his faith in these words:

"External circumstances may be so formed as to have an overwhelming and irresistible influence over every infant that comes into existence, either for good or evil; to compel him to receive any particular sentiments or habits, to surround him through life, with the most agreeable or disagreeable objects, and thus at pleasure make any portion, or the whole of the human race, poor, ignorant, vicious and wretched; or affluent, intelligent, virtuous and happy."

Where does the truth lie? Probably not at either extreme. The

A. Gesell, Growth potential and infant personality, *Infancy and Human Growth* (Chapter XVII), New York: Macmillan, 1928. Reprinted with permission.

opposition of doctrines of development has led to an overrigid distinction between intrinsic and extrinsic factors. Proverbs, metaphors, and epigrams have conspired to widen the cleavage between nature versus nurture, instinct versus habit, inheritance versus training, original versus acquired capacity. We have so overconventionalized the concepts of heredity and environment even in scientific textbooks that these concepts have become antithetical when they are in fact supplementary and reciprocal. In the field of mental inheritance there are further sources of confusion. The geneticist tends to speak of mental traits as though they were discrete faculties and lumps them with physical unit characters. The psychologist on the other hand is prone to argue in terms of a discrete, hormic mind independent of the bodily structure.

Here again the concept of growth proves it value. It leads to a depolarization of the two opposing categories of heredity and environment. Growth always represents a continuum; it therefore becomes unnecessary to draw a sharp distinction between physical and mental manifestation. Growth is also a process of integrative organization; it thus becomes desirable to consider *conjointly* the factors which enter into the shaping of the individual. From this point of view the organic mechanism of development and the reciprocal rather than the contrastive influence of heredity and environment is of chief concern. The interest shifts to the *conditions* of development, and to the projective influence of one stage of development upon another stage. Growth is constantly creating its own conditions. It is important not only to recognize the germinal determinations which underlie the growth process, but the regulatory influence of the very products of growth.

The supreme genetic law appears to be this: All present growth hinges on past growth. Growth is not a simple function neatly determined by X units of inheritance plus Y units of environment, but is an historical complex which reflects at every stage the past which it incorporates. In other words we are led astray by an artificial dualism of heredity and environment, if it blinds us to the fact that growth is a continuous self-conditioning process, rather than a drama controlled, *ex machina,* by two forces.

It follows from these considerations that it is impossible to determine in any precise way the exact degree of hereditary versus environmental influence in early mental development. At the present stage of knowledge it is important to avoid any over simplification of the problem. Bearing these difficulties and reservations in mind, we may, however, presently examine the drift of our available data, and venture some suggestions as to the relative rôle of inherent and induced factors in the mental growth of the infant. It will be understood that the so-called inherent factors may from a strict biological point of view often have a secondary or derived aspect. For example, the genesis of the eye in the embryo is due to an inherent, specific organ-forming substance in the genes. This is a primary chemical differentiation; but even this self-differentiation is under the influence of an organizing center and of gradients from which influences spread. The early development of the organ is furthermore regulated by its position in relation to other organs. This is a form of dependent differentiation, in which mechanical and physical influences come into play. After the attainment of histological differentiation of the tissues, the organism begins to function as a more or less integrated individual. From then on four new processes come into operation—"the trophic influence of nerves; the circulation of growth-modifying internal secretions; differential growth along different axes; and the adaptational effect of function."

Although these refinements belong to the field of experimental biology and cannot enter into a discussion of mental inheritance, they should at least figure in the background of such discussion, as a corrective against uncritical generalization and "inspired thinking." It is apparent that biometry, although it must supply the measurements and statistics of individual differences, cannot elucidate the actual mechanism of individual differentiation. This is a problem of physiology, and the pioneer investigations of developmental physiology are already putting the traditional question of Nature vs. Nurture in a new light. The genes initiate the process of devolment and determine its sphere and limits; but the process continuously creates its own inner control.

[Gesell describes Carmichael's (1926) study of anesthetized salamanders and Coghill's (1926) studies of maturation and behavior in Amblystoma.]

The Inherent Basis of Developmental Trend and Tempo

Recognizing, then, the intimate interplay of innate, induced, and environmental factors, we may inquire into the rôle of heredity in some of the major aspects of mental growth. . .

The tempo and trend of development in each infant appear to be constitutional characteristics, for the most part hereditary in nature. In cases of secondary amentia the retardation of developmental rate is, of course, acquired. The deficiency then becomes part of the constitution of the child, and the "retardation" is symptomatic of impairment of structure and reduction of developmental potency. Such potency as remains, however, is part of the original nature of the child. The reduction of potency may occur in utero, at time of birth, or postnatally. The reduction may be complete or partial, selective or symmetrical; and in any given case the developmental end-results depend chiefly upon the original deprivation rather than the later environmental opportunity. In certain injuries to the central nervous system, however, there is an indeterminate reserve of nerve-cell tissue, which can undergo substitutive or compensatory development. The effectuality of training and environment will then depend upon the age at which the damage occurred, the amount of available compensating tissue, and the intensity of the demand upon it. When these factors conspire favorably, certain "hopeless" cases of motor disability undergo remarkable improvement under the stress of effort and training. Here the rôle of environment is critical.

It is significant that for many cases of mental deficiency the cause is quite obscure. In the absence of a frank illness, injury, or trauma, the temptation is to ascribe the deficiency to germinal defect. The possibilities of defective growth regulation in the early embryonic period are however, theoretically, so numerous that many of these instances of congenital defect cannot be safely ascribed to faulty genes. The defect, however, is constitutional and the lowered tempo and lowered trend of development are as ineradicably part of the physiological equipment of the individual as the skin pattern of his hands.

The mental growth curves of the six siblings reported [earlier] . . . are strongly suggestive of underlying hereditary determination. The curves represent two highly contrastive types of growth. It is scarcely conceivable that such a consistent disparity could arise out of some subtle difference in nutrition, hygiene, or household conditions for the two groups. The children were reared in the same home by the same hand. It is more conceivable that a decisive difference in the germinal determinations account for both the average and the reduced growth potency.

Acceleration of development, likewise, is typically an inherent biological characteristic of the individual, most probably hereditary in nature. There is no convincing evidence that fundamental acceleration of development can be readily induced by either pernicious or enlightened methods of stimulation. Through sheer conditioning and training it is possible to teach both infants and animals prodigious tricks: It is possible, also, that certain kinds of conditioning may exert a deep augmenting effect upon the dynamics of individual growth, reaching the endocrine constitution. This would be a secondary, derived kind of acceleration, comparable to the reduction of development in secondary amentia. It is a theoretical possibility rather than a frequent clinical manifestation. Abnormal forms of precocity encountered clinically are likely to be partial and unsymmetrical. They constitute atypical deviations; they may be associated with infantilism and with unusual or pathological glandular conditions. The wholesome variety of acceleration found with superior endowment, is really part and parcel of that endowment, a symptom of intensified growth, a fundamental individual difference, characteristic of, because necessary to, the developmental mechanics of certain kinds of ability. If the methods of biochemical measurement were available, it might be possible to determine certain differences in the energetics or dynamics of these rapidly growing infants, even in the first months of existence, when we could scarcely attribute their precocity to special educational or environmental stimulation.

If the superior individual as a rule mentally grows not only faster but for a longer time, this lengthened span may be regarded as primarily a manifestation of inherent endowment.

That secondary, derived factors also come into play will be presently noted. The interspecies and interracial differences in the duration of plasticity are doubtless correlated with differences in organic constitution. Within limits, comparable individual differences in the growth cycle of man may be presumed to have a similar basis.

This does not, however, exclude the operation of extrinsic influences. Whether one regards thyroid extract as an article of diet, or as a biochemical activator, it is certain that in some instances it affects the metabolism of the body so profoundly as to have a demonstrable effect upon both physical and mental growth. Here, then, an extrinsic factor modifies the tempo and trend of development. It is also possible that future insight into endocrine physiology will actually lead to a postponement and amelioration of senility. Then again the dominance of hereditary determination would give way to environmental regulation. For similar reasons it is probable that superior physical hygiene will continue to have a favorable effect upon growth, particularly in cases of previous neglect or partial deprivation. In one or two of the "atypical" growth cases reported in the foregoing section, it is possible that obscure but genuine alterations of the physiological economy were responsible for the psychodevelopmental improvement. On the whole, the stability of the developmental trend and tempo is more conspicuous than its sensitiveness to "external" influences. The case of puberty praecox described [earlier] . . . is particularly impressive. Here adolescence was precociously displaced to the extent of a whole decade; the morphology of the body was definitely responsive to this glandular deviation; but the nervous system was only mildly deflected in its course of growth.

To what extent endocrine complexes are to be construed as genuinely hereditary is a significant genetic question. They may be in the nature of adaptations to climatic and nutritional conditions, rather than evidences of fundamental germinal variations. Shirokogoroff [*The Chinese of Chekiang and Kinagsu*] in his elaborate study of the process of physical growth among the Chinese holds that growth is controlled by the complex of glands of internal secretion on the one hand and the inherent peculiarities of ethnical groups on the other. The latter peculiarities are more clearly hereditary than the former. He came to the general conclusion that "The endocrine complexes define not only the process of physical growth, but the psychic behavior of ethnical units, so that the peculiarities of Chinese psychology and behavior may be explained as the result of their glandular complexes." The study of the process of growth, it is suggested, may even serve as a method of discovering the chemical components of the ethnical units. Are these components laid down in the chromosomal packets?

Clinical mongolism, which, of course, is in no way to be confused with ethnical differentiation, raises similar questions concerning the rôle of early glandular secretion. The cause of mongolism is unknown. Neuropathic heredity, familial characteristics, syphilitic, alcoholic, tuberculous and arthritic lesions are rarely and irregularly involved. More frequent are influences which disturb pregnancy such as advanced age or exhaustion of mothers, numerous previous pregnancies, privations, violent emotion, etc. But even these influences are subject to exception and to error of interpretation. The fact that mongolism may occur in one of fraternal twins, and has not been reported in only one of identical twins, suggests the existence of a germinal defect. To be so much in the dark as to the etiology of such a well-defined clinical entity as mongolism suggests the need of great caution in assigning the cause of congenital defect.

Congenital total hemihypertrophy, particularly when found in association with mental defect, would naturally suggest a defective germ plasm. The available evidence does not support this suggestion, but favors the view that some epigenetic factors relating to regulation of symmetry are responsible for the anomaly and all its correlated disturbances in tissue development, including partial cerebral agenesis. To be sure, the imbalance in twinning may itself be ascribed to an original defect in the genes; but it is more in accord with the law of parsimony to ascribe it to some failure in the mechanism of growth regulation. However, whether germinal or epigenetic in origin, the anomaly becomes established at an extremely early embryonic period, and projects itself irrevocably into the entire growth cycle. It becomes an inherent even if not inherited character, and is an excellent illustration of projective importance of early developmental deviations.

Inherent Factors in Handedness

Handedness is a form of asymmetry which likewise may be interpreted in terms of the physiology of twinning. Perfect ambidexterity would assume ideal symmetry in body build, and complete ambivalence in the two cerebral hemispheres. Such perfect balance, theoretically and actually, must be a rarity, which, if it ever exists, tends to be overthrown even in the intra-uterine stage of development with postural and gravitational adaptations. In the great majority of instances the balance is thrown in favor of the right hand and the right eye. Accompanying, following, or determining this unidextrality is a dominance of one of the cerebral hemispheres. Is this cerebral dominance strictly hereditary, or is it an epigenetic by-product of developmental mechanics comparable in a broad way in its genesis to hemihypertrophy? At any rate handedness becomes inherent, and becomes part of the constitutional make-up of the individual.

The fact that left-handedness is sometimes a familial trait suggests the existence of germinal factors; but not conclusively, because the sinistrality may still be a secondary by-product of a more fundamental familial trait involving vascular or anatomical peculiarities. The frequency of left-handedness in twins suggests an epigenetic factor of a regulatory nature. The increment of unidextrality at adolescence as shown by increased disparity in dynamometer records again suggests basic germinal determiners. The fact that even among left-handed and right-handed individuals there is a wide range of variation with respect to the intensity or degree of the handedness suggests that unidextrality is based on inherent constitutional rather than cultural factors.

All these considerations cast doubt on the theory that handedness is a result of social conditioning. Suppose that all the left-handed individuals in the world arose in their might and imposed a left-handed civilization for a period of fifty years. Is it probable that the infants of that era would be relatively bidextrous for six months, reach for the cube with the left hand at nine months, and be consistently left-handed at one year? Under extremely diverse, ambiguous and intermittent social suggestions, we have found that the great majority of infants of the present day show a progressive tendency toward right-handedness which becomes well established in the second half of the first year. The fact that under similar conditions a significant minority of infants show equally well defined left-handedness, is itself suggestive of more deep-seated physiological if not hereditary factors.

We may cite briefly the case of an infant who showed evidence of left-handedness in the very first day of his postnatal existence. He amused the nurses by the vigorous manner in which he sucked his left hand. When questioned the nurses reported that it was always his *left* hand which went to his mouth. His mother, a good observer, does not recall that he ever used the right hand instead. When the time came to use the domestic implements of culture, spoon, crayon, cup, toys, handkerchief, etc., he consistently showed preference for the left hand. Pictures at this time indicate that he consistently crossed his legs in sitting posture in a manner different from his right-handed sister. His parents, persuaded that handedness was the result of social conditioning, used judicious and persistent suggestion to favor the right hand. The porridge might be eaten with the left hand, but dessert must always be eaten with the right hand. Hedonic association could not be better planned. When ready for school entrance this boy was psychologically examined. He proved to be a boy of superior intelligence, but with relatively inferior output in drawing, even though his father is an artist.

In all his manual activities he showed an inveterate preference for right to left, and contraclockwise movements. When it came to drawing a locomotive with crayon, the smoke streamed to the left; likewise, when it came to reading his first letters on signs and in books, he proceeded from right to left. K.I. was read as I.K. Letters and numbers were mirror written. There can be no doubt that this boy has a constitutional flare toward left-handed performance, and would be more comfortable in a sinistral society. He is reported in this detail to show that systematic social conditioning cannot overcome inherent left-handedness; and to indicate that its inherency may date from birth.

The Early Genesis of Individual Differences

Concerning the inheritance of specific abilities, our data furnish only indirect suggestion. Specific ability in drawing, special interest in music, marked sociality, early facility in language, precocity in the use of generalizations and abstractions, all these manifest themselves in infancy in a way suggestive of native gifts or predispositions. If conditioning during infancy were responsible for such individual differences, there would be much more similarity between siblings and twins than is actually found. The extreme form of the theory of conditioning proves too much; for if it held, there would be numerous instances of bizarre ability and grotesque psychological resemblance between brothers and sisters.

Our data as a whole and clinical experience with infants give no confirmation to the theory that infants start abreast at a straight base line parallel with the threshold of birth, and that psychological differences among individuals rise by cumulative and selective action on a homogeneous protoplasmic Urstoff which in quality and amount is equally apportioned. Minute anthropometric measurements of foetuses show that racial and individual peculiarities of structure in face, hand, foot, are demonstrable in the prenatal stage. If this is true of bones, muscles, and skin, there is no reason why it should not be true of the internal structure of the nervous system. The plasticity of the nervous system is not in itself inconsistent with a considerable degree of native differentiation. The "appalling" resemblance between man and the ape in the prenatal period has been exaggerated; because beneath and beyond the resemblance are differences, less obvious but of extreme developmental importance. Indeed in this field of comparative anatomy and comparative psychology the differences are almost more in need of scientific definition than the more easily discoverable correspondences. The study of such differences shows that the distinctive human and individual traits come not by way of addition to a common substructure, but are laid down in the substructure itself.

If we are to ascertain the genesis of human deviations we must first of all determine how early in life such deviations assert themselves. Investigation must be directed more and more to the period of infancy. The time of the genesis of individual differences is part of the question of the mode of genesis.

Bearing on this point, brief reference may be made to a study in which Miss Elizabeth Lord and the writer reported a psychological comparison of eleven pairs of nursery school children who were comparable as to age and school experience but contrastive as to the socio-economic status of their homes. One child in each pair came from an underprivileged home, the other from a favored home with father or mother occupationally at the professional level. Individual tests, measurements, and clinical estimates were made of each child on fifteen items yielding 330 comparative findings. There was a definite bimodal tendency in the distribution of these findings, the higher ratings gravitating strongly to the favored group. The data suggest that the basic growth factors which will differentiate the abilities and personalities of these twenty-two children in adult years were in operation at least as early as the age of two or three years.

These differentiating growth characteristics began to operate when? The difficulty of fixing the zero point in answer to this question is itself a partial answer to the question. There is no conclusive control experiment. The same infants would have to be rereared in converse homes and converse schools to furnish complete evidence. It is probable that in the field of personality characteristics, emotional attitudes, interests, and preferences, the greatest reversal of ratings would occur. But this would not argue that the fundamental growth potency can be radically altered by a change of milieu.

It is doubtful whether the basic temperamental qualities of infants can be measurably altered by environmental influence. Training and hygiene may exert very palpable and important influence in the organization of the personality without necessarily altering the underlying naturel or habitus. We have been particularly impressed with a difference in temperamental reactions in a pair of twins, of the fraternal type, who have been under close observation for a period of several months dating from birth. Even in these early months mother and examiner are agreed that there is a consistent difference between the twins with respect to such matters as placidity, length of crying, vigor of protest, tolerance of physical discomfort, readiness of smiling, social responsiveness, etc. With the same home, the same mother, similar physical health, it is highly probable that these differences in emotivity bespeak an inherent if not inborn difference in temperamental make-up. Experience and education will not so much modify as they will (and should) be modified by this native difference.

The temperamental characteristics of C. D.. . . . may be recalled here. This girl exhibited a striking degree of amenability, sociality, and good nature as early as the age of nine months. We have followed her career closely. She is now five years of age, and in spite of a varied experience in boarding homes and institutions she has not lost these engaging characteristics. They are part and parcel of her make-up quite as much as the lowered tempo and the lowered trend of her general development. It can be predicted with much certainty that she will retain her present emotional equipment when she is an adolescent and an adult. But more than this cannot be predicted in the field of personality. For whether she becomes a delinquent, and she is potentially one, will depend upon her subsequent training, conditioning, and supervision. She is potentially, also, a willing, helpful, productive worker. Environment retains a critical rôle even though heredity sets metes and bounds.

The very essence of mental growth lies in this mixture of determinateness and indeterminateness. Tempo, trend, and temperament are in large measure determined by inherent or hereditary factors; but the wealth of detail in the dynamic patterns which we call personality is indeterminate until it is defined through experience. Growth potency is fundamentally dependent on original equipment; but the personality make-up is almost literally fabricated by the social conditions in which the young mind grows.

Personality Formation and the Web of Life

Indeed, the child's "personality make-up," so far as it is a describable subsisting reality, consists in the countless conditioned reflexes, associative memories, habits and attitudes which it acquires as a result of being reared by personal beings. If he were never touched by ministering hands, if he did not see and hear the evidences of humanity, if he could grow up in an absolutely asocial vacuum, it is difficult to believe that he would have any recognizable "personality make-up" at all. The balance, the topography, the well-being of personality depend to a remarkable degree upon the impress of other personalities.

The biologist emphasizes the marvelous interrelation and integration of all the organic world or the web of life. Through the sensitive, sifting processes of evolution, all forms of life have in some way become interdependent. All species are thus adapted to each other.

This conceptual image of the web of life, Thomson considers one of the four great ideas in Darwinism. "To put it in the coldest way, there seems to be a tendency in animate nature towards the correlation of organisms." "Nature is seen more and more vividly as a fabric." "The circle of one creature's life cuts into many other circles." The relationships are not in static completion or stable design. On a majestic scale which comprises the whole organic world, evolution continues to slowly modify both the organisms and the total pattern of mutual adaptations. This complex system of interrelations "forms an external registration of evolutionary gains and a sieve by which variations, sometimes subtle nuances, one might think, are effectually sifted."

The mechanism of evolution and the mechanism of growth, after all, have much in common. The most striking difference relates to time. What evolution achieves in ages, the infant in his growth accomplishes in brief moments. But he grows and adapts in a manner which is measurably comparable to the evolutionary process.

The image of the web of life is, in fact, applicable to the mechanics of personality formation. It is possible to think of each personal complex of mental growth as a brief compression of events staged in a little theater in which the individual achieves a unique but conditioned system of adaptations to the whole human family. Here again is a correlation of organisms, based on the interactions and the interdependencies of contiguous personalities. Here, too, in the mental development of each new infant we glimpse the strands of nature's vast web of life, a ceaseless process of adaptation to other individuals, an interplay which inevitably registers itself in the delicate tissue of the child's growing personality.

All children are thus, through correlation, adapted to their parents and to each other. Even the maladjustments between parent and child are adaptations in a psycho-biological sense and can only be comprehended if we view them as lawfully conditioned modes of adaptation. Growth is again the key concept. For better or for worse, children and their elders must grow up with each other, which means in interrelation one to the other. The roots of the growth of the infant's personality reach into other human beings.

These considerations give great emphasis to the environmental or psychodynamic importance of the parent-infant relationship. This relationship is so fundamental that it may be construed in biological as well as cultural terms. Indeed even in infrahuman family life there are noteworthy manifestations of parental behavior. The more basic principles of interaction between child and parent can be fruitfully analyzed by means of such biological categories as *parasitism, symbiosis,* and *commensalism.* In the present volume, no space will be devoted to these details. It is sufficient to point out that the personality configuration of the child is not determined by germinal constitution, and that it is a product of growth regulation. The regulation is accomplished both consciously and unconsciously through the social interaction between the young child and his household. The association of parent and child is a kind of psychobiological partnership. It is infinitely more complicated than a mere nutritional arrangement, but it obeys similar laws of nature, and lies equally in the sphere of human control.

It appears, then, in summary, that there is a profound interdependence between "heredity" and "environment" in the control of development. These terms, from tradition, are dualistic in connotation, but growth itself is integrative and resolves the antithesis. The ancient antinomy of determinism versus freedom likewise seems inapplicable to the facts of growth. All growth is lawful and in that sense determined. The intrinsic determiners of development work in conformance to genetic laws, the extrinsic factors work in similar and coördinated conformance. The spheres of intrinsic and extrinsic influence are not separate but interpenetrate, and scientifically, if not metaphysically, it is impossible to assign a unique and absolute autonomy to any factor which enters into the growth complex. Even the originative and mutational manifestations always emerge in and out of a zone of growth. They may be unpredictable; but they are not pure miracles. From the standpoint of scientific policy they must be brought within the scope of developmental law.

There is after all a difference between predeterminism and determinism. Scientific determinism does not spell foreordination; but aims to bring even "freedom" within the limits of law and therefore also within the limits of comprehension. An absolutely whimsical and fortuitous freedom would be as offensive to understanding as a stereotyped predestination. In organic evolution and in the growth of the individual these divergent extremes are kept in progressive check and balance. Viewed from one aspect, the phenomena of growth are impressive for their conservative stability; viewed from another aspect they are impressive for their productive fertility. Plasticity is neither a negative nor a passive character. It is a positive "function of growth," a method of transconstruction or assimilation.

The concept of heredity in its classic simplicity is contradicted by the existence of this kind of plasticity. Apparently there is a process of competition and selection in the formative complex of growth. Even native endowment comes not as a discrete bequest, but is built up through the sifting influences of competition among variable components. Some of these survive, others give way. The native endowment is thus built up through the screening stress of growth, and is a product of growth as well as of germinal constitution. Not all potentialities are realized, but only those which pass the mesh of already attained organization. All growth is self limited. Growth is mainly determined by previous growth. But this is a progressive kind of determinism which in the field of behavior, at least, comes under human control, and is inconsistent with a fatalistic view of infancy.

These considerations are general. They may be given concreteness if we formulate them briefly in terms of growth potency, personality, and the nervous system. Growth potency is broadly and fundamentally determined by inheritance. The basic developmental tempo, trend, and temperament are mainly inherent individual characteristics. Personality in its most pervasive and inclusive sense is mainly a product of the conditions of development. Maturation proceeds from intrinsic potentiality; organization issues from extrinsic and experiential determinants. But utmost realization of growth potency depends upon maximum organization.

The nervous system stands supreme among the federation of organs which together constitute the human individual. Its supremacy consists in the function of maintaining and furthering the integrity of the body and its behavior. By virtue of this function nature has safeguarded it with certain distinctive growth characteristics. Among all the organs of the body the nervous system manifests a high degree of autonomy in paradoxical union with a high degree of impressionability. It is remarkably resistant to adversity. It withstands much deprivation. When other organs of the body starve, it does not starve as much as they do. This relative invulnerability gives it a certain stability in the somatic competition between organ systems. It tends to grow in obedience to inborn determiners, whether saddled with handicap or favored with opportunity. It responds to opportunity and capitalizes it; but its supreme function is the optimum integration of the individual in all circumstances.

All things considered, the inevitableness and surety of maturation are the most impressive characteristic of early development. It is the hereditary ballast which conserves and stabilizes the growth of each individual infant. It is indigenous in its impulsion; but we may well be grateful for this degree of determinism. If it did not exist the infant would be a victim of a flaccid malleability which is sometimes romantically ascribed to him. His mind, his spirit, his personality would fall a ready prey to disease, to starvation, to malnutrition, and worst of all to misguided management. As it is, the inborn tendency toward optimum development is so inveterate that he benefits liberally from what is good in our practice, and suffers less than he logically should from our unenlightenment. Only if we give respect to this inner core of inheritance can we respect the important individual differences which distinguish infants as well as men.

*　*　*

In 1928, Gesell was in mid-career; for another two decades he would continue his work of measurement and diagnosis, changing his attitudes toward the child hardly at all in the interval but adding steadily to our knowledge of man developing. The stability of the Gesellian position is even more noteworthy in consideration of the turmoil—or, better, the several turmoils—through which psychology passed between the award of his Ph.D. in 1906 and his retirement from Yale in 1948. While Gesell was completing his work on jealousy, Freud was watching the reaction of his colleagues to the publication of *Three Contributions to a Theory of Sex,* an event which marked, at least for studies of the child, what may be called the Greater Turmoil of twentieth-century psychology. But the Lesser Turmoil was also brewing in 1906 as John Watson, fresh from his dissertation on rat education, was beginning to consider how far he might extend the procedures of animal psychology. His conclusions were far-reaching.

Watson was by no means the only American psychologist who was wearied and frustrated by the self-conscious esoterica of Wundt's students. With notable irony, in the same journal in which Watson published his manifesto on behaviorism there appears a sober and moderate paper by James Rowland Angell on behavior as a category of psychology.* For years, Angell and his students at Chicago—Watson among them—had sought a way of escaping the antiseptic introspective analysis of consciousness that was "experimental psychology" without losing the problems of perception, imagination, learning, and thinking that seemed appropriate to psychological study. But whether or not the times were ready for functionalist moderation, Watson was not; between 1913 and 1920, he shook the house of psychology to its foundations and, along the way, invented a new kind of child.

The beginnings of the Watsonian revolt were embedded in the fact that the procedures of observation and description used in the study of human adults seemed artificial and misleading when applied to the study of animals and young children. More-

* J. R. Angell, Behavior as a category of psychology, *Psychol. Rev.,* **20**, 1913, 255–270.

over, Watson was unwilling to accept variation in method to fit
the subject; in his view it was necessary to adopt a single and
consistent position on the nature of psychology. The first premise
of his revision of psychology announced the subject matter of
the field and the words of his announcement were as clear as
Gabriel's trumpet and as sharp as a knife.

Psychology as the behaviorist views it is a purely objective experimental
branch of natural science. Its theoretical goal is the prediction and control of behavior. Introspection forms no essential part of its methods,
nor is the scientific value of its data dependent upon the readiness with
which they lend themselves to interpretation in terms of consciousness.
The behaviorist, in his efforts to get a unitary scheme of animal response,
recognizes no dividing line between man and brute. The behavior of
man, with all its refinement and complexity, forms only a part of the
behaviorist's total scheme of investigation.*

It was an exhilarating message to young American psychologists,
and the transformation of the discipline from the science of mind
to the science of behavior took place, not without argument, but
with a speed remarkable for the usually conservative pace of
academic change. Whatever its intellectual justification, the behaviorist revision was hurried into the lives of psychologists and
citizens for several rather diverse reasons. The two men who
might have controlled Watson's excess were lost to psychology;
James died in 1910 and Baldwin went into exile in 1909. Psychologists showed during the First World War that they could
make important contributions to such practical problems as selection and administration, and not by means of introspective
analysis. The war marked a turn in American culture, and Watson's
simple dogma of the limitless power of man to change his fellow
man was met with the unreasoning support and unreasoning
opposition that builds cults and newspaper copy. It was Watson's
dedication to the principle of man's modifiability by experience
that made him a child psychologist and changed the tone of
child study in the United States for several decades. Watson was

* J. B. Watson, Psychology as the behaviorist views it, *Psychol. Rev.*, **20**,
1913, 158–177. The quotation is the article's first paragraph.

blessed too by the discovery of the work of Pavlov; by 1915, he had not only a program but a mechanism—the conditioned reflex.*

It was at about this time that Watson began his first systematic observations of children, cataloging the reflex equipment of the newborn infant, elaborating a theory of emotional development based on three unconditioned reflexes (fear, rage, and love) and demonstrating the experimental learning and extinction of fear in a child by procedures of classical conditioning.† In the midst of this work—which Watson clearly saw as the direction of his career—he resigned from Johns Hopkins and began his second life as advertising executive and psychological polemicist.‡

Watson never saw clearly—and he left this weakness as a legacy to his most enthusiastic heirs—that the behavioristic revolution was essentially a revolution of method. The decision to study behavior by objective methods does not carry in its train any particular view of man or society; certainly it does not impose an ethic. Yet the radical behaviorists—and Watson was not the last —have moved from considerations of method and research procedure to considerations of the values of society with less visible transition and less restraint than their colleagues. Almost simultaneously with his call to the contest in 1913, Watson made the leap to a theory of man that emphasized the contribution of specific environmental experience as against the mark of heredity.

But Watson was to go further; the selection which follows is from his book of advice to parents based on psychological research. The restraint of the researcher is abandoned and Watson gives himself over to an angry commentary on the evils of mothers in our society; reading these fulminations now, one can understand why Bertrand Russell concluded that Watson must be the only behaviorist. Unhappily for psychology and for children born

* J. B. Watson, The place of the conditioned-reflex in psychology, *Psychol. Rev.*, **23**, 1916, 89–116.

† The best summary of this work, together with the later studies Watson carried out with Mary Cover Jones, appears in his Powell lectures, in C. Murchison (Ed.) *Psychologies of 1925*, Worcester, Mass.: Clark University Press, 1926, pp. 1–81.

‡ The course of child psychology would almost certainly have been different— though in incalculable ways—had Baldwin and Watson continued at Hopkins to the natural end of their academic careers, 1929 for Baldwin and 1946 for Watson.

between 1925 and 1940, Russell was wrong. Watson's views, cruel and silly as they must have appeared to considerate men at all times, exerted a strong influence on child-rearing procedures, through his own books and articles (a series appeared in *Harper's* in 1927*) and through his voice in the Children's Bureau. Yet it is not merely as a polemecist that Watson takes his place in the history of child psychology. His productive criticism of psychological method carried with it a change in attitudes toward psychological theory. Not only were the descriptive terms of mentalistic psychology foresworn, but it was also necessary to confine psychological theory to the words of physics and associationistic philosophy. The result, as Watson's doctrines became models for research on the behavior of the child, was a theoretical language and a range of method too narrow to contain the child's variety and almost prohibitive of sensitive investigation of emotion and thinking in the child. Slowly over the last half-century, there has been a return to these difficult and provocative problems of child behavior with the skeptical and tough-minded attitude that Watson taught, but restoring the balance has probably been slowed by the remembered model of Watson's scientism and his overextension of a revision in method. Certainly, child psychology is not yet free of the Watsonian *non sequitur*—that the objective study of behavior entails a particular theory of the child.

Watson's lasting contribution to our knowledge of children is centered on his studies of the infant and on his startling and exciting proposal that parents could make of their children what they willed. His experimental reports, never insipid or pussyfooting, are serious, courteous to his opponents, and scientifically restrained. Only when he spoke at large did his voice become strident. Watson said, of the book from which the following passages come, *"Psychological Care of Infant and Child* was another book I feel sorry about—not because of its sketchy form, but because I did not know enough to write the book I wanted to write."† Nonetheless, the passages accurately reflect Watson's beliefs about children and research with children. Barred from

---

* These articles were put in a book "frankly directed to the public," J. B. Watson, *The Ways of Behaviorism*, New York: Harper, 1928.

† J. B. Watson [Autobiography], in C. Murchison's *A History of Psychology in Autobiography*, Vol. III, pp. 271–281. The quotation is from p. 280.

his laboratory and the audience of his professional colleagues, Watson could not extend and modify the beginnings he made in the study of children. As a consequence, his work grew only in bulk and rancor, never in form, and his dogmatism imposed constraints on academic child psychology that it did not throw off for many years.

*   *   *

John Broadus Watson (1878–1958)

Fears of Children and the Love of Mothers

Children's fears are home grown just like their loves and temper outbursts. The parents do the emotional planting and the cultivating. At three years of age the child's whole emotional life plan has been laid down, his emotional disposition set. At that age the parents have already determined for him whether he is to grow into a happy person, wholesome and good-natured, whether he is to be a whining, complaining neurotic, an anger driven, vindictive, over-bearing slave driver, or one whose every move in life is definitely controlled by fear.

But How do Parents Build in Fears?

. . . I [have] brought out the fact that all we have to start with in building a human being is a lively squirming bit of flesh, capable of making a few simple responses such as movements of the hands and arms and fingers and toes, crying and smiling, making certain sounds with its throat. I [have said] that parents take this raw material and begin to fashion it in ways to suit themselves.

J. B. Watson, *Psychological Care of Infant and Child*, New York: Norton, 1928, Chapters 2 and 3. Reprinted with permission of the publisher.

This means that parents, whether they know it or not, start intensive training of the child at birth.

It is especially easy to shape the emotional life at this early age. I might make this simple comparison: The fabricator of metal takes his heated mass, places it upon the anvil and begins to shape it according to patterns of his own. Sometimes he uses a heavy hammer, sometimes a light one; sometimes he strikes the yielding mass a mighty blow, sometimes he gives it just a touch. So inevitably do we begin at birth to shape the emotional life of our children. The blacksmith has all the advantage. If his strokes have been heavy and awkward and he spoils his work, he can put the metal back on the fire and start the process over. There is no way of starting over again with the child. Every stroke, be it true or false, has its effect. The best we can do is to conceal, skillfully as we can, the defects of our shaping. We can still make a useful instrument, an instrument that will work, but how few human instruments have ever been perfectly shaped to fit the environments in which they must function!

I think I can take you into the laboratory and give you a clear picture of the kinds of sledge hammers you are using in fashioning the fear life of your child.

Our laboratory work shows the fear life of the newborn infant is simplicity itself. From birth the child will show fear whenever a sudden loud sound is made close to its head and whenever it is thrown off its balance, as for example, when its blanket is quickly jerked. No other fears are natural, all other fears are built in.

And yet, think how complicated is the fear life of the three-year-old, the adolescent, the timid adult. Study the fears of the adults around you. I have seen a grown man cower and cringe and literally blanch with fear at the sight of a gun. I have seen a man stay all night in a hotel rather than enter his dark home when family and servants are away. I have seen a woman go into hysterics when a bat flew into a room. I have seen a child so torn by fear of moving animal toys that his whole organized life was in danger. Think of our fear of lightning, wind, railway trains, automobile accidents, ocean travel, burglars, fire, electricity and the thousands of other things that literally torture us even in this modern, supposedly secure life we lead. Think how peaceful, how calm, how efficient our lives would be if we were no more fearful than the newborn baby.

What Can the Laboratory Say About the Way Fears Grow Up?

Suppose I put before you a beautiful, healthy, well-formed baby nine months of age. On his mattress I place a rabbit. I know this baby's history; I know he has never seen a rabbit before. He reaches for the rabbit first with one hand, then the other the moment his eyes light upon it. I replace the rabbit with a dog. He behaves the same way. I next show him a cat, then a pigeon. Each new object is gleefully welcomed and equally gleefully handled. Afraid of furry objects? Not at all. But how about slimy objects? Surely he is afraid of cold, clammy, squirmy animals. Surely he is afraid of fish and frogs. I hand him a gold fish, alive and squirming. I put a green frog in front of him. Something new, again for the first time. Yes, a new world to work at. Immediately he goes after it as vigorously as after the other members of the animal kingdom. But surely all ancient history tells us that man instinctively avoids the snake. Literature is full of references to the fact that man's natural enemy is the snake. Not so with our lusty nine months infant. The boa constrictor I put in front of him—when young the most harmless of snakes—calls out the most vigorous of all those favorable friendly responses.

But won't our infant cry out in fear when I put him in the total darkness of a lightproof room? Not at all. But won't flame, that most terrifying of all physical agents, when seen for the first time at this tender age throw him almost into a fit? Let us take an iron pan and make a little bonfire of newspapers, being careful to keep it far enough away to keep the child from harm.

This infant must be phlegmatic, without emotional life. Not at all. I can convince you easily otherwise. In my hands I have a steel bar about an inch in diameter and about four feet long, and a carpenter's hammer. The child is sitting up looking at the attendant. I hold the steel bar about a foot behind his head where he can't see me. I rap the steel bar sharply with the hammer. The picture changes immediately. First a whimper, a sudden catching of the breath, a stiffening of the whole body, a pulling of the hands to the side, then a cry, then tears. I bang it again. The reaction becomes still more pronounced. He cries out loud, rolls over to his side and begins to crawl away as rapidly as possible.

Suppose I let him sit quietly on a blanket over his mattress. He may be very still, just dozing, or he may be playing eagerly with a toy. Suddenly I jerk the blanket, pull his support from under him. This sudden loss of support produces almost the same reaction as the loud sound. I haven't hurt him by pulling the blanket, he falls over from his sitting position fifty times a day and never whimpers. Your training has nothing to do with the fear he shows at loud sounds and loss of support, nor will any training ever completely remove the potency of these things to call out fears. I have seen the most seasoned hunter when dozing, jump violently when his comrade strikes a match to kindle the camp fire. You have seen the most intrepid of women show terror in crossing a perfectly safe foot bridge that sways with her weight.

Fear of all other objects is home-made. Now to prove it. Again I put in front of you the nine months old infant. I have my assistant take his old playmate, the rabbit, out of its pasteboard box and hand it to him. He starts to reach for it. But just as his hands touch it I bang the steel bar behind his head. He whimpers and cries and shows fear. Then I wait awhile. I give him his blocks to play with. He quiets down and soon becomes busy with them. Again my assistant shows him the rabbit. This time he reacts to it quite slowly. He doesn't plunge his hands out as quickly and eagerly as before. Finally he does touch it gingerly. Again I strike the steel bar behind his head. Again I get a pronounced fear response. Then I let him quiet down. He plays with his blocks. Again the assistant bring in the rabbit. This time something new develops. No longer do I have to rap the steel bar behind his head to bring out fear. *He shows fear at the sight of the rabbit.* He makes the same reaction to it that he makes to the sound of the steel bar. He begins to cry and turn away the moment he sees it.

I have started the process of fear building. And this fear of the rabbit persists. If you show the rabbit to him one month later you get the same reaction. There is good evidence to show that such early built in fears last throughout the lifetime of the individual.

We have a name in the laboratory for fears built up in this experimental way. We call them *conditioned* fears and we mean by that "home-made fears." By this method we can, so far as we know, make any object in the world call out a *conditioned* fear response. All we have to do is to show the infant any object and make a loud sound at the same moment.

But this fear of the rabbit is not the only building stone we have laid in the child's life of fear. After this one experience, and with no further contact with animals, all furry animals such as the dog, the cat, the rat, the guinea pig, may one and all call out fear. He becomes afraid even of a fur coat, a rug or a Santa Claus mask. He does not have to touch them; just seeing them will call out fear. This simple experiment gives us a startling insight into the ways in which our early home surroundings can build up fears. You may think that such experiments are cruel, but they are not cruel if they help us to understand the fear life of the millions of people around us and give us practical help in bringing up our children more nearly free from fears than we ourselves have been brought up. They will be worth all they cost if through them we can find a method which will help us remove fear.

How We Build Up Fears in the Home

But, you say, these are laboratory experiments. What have they to do with the home? How do the parents build in these fears? In the simplest kinds of ways. Just think of the noises in the home; and the younger the child, the less organized it is, the more likely are these noises to produce fear reaction. Let me enumerate a few of them. Your child has shown a litttle unwillingness to go to bed. This has hampered your own movements a bit and you slam the door when you go out. You want your child to live in a well ventilated room; you open all the windows on a breezy night. Before you get to the door, it slams. In the night when the child is sleeping soundly the shade falls down or the screen placed around its crib falls over. Doors slam all over the house on windy nights, pots and pans are dropped. All of these things are powerful agents, they are sledge hammers in the shaping of your child. No flash of lightning can ever scare your child; even a beam of bright sunlight flashed upon its face in its darkened room will cause only a squinting of the eye. But the loud sizzling crack of thunder overhead will call out a scream of terror and thereafter the flash of lightning may call out the most pronounced fit of terror. If the child happens to be in a darkened room when the peal of thunder occurs it may become afraid of the dark for days and weeks.

— — —

Now the simple word "don't" has no power in itself to produce either a negative or a fear reaction in the child. It must borrow this power. Where does it get it? In two ways. The father has a powerful voice. Just at the moment the child starts to reach for something or to perform some act not desired by the father, he yells "Don't!" You have everything ready to produce a conditioned fear reaction. The powerful word "don't" takes the place of the steel bar in our laboratory experiment. In a short time the child shows a fear reaction when in that situation. "Don't" derives its sledge hammer power in another way. Often when the child reaches for an object one of the parents slaps its fingers and says "don't" at the same time. Now the slapping or painful stimulus will make the child jerk back its hand. Again we have a situation at hand for setting up a conditioned negative response. "Don't" soon takes on the same power to produce fear and negative reactions as loud sounds and painful objects. Because of the frequency with which we use them, "don't" and words like it soon become the ruling forces in the life of every child. The power of the state, church and society is built upon this simple principle. They all teach us to live a life of fear. I quarrel with them not as institutions but because of their methods of instruction. In a similar way, hundreds of other words and sentences take on the same powerful significance. Even as adults we feel the potency of: "Don't touch that dog, it will bite you!" "That thing might explode!" "The match will burn you up!" "Don't touch fire, it is hot!" "That water is deep—there is a heavy undertow!" The terms "wicked," "wrong," "sin," "pirate," "enemy," "the devil," "Satan," all get their reaction-producing effects in this simple way.

[Watson comments on the need for *some* fear-training in the home.]

To get the right psychological conditions, the parent should always apply this painful stimulus just at the moment the undesirable act is taking place. If you wait for father to spank when he gets home it is practically impossible to establish a conditioned negative response. Unless negatively conditioned in this way how else will children learn not to reach for glasses and vases? How can they learn not to touch strange dogs, fondle strange cats, to walk out into the water? But the building in of these necessary negative responses and gentler fear responses, both by the word "don't" and by rapping the fingers smartly, must not be looked upon as punishing the child in the old sense. The word punishment should not appear in our dictionaries except as an obsolete word, and I believe this should be just as true in the field of criminology as in that of child rearing. The parents' object in rapping the child with a pencil is to get it to react in conformity with certain social usages—to behave itself. Why then should the parents ever be angry? Why should they ever punish in the old biblical sense? Such things as beating and expiation of offences, so common now in our schools and homes, in the church, in our criminal law, in our judicial procedure, are relics of the Dark Ages. The parents' attitude should be positive, should be that of the instructor. We can sum it all up by saying that the behaviorist advocates the early building in of appropriate common sense negative reactions by the method of gently rapping the fingers or hand or other bodily part when the undesirable act is taking place, *but as an objective experimental procedure*—never as punishment.

[Watson discusses ineffective techniques for getting rid of inappropriate fear.]

When all other methods fail, try this method which was developed in the laboratory by Mrs. Mary Cover Jones. Work it only once per day, at noontime, when the child is hungry. Just as the child sees its food, let some one show the rabbit as far away as possible. You may have to open the hall door if the dining room is not large enough to get the rabbit far enough away. When the rabbit is far enough away the child will begin to eat. Do not let it ever see the rabbit except at this one time during the day. The next day when the child begins to eat show the rabbit first at the same point where it was shown the day before. Then bring it a little nearer. When the child begins to show fear stop the advance. Repeat this procedure every day. Soon the child can tolerate the *rabbit on the table*, then in its lap. Tranquillity descends; the fear is gone permanently. We call this process *unconditioning*. Retraining by this method has a widespread effect. It removes the fear of other furry animals, or at least greatly modifies it.

Suppose your child has suddenly been made afraid of the dark, don't rave and storm at it. Start unconditioning at once. Put the child to bed at its usual time. Leave a faint light in the hall and leave the door open. Then every night after putting the child to bed close the door a little more and dim the light still more. Three or four nights usually suffice.

Suppose your child has lost its balance in the water or has been made negative to its bath by slipping and falling so that the morning bath becomes a terror—not an unusual thing. Don't take the child to the bathroom for a time. Give it a sponge bath in the nursery for a day or two; then use a wash basin with a little water in it. Increase the water in the basin. Begin to use a wetter sponge. In a few days you can take the child back again to its regular bath. I have seen fathers especially almost ruin their children's chances of learning to swim and dive by forcing them into the water.

Just ordinary *common sense*—this helps us to prevent fears in the home. By unconditioning as soon as fear of any object did develop, I have seen several sets of children grow up practically without fear of animals (although they would not touch strange ones), without fear, timidity or shyness in the presence of strangers, without fears of the dark, fire or any other object animate or inanimate. Fear behavior can be taught just as easily as reading and writing, building with blocks or drawing. It can be taught well or badly. When taught scientifically the emotional life is then under "control."

Surely every mother with a timid, fearful child will be more than willing, now that she knows how to start, to take the time and trouble necessary sensibly to shape *the fear life* of her child.

The Dangers of Too Much Mother Love

Once at the close of a lecture before parents, a dear old lady got up and said, "Thank God, my children are grown and that I had a chance to enjoy them before I met you."

Doesn't she express here the weakness in our modern way of bringing up children? We have children to enjoy them. We need to express our love in some way. The honeymoon period doesn't last forever with all husbands and wives, and we eke it out in a way we think is harmless by loving our children to death. Isn't this especially true of the mother today? No matter how much she may love her husband, he is away all day; her heart is full of love which she must express in some way. She expresses it by showering love and kisses upon her children—and thinks the world should laud her for it. *And it does.*

Not long ago, I went motoring with two boys, aged four and two, their mother, grandmother and nurse. In the course of the two-hour ride, one of the children was kissed thirty-two times— four by his mother, eight by the nurse and twenty times by the grandmother. The other child was almost equally smothered in love.

But there are not many mothers like that, you say—mothers are getting modern, they do not kiss and fondle their children nearly so much as they used to. Unfortunately this is not true. I once let slip in a lecture some of my ideas on the dangers lurking in the mother's kiss. Immediately, thousands of newspapers wrote scathing editorials on "Don't kiss the baby." Hundreds of letters poured in. Judging from them, kissing the baby to death is just about as popular a sport as it ever was, except for a very small part of our population.

Is it just the hard heartedness of the behaviorist—his lack of sentiment—that makes him object to kissing? Not at all. There are serious rocks ahead for the over-kissed child. Before I name them I want to explain how love grows up.

Our laboratory studies show that we can bring out a love response in a newborn child by just one stimulus—*by stroking its skin*. The more sensitive the skin area, the more marked the response. These sensitive areas are the lips, ears, back of the neck, nipples and the sex organs. If the child is crying, stroking these areas will often cause the child to become quiet or even to smile. Nurses and mothers have learned this method of quieting an infant by the trial and error process. They pick the child up, pat it, soothe it, kiss it, rock it, walk with it, dandle it on the knee, and the like. All of this kind of petting has the result of gently stimulating the skin. Unscrupulous nurses have learned the very direct result which comes from stroking the sex organs. When the child gets older, the fondling, petting, patting, rocking of the body will bring out a gurgle or a coo, open laughter, and extension of the arms for the embrace.

The *love life* of the child is *at birth* very simple as is all of its other emotional behavior. Touching and stroking of the skin of the young infant brings out a love response. No other stimulus will.

This means that there is no "instinctive" love of the child for the parents, nor for any other person or object. It means that all affection, be it parental, child for parent or love between the sexes, is built up with such bricks and mortar. A great many parents who have much too much sentiment in their makeup, feel that when the behaviorist announces this he is robbing them of all the sacredness and sweetness in the child-parent relationship. Parents feel that it is just natural that they should love their children in this tangible way and that they should be similarly loved by the child in return. Some of the most tortured moments come when the parents have had to be away from their nine-months old baby for a stretch of three weeks. When they part from it, the child gurgles, coos, holds out its arms and shows every evidence of deepest parental love. Three weeks later when they return the child turns to the attendant who has in the interim fondled and petted it and put the bottle to the sensitive lips. The infant child loves anyone who strokes and feeds it.

It is true that parents have got away from rocking their children to sleep. You find the cradle with rockers on it now only in exhibits of early American furniture. You will say that we have made progress in this respect at any rate. This is true. Dr. Holt's book on the care of the infant can take credit for this education. But it is doubtful if mothers would have given it up if home economics had not demanded it. Mothers found that if they started training the infant at birth, it would learn to go to sleep without rocking. This gave the mother more time for household duties, gossiping, bridge and shopping. Dr. Holt suggested it; the economic value of the system was easy to recognize.

But it doesn't take much time to pet and kiss the baby. You can do it when you pick him up from the crib after a nap, when you put him to bed, and especially after his bath. What more delectable to the mother than to kiss her chubby baby from head to foot after the bath! And it takes so little time!

To come back to the mechanics of love and affection. Loves grow up in children just like fears. _Loves_ are home made, built in. In other words loves are _conditioned_. You have everything at hand all day long for setting up conditioned love responses. The touch of the skin takes the place of the steel bar, the sight of the mother's face takes the place of the rabbit in the experiments with fear. The child _sees_ the mother's face when she pets it. Soon, _the mere sight of the mother's face_ calls out the love response. The touch of the skin is no longer necessary to call it out. A conditioned love reaction has been formed. Even if she pats the child in the dark, the _sound_ of her voice as she croons soon comes to call out a love response. This is the psychological explanation of the child's joyous reactions to the sound of the mother's voice. So with her footsteps, the sight of the mother's clothes, of her photograph. All too soon the child gets shot through with too many of these love reactions. In addition the child gets honeycombed with love responses for the nurse, for the father and for any other constant attendant who fondles it. Love reactions soon dominate the child. It requires no instinct, no "intelligence," no "reasoning" on the child's part for such responses to grow up.

The Adult Effects of Too Much Coddling in Infancy

To understand the end results of too much coddling, let us examine some of our own adult behavior. Nearly all of us have suffered from over-coddling in our infancy. How does it show? It shows as *invalidism*. As adults we have too many aches and pains. I rarely ask anybody with whom I am constantly thrown how he feels or how he slept last night. Almost invariably, if I am a person he doesn't have to keep up a front around, I get the answer, "Not very well." If I give him the chance, he expatiates along one of the following lines—"my digestion is poor; I have a constant headache; my muscles ache like fire; I am all tired out; I don't feel young any more; my liver is bad; I have a bad taste in my mouth"—and so on through the whole gamut of ills. Now these people have nothing wrong with them that the doctors can locate—and with the wonderful technique physicians have developed, the doctor can usually find out if anything is wrong. The individual who was not taught in his youth by his mother to be dependent, is one who comes to adult life too busy with his work to note the tiny mishaps that occur in his bodily makeup. When we are deeply engaged in our work, we never note them. Can you imagine an aviator flying in a fog or making a landing in a difficult field wondering whether his luncheon is going to digest.

[Watson continues on the theme of invalidism.]

Now over conditioning in love is the rule. Prove it yourself by counting the number of times your child whines and wails "Mother." All over the house, all day long, the two-year-old, the three-year-old and the four-year-old whine "Mamma, Mamma," "Mother." Now these love responses which the mother or father is building in by over conditioning, in spite of what the poet and the novelist may have to say, are not constructive. They do not fight many battles for the child. They do not help it to conquer the difficulties it must meet in its environment. Hence just to the extent to which you devote time to petting and coddling— and I have seen almost all of the child's waking hours devoted to it—just to that extent do you rob the child of the time which he should be devoting to the manipulation of his universe, acquiring a technique with fingers, hands and arms. He must have time to pull his universe apart and put it together again. Even from this standpoint alone—that of robbing the child of its opportunity for conquering the world, coddling is a dangerous experiment.

The mother coddles the child for two reasons. One, she admits; the other, she doesn't admit because she doesn't know that it is true. The one she admits is that she wants the child to be happy, she wants it to be surrounded by love in order that it may grow up to be a kindly, goodnatured child. The other is that her own whole being cries out for the expression of love. Her mother before her has trained her to give and receive love. She is starved for love—affection, as she prefers to call it. It is at bottom a sex-seeking response in her, else she would never kiss the child on the lips. Certainly, to satisfy her professed reason for coddling, kissing the youngster on the forehead, on the back of the hand, patting it on the head once in a while, would be all the petting needed for a baby to learn that it is growing up in a kindly home.

But even granting that the mother thinks she kisses the child for the perfectly logical reason of implanting the proper amount of affection and kindliness in it, does she succeed? The fact I brought out before, that we rarely see a happy child, is proof to the contrary. The fact that our children are always crying and always whining shows the unhappy, unwholesome state they are in. Their digestion is interfered with and probably their whole glandular system is deranged.

Should the Mother Never Kiss the Baby?

There is a sensible way of treating children. Treat them as though they were young adults. Dress them, bathe them with care and circumspection. Let your behavior always be objective and kindly firm. Never hug and kiss them, never let them sit in your lap. If you must, kiss them once on the forehead when they say good night. Shake hands with them in the morning. Give them a pat on the head if they have made an extraordinarily good job of a difficult task. Try it out. In a week's time you will find how easy it is to be perfectly objective with your child and at the same time kindly. You will be utterly ashamed of the mawkish, sentimental way you have been handling it. . . .

6

Workers of a Grand Design:
Freud and Piaget

Once the notion of development is accepted and the child is no longer seen as a malformed adult, the two central tasks of the child psychologist are set. He must describe the beginnings of development—the problem of origins—and he must propose a mechanism for further development—the problem of change. Gesell and Watson solved these problems with simplicity and elegance. For Gesell, reliably observable responses common to all members of the species and of common appearance in time were the raw materials of development; maturation was his mechanism. Watson, in his later writings, began his story of development with the "squirmings" of the infant; change took place through classical conditioning. Appealing as these models of development were in their clarity and forthrightness, applying them to the behavior of children was rather like dissecting butterflies with a hammer. Alternatives were sought and, as always will happen in a science that has not yet become cumulative, alternatives were found. In almost every case, the proposals for an understanding of child behavior that claim the field once occupied by Watson and Gesell portray a far more complicated and more hidden child than was known heretofore. In vastly different ways, the men we shall meet in this chapter—Freud and Piaget— gave texture and range to the definition of the child. Freud, speaking of the child's affects, and Piaget, speaking of his knowl-

245

edge, sketched out portraits of the child that remain, like the child they depict, incomplete, provocative, and of uncertain promise.

While Watson was wrestling with the problem of the relation between his observations of animals and his colleagues' concern with consciousness, and while Gesell was collecting data for his dissertation, Sigmund Freud, older than both by twenty years, was preparing *Three Contributions to the Theory of Sex.* Even more than his theory of dreams, in which some of the assaulting implications of psychoanalysis were muted or could be seen only as prologue to a discussion of levels of consciousness, the papers on sex put Freud clearly among the destroyers. Nowhere in the Freudian writ would he be more at variance with common belief than in the second essay, on infantile sexuality.

What poets and students of human nature had always asserted turned out to be true: the impressions of that remote period of life, though they were for the most part buried in amnesia, left ineradicable traces upon the individual's growth and in particular laid the foundations of any nervous disorder that was to follow. But since these experiences of childhood were always concerned with sexual excitations and the reaction against them, I found myself faced by the fact of infantile sexuality —once again a novelty and a contradiction of one of the strongest of human prejudices. Childhood was looked upon as 'innocent' and free from the lusts of sex, and the fight with the demon of 'sensuality' was not thought to begin until the troubled age of puberty. Such occasional sexual activities as it had been impossible to overlook in children were put down as signs of degeneracy and premature depravity or as a curious freak of nature. Few of the findings of psychoanalysis have met with such universal contradiction or have aroused such an outburst of indignation as the assertion that the sexual function starts at the beginning of life and reveals its presence by important signs even in childhood. And yet no other finding of analysis can be demonstrated so easily and so completely.*

Sixty years after the publication of *Three Contributions*, infantile sexuality is a sophomore cliché and psychoanalysis the property of playwrights, English professors, and movie stars, but some sense of Freud's impact on psychology can be seen in a

* S. Freud, *An Autobiographical Study* (Translated by J. Strachey), London: Hogarth, 1935, pp. 58ff. First published in Vol. IV of *Die Medizin der Gegenwart in Selbtsdarstellungen*, Leipzig: Meiner, 1925.

brief review given by an American psychologist to the publication of the case of little Hans.*

Acquaintances of Freud working under his direction have studied a remarkable case of sexual precocity of a boy who at the age of three began to be interested above all things in the Wiwimacher [Hans' name for his penis] and was eagerly concerned as to whether chairs, animals, men and women, etc., possessed this part, and could not be withheld from incessant interest and conversation on the topic. The child was plainly hereditarily *belastet* [tainted], but was cured by hypnotic treatment modified in form to be applicable to children.†

Quite apart from the distortions of fact in this note, it represents well the attitude of assimilation to the pathological that met Freud's early discussions of children. The passage that follows is capable of Freudian shock even today, if it is read without the protection of segregation ("Oh, yes, that's psychoanalysis") that insulates us from Freud's vision. Glance back to Preyer's account of the child, or even Hall's, to understand better the serenity that Freud destroyed by reviving a demonic view of the child, a view absent from psychology for a century and a half.

*   *   *

Sigmund Freud (1856–1939)

Infantile Sexuality

It is a part of popular belief about the sexual impulse that it is absent in childhood and that it first appears in the period of life

S. Freud, *Three Contributions to the Sexual Theory* (Translated by A. A. Brill), Nervous and Mental Disease Monograph Series, No. 7, 1910. First published by Deuticke in 1905 in Vienna as *Drei Abhandlungen der Sexualtheorie*. This selection is the second contribution; footnotes have been deleted.

* S. Freud, *Analyse der Phobie eines 5–jährigen Knaben,* Vienna: Deuticke, 1909.
† [T. Walters (?)] [Reviews], *Amer. J. Psychol.,* **20**, 1909, 466.

known as puberty. This, though an obvious error, is a serious one in its consequences and is chiefly due to our present ignorance of the fundamental principles of the sexual life. A comprehensive study of the sexual manifestations of childhood would probably reveal to us the existence of the essential features of the sexual impulse, and would make us acquainted with its development and its composition from various sources.

The Neglect of the Infantile

It is remarkable that those writers who endeavor to explain the qualities and reactions of the adult individual have given so much more attention to the ancestral period than to the period of the individual's own existence—that is, they have attributed more influence to heredity than to childhood. As a matter of fact, it might well be supposed that the influence of the latter period would be easier to understand, and that it would be entitled to more consideration than heredity. To be sure, one occasionally finds in medical literature notes on the premature sexual activities of small children, about erections and masturbation and even actions resembling coitus, but these are referred to merely as exceptional occurrences, as curiosities, or as deterring examples of premature perversity. No author has to my knowledge recognized the lawfulness of the sexual impulse in childhood, and in the numerous writings on the development of the child the chapter on "Sexual Development" is usually passed over.

Infantile Amnesia

This remarkable negligence is due partly to conventional considerations, which influence the writers on account of their own bringing up, and partly to a psychic phenomenon which has thus far remained unexplained. I refer to the peculiar amnesia which veils from most people (not from all!) the first years of their childhood, usually the first six or eight years. So far it has not occurred to us that this amnesia ought to surprise us, though we have in fact good reasons for surprise. For we are informed that in those years from which we later obtain nothing except a few incomprehensible memory fragments, we have vividly reacted to impressions, that we have manifested pain and pleasure like any human being, that we have evinced love, jealousy, and other passions as they then affected us; indeed we are told that we have uttered remarks which proved to grown-ups that we possessed understanding and a budding power of judgment. Still we know nothing of all this when we become older. Why does our memory lag behind all our other psychic activities? We really have reason to believe that at no time of life are we more capable of impressions and reproductions than during the years of childhood.

On the other hand we must assume, or we may convince ourselves through psychological observations on others, that the very impressions which we have forgotten have nevertheless left the deepest traces in our psychic life, and acted as determinants for our whole future development. We conclude therefore that we do not deal with a real forgetting of infantile impressions but rather with an amnesia similar to that observed in neurotics for later experiences, the nature of which consists in their being detained from consciousness (repression). But what forces bring about this repression of the infantile impressions? He who can solve this riddle will also explain hysterical amnesia.

We shall not, however, hesitate to assert that the existence of the infantile amnesia gives us a new point of comparison between the psychic states of the child and those of the psychoneurotic. We have already encountered another point of comparison when confronted by the fact that the sexuality of the psychoneurotic preserves the infantile character or has returned to it. May there not be an ultimate connection between the infantile and the hysterical amnesias?

The connection between the infantile and the hysterical amnesias is really more than a mere play of wit. The hysterical amnesia which serves the repression can only be explained by the fact that the individual already possesses a sum of recollections which have been withdrawn from conscious disposal and which by associative connection now seize that which is acted upon by the repelling forces of the repression emanating from consciousness. We may say that without infantile amnesia there would be no hysterical amnesia.

I believe that the infantile amnesia which causes the individual to look upon his childhood as if it were a prehistoric time and conceals from him the beginning of his own sexual life—that this amnesia is responsible for the fact that one does not usually attribute any value to the infantile period in the development of the sexual life. One single observer cannot fill the gap which has been thus produced in our knowledge. As early as 1896 I had already emphasized the significance of childhood for the origin of certain important phenomena connected with the sexual life, and since then I have not ceased to put into the foreground the importance of the infantile factor for sexuality.

The Sexual Latency Period of Childhood and its Emergence

The extraordinary frequent discoveries of apparently abnormal and exceptional sexual manifestations in childhood, as well as the discovery of infantile reminiscences in neurotics, which were hitherto unconscious, allow us to sketch the following picture of the sexual behavior of childhood.

It seems certain that the newborn child brings with it the germs of sexual feelings which continue to develop for some time and then succumb to a progressive suppression, which is in turn broken through by the proper advances of the sexual development and which can be checked by individual idiosyncrasies. Nothing definite is known concerning the lawfulness and periodicity of this oscillating course of development. It seems, however, that the sexual life of the child mostly manifests itself in the third or fourth year in some form accessible to observation.

The Sexual Inhibition

It is during this period of total or at least partial latency that the psychic forces develop which later act as inhibitions on the sexual life, and narrow its direction like dams. These psychic forces are loathing, shame, and moral and esthetic ideation masses. We may gain the impression that the erection of these dams in the civilized child is the work of education; and surely education contributes much to it. In reality, however, this development is organically determined and can occasionally be produced without the help of education. Indeed education remains properly within its assigned realm only if it strictly follows the path sketched for it by the organic determinant and impresses it somewhat cleaner and deeper.

Reaction Formation and Sublimation

What are the means that accomplish these very important constructions so significant for the later personal culture and normality? They are probably brought about at the cost of the infantile sexuality itself, the influx of which has not stopped even in this latency period—the energy of which indeed has been turned away either wholly or partially from sexual utilization and conducted to other aims. The historians of civilization seem to be unanimous in the opinion that such deviation of sexual motive powers from sexual aims to new aims, a process which merits the name of *sublimation,* has furnished powerful components for all cultural accomplishments. We will therefore add that the same process acts in the development of every individual, and that it begins to act in the sexual latency period.

We can also venture an opinion about the mechanisms of such sublimation. The sexual feelings of these infantile years on the one hand could not be utilizable, since the procreating functions are postponed,—this is the chief character of the latency period; on the other hand, they would in themselves be perverse, as they would emanate from erogenous zones and would be born of impulses which in the individual's course of development could only evoke a feeling of displeasure. They therefore awaken contrary forces (feelings of reaction), which in order to suppress such displeasure, build up the above mentioned psychic dams: loathing, shame, and morality.

The Emergence of the Latency Period

Without deluding ourselves as to the hypothetical nature and deficient clearness of our understanding regarding the infantile period of latency and delay, we will return to reality and state that such a utilization of the infantile sexuality represents an ideal bringing up from which the development of the individual usually deviates in some measure and often very considerably. A portion of the sexual manifestation occasionally breaks through which has withdrawn from sublimation, or a sexual activity remains throughout the whole duration of the latency period until the reinforced breaking through of the sexual impulse in puberty. In so far as they have paid any attention to infantile sexuality the educators behave as if they shared our views concerning the formation of the moral forces of defence at the cost of sexuality, and as if they knew that sexual activity makes the child uneducable; for the educators consider all sexual manifestations of the child as an "evil" in the face of which little can be accomplished. We have, however, every reason for directing our attention to those phenomena so much feared by the educators, for we expect to find in them the solution of the primitive formation of the sexual impulse.

The Manifestations of the Infantile Sexuality

For reasons which we shall discuss later we will take as a model of the infantile sexual manifestations thumbsucking (pleasure-sucking), to which the Hungarian pediatrist, Lindner, has devoted an excellent essay.

Thumbsucking

Thumbsucking, which manifests itself in the nursing baby and which may be continued till maturity or throughout life, consists in a rhythmic repetition of sucking contact with the mouth (the lips), wherein the purpose of taking nourishment is excluded. A part of the lip itself, the tongue, which is another preferable skin region within reach, and even the big toe—may be taken as objects for sucking. Simultaneously, there is also a desire to grasp things, which manifests itself in a rhythmical pulling of the ear lobe and which may cause the child to grasp a part of another person (generally the ear) for the same purpose. The pleasure-sucking is connected with an entire exhaustion of attention and leads to sleep or even to a motor reaction in the form of an orgasm. Pleasure-sucking is often combined with a rubbing contact with certain sensitive parts of the body, such as the breast and external genitals. It is by this road that many children go from thumb-sucking to masturbation.

No investigator has yet doubted the sexual nature of this action. Still, the best theories based on the observations of adults leave us in the lurch in the face of this manifestation of infantile sexual activity. If we think of Moll's division of the sexual impulse, the detumescence and contrectation impulses, we find that the first factor is here out of question, and that the second can be recognized only with difficulty, as Moll later apparently describes this also as a detumescence impulse directed against other persons.

Autoerotism

It is our duty here to arrange this state of affairs differently. Let us insist that the most striking character of this sexual activity is that the impulse is not directed against other persons but that it gratifies itself on its own body; to use the happy term invented by Havelock Ellis, we will say that it is autoerotic.

It is, moreover, clear that the action of the thumbsucking child is determined by the fact that it seeks a pleasure which has already been experienced and is now remembered. Through the rhythmic sucking on a portion of the skin or mucous membrane it finds the gratification in the simplest way. It is also easy to conjecture on what occasions the child first experienced this pleasure which it now strives to renew. The first and most important activity in the child's life, the sucking from the mother's breast (or its substitute), must have acquainted it with this pleasure. We would say that the child's lip behaved like an erogenous zone, and that the excitement through the warm stream of milk was really the cause of the pleasurable sensation. To be sure, the gratification of the erogenous zone was at first united with the gratification of taking nourishment. He who sees a satiated child sink back from the mother's breast, and merge into sleep with reddened cheeks and blissful smile, will have to admit that this picture remains as a guide for the expression of sexual gratification in later life. But the desire for repetition of the sexual gratification is separated from the desire for taking nourishment; a separation which becomes unavoidable with the appearance of the teeth when the nourishment is no longer sucked in but chewed. The child does not make use of a strange object for sucking but prefers its own skin because it is more convenient, because it thus makes itself independent of the outerworld which it cannot yet control, and because in this way it creates for itself, as it were, a second, even if an inferior, erogenous zone. The inferiority of this second region urges it later to seek the same parts, the lips of another person. ("It is a pity that I cannot kiss myself," might be attributed to it.)

Not all children suck their thumbs. It may be assumed that it is found only in children in whom the erogenous significance of the lip-zone is constitutionally reënforced. Children in whom this is retained are habitual kissers as adults and show a tendency to perverse kissing, or as men they have a marked desire for drinking and smoking. But if repression comes into play they experience disgust for eating and evince hysterical vomiting. By virtue of the community of the lip-zone the repression encroaches upon the impulse of nourishment. Many of my female patients showing disturbances in eating, such as hysterical globus, choking sensations, and vomiting, have been energetic thumbsuckers during infancy.

In the thumbsucking or pleasure-sucking we have already been able to observe the two essential characters of one infantile sexual manifestation. This manifestation does not yet know any sexual object, it is autoerotic and its sexual aim is under the control of an erogenous zone. Let us assume for the present that these characters also hold true for most of the other activities of the infantile sexual impulse.

The Sexual Aim of the Infantile Sexuality

The Characters of the Erogenous Zones

From the example of thumbsucking we may gather a great many points useful for the distinguishing of an erogenous zone. It is a portion of skin or mucous membrane in which the stimuli produce a feeling of pleasure of definite quality. There is no doubt that the pleasure-producing stimuli are governed by special determinants which we do not know. The rhythmic characters must play some parts in them and this strongly suggests an analogy to tickling. It does not, however, appear so certain whether the character of the pleasurable feeling evoked by the stimulus can be designated as "peculiar," and in what part of this peculiarity the sexual factor exists. Psychology is still groping in the dark when it concerns matters of pleasure and pain, and the most cautious assumption is therefore the most advisable. We may perhaps later come upon reasons which seem to support the peculiar quality of the sensation of pleasure.

The erogenous quality may adhere most notably to definite regions of the body. As is shown by the example of thumb-sucking, there are predestined erogenous zones. But the same example also shows that any other region of skin or mucous membrane may assume the function of an erogenous zone; it must therefore carry along a certain adaptability. The production of the sensation of pleasure therefore depends more on the quality of the stimulus than on the nature of the bodily region. The thumb-sucking child looks around on his body and selects any portion of it for pleasure-sucking, and becoming accustomed to it, he then prefers it. If he accidentally strikes upon a predestined region, such as breast, nipple or genitals, it naturally has the preference. A quite analogous tendency to displacement is again found in the symptomatology of hysteria. In this neurosis the repression mostly concerns the genital zones proper; these in turn transmit their excitation to the other erogenous zones, usually dormant in mature life, which then behave exactly like genitals. But besides this, just as in thumbsucking, any other region of the body may become endowed with the excitation of the genitals and raised to an erogenous zone. Erogenous and hysterogenous zones show the same characters.

The Infantile Sexual Aim

The sexual aim of the infantile impulse consists in the production of gratification through the proper excitation of this or that selected erogenous zone. In order to leave a desire for its repeti-

tion this gratification must have been previously experienced, and
we may be sure that nature has devised definite means so as not
to leave this occurrence to mere chance. The arrangement which
has fulfilled this purpose for the lip-zone we have already discussed; it is the simultaneous connection of this part of the
body with the taking of nourishment. We shall also meet other
similar mechanisms as sources of sexuality. The state of desire for
repetition of gratification can be recognized through a peculiar
feeling of tension which in itself is rather of a painful character,
and through a centrally determined feeling of itching or sensitiveness which is projected into the peripheral erogenous zone. The
sexual aim may therefore be formulated as follows: the chief
object is to substitute for the projected feeling of sensitiveness
in the erogenous zone that outer stimulus which removes the
feeling of sensitiveness by evoking the feeling of gratification.
This external stimulus consists usually in a manifestation which
is analogous to sucking.

It is in full accord with our physiological knowledge if the
desire happens to be awakened also peripherally through an actual
change in the erogenous zone. The action is only to some extent
strange, as one stimulus for its suppression seems to want another
applied to the same place.

The Masturbatic Sexual Manifestations

It is a matter of great satisfaction to know that there is nothing
further of greater importance to learn about the sexual activity
of the child after the impulse of one erogenous zone has become
comprehensible to us. The most pronounced differences are found
in the action necessary for the gratification, which consists in
sucking for the lip-zone and which must be replaced by other
muscular actions according to the situation and nature of the
other zones.

The Activity of the Anal Zone

Like the lip zone the anal zone is, through its position, adapted
to conduct the sexuality to the other functions of the body. It

should be assumed that the erogenous significance of this region of the body was originally very large. Through psychoanalysis one finds, not without surprise, the many transformations that are normally undertaken with the usual excitations emanating from here, and that this zone often retains for life a considerable fragment of genital irritability. The intestinal catarrhs so frequent during infancy produce intensive irritations in this zone, and we often hear it said that intestinal catarrh at this delicate age causes "nervousness." In later neurotic diseases they exert a definite influence on the symptomatic expression of the neurosis, placing at its disposal the whole sum of intestinal disturbances. Considering the erogenous significance of the anal zone which has been retained at least in transformation, one should not laugh at the hemorrhoidal influences to which the old medical literature attached so much weight in the explanation of neurotic states.

Children utilizing the erogenous sensitiveness of the anal zone can be recognized by their holding back of fecal masses until through accumulation there result violent muscular contractions; the passage of these masses through the anus is apt to produce a marked irritation on the mucous membrane. Besides the pain this must produce also a sensation of pleasure. One of the surest premonitions of later eccentricity or nervousness is when an infant obstinately refuses to empty his bowel when placed on the chamber by the nurse and reserves this function at its own pleasure. It does not concern him that he will soil his bed; all he cares for is not to lose the subsidiary pleasure while defecating. The educators have again the right inkling when they designate children who withhold these functions as bad.

The retention of fecal masses, which is at first intentional in order to utilize them, as it were, for masturbatic excitation of the anal zone, is at least one of the roots of constipation so frequent in neuropaths. The whole significance of the anal zone is mirrored in the fact that there are but few neurotics who have not their special scatologic customs, ceremonies, etc., which they retain with cautious secrecy.

Real masturbatic irritation of the anal zone by means of the fingers, evoked through either centrally or peripherally supported itching, is not at all rare in older children.

The Activity of the Genital Zone

Among the erogenous zones of the child's body there is one which certainly does not play the main rôle, and which cannot be the carrier of earliest sexual feeling—which, however, is destined for great things in the later life. In both male and female it is connected with the voiding of urine (penis, clitoris), and in the former it is enclosed in a sack of mucous membrane, probably in order not to miss the irritations caused by the secretions which may arouse the sexual excitement at an early age. The sexual activities of this erogenous zone, which belongs to the real genitals, are the beginning of the later normal sexual life.

Owing to the anatomical position, the overflowing of secretions, the washing and rubbing of the body, and to certain accidental excitements (the wandering of intestinal worms in the girl), it happens that the pleasurable feeling which these parts of the body are capable of producing makes itself noticeable to the child even during the sucking age, and thus awakens desire for its repetition. When we review all the actual arrangements, and bear in mind that the measures for cleanliness have the same effect as the uncleanliness itself, we can then scarcely mistake nature's intention, which is to establish the future primacy of these erogenous zones for the sexual activity through the infantile onanism from which hardly an individual escapes. The action removing the stimulus and setting free the gratification consists in a rubbing contiguity with the hand or in a certain previously-formed pressure reflex effected by the closure of the thighs. The latter procedure seems to be the more primitive and is by far the more common in girls. The preference for the hand in boys already indicates what an important part of the male sexual activity will be accomplished in the future by the acquisition impulse (Bemächtigungstrieb).

The infantile onanism seems to disappear with the onset of the latency period, but it may continue uninterruptedly till puberty and thus represent the first marked deviation from the development desirable for civilized man. At some time during childhood after the nursing period, the sexual impulse of the genitals reawakens and continues active for some time until it is again suppressed, or it may continue without interruption. The possible relations are very diverse and can only be elucidated through a more precise analysis of individual cases. The details, however, of this second infantile sexual activity leave behind the profoundest (unconscious) impressions in the person's memory; if the individual remains healthy they determine his character and if he becomes sick after puberty they determine the symptomatology of his neurosis. In the latter case it is found that this sexual period is forgotten and the conscious reminiscences pointing to them are displaced; I have already mentioned that I would like to connect the normal infantile amnesia with this infantile sexual activity. By psychoanalytic investigation it is possible to bring to consciousness the forgotten material, and thereby to remove a compulsion which emanates from the unconscious psychic material.

The Return of the Infantile Masturbation

The sexual excitation of the infantile period returns during childhood (we have not yet succeeded in establishing definite periods), either as a centrally determined tickling sensation demanding onanistic gratification, or as a pollution-like process which, analogous to the pollution of maturity, may attain gratification without the aid of any action. The latter case is more frequent in girls and in the second half of childhood; its determinants are not well understood, but it often, though not regularly seems to have as a basis a period of early active onanism. The symptomatology of this sexual manifestation is poor; the genital apparatus is still undeveloped and all signs are therefore displayed by the urinary apparatus which is, so to say, the guardian of the genital apparatus. Most of the so-called bladder disturbances of this period are of a sexual nature; whenever the enuresis nocturna does not represent an epileptic attack it corresponds to a pollution.

The return of the sexual activity is determined by inner and outer causes which can be conjectured from the formation of the symptoms of neurotic diseases and definitely revealed by psychoanalytic investigations. The internal causes will be discussed later; the accidental outer causes attain at this time a great and permanent significance. As the first outer cause we have the influence of seduction which prematurely treats the child as a sexual object;

under conditions favoring impressions this teaches the child the gratification of the genital zones, and thus usually forces it to repeat this gratification in onanism. Such influences can come from adults or other children. I cannot admit that I over-estimated its frequency or its significance in my contributions to the etiology of hysteria, though I did not know then that normal individuals may have the same experiences in their childhood, and hence placed a higher value on seductions than on the factors found in the sexual constitution and development. It is quite obvious that no seduction is necessary to awaken the sexual life of the child, that such an awakening may come on spontaneously from inner sources.

Polymorphous-perverse Disposition

It is instructive to know that under the influence of seduction the child may become polymorphous-perverse and may be misled into all sorts of transgressions. This goes to show that it carries along the adaptation for them in its disposition. The formation of such perversions meets but slight resistance because the psychic dams against sexual excesses, such as shame, loathing and morality —which depend on the age of the child—are not yet erected or are only in the process of formation. In this respect the child perhaps does not behave differently from the average uncivilized woman in whom the same polymorphous-perverse disposition exists. Such a woman may remain sexually normal under usual conditions, but under the guidance of a clever seducer she will find pleasure in every perversion, and will retain the same as her sexual activity. The same polymorphous or infantile disposition fits the prostitute for her professional activity, and in the enormous number of prostitutes and of women to whom we must attribute an adaptation for prostitution, even if they do not follow this calling, it is absolutely impossible not to recognize in their uniform disposition for all perversions the universal and primitive human.

Partial Impulses

For the rest, the influence of seduction does not aid us in unravelling the original relations of the sexual impulse, but rather confuses our understanding of the same, inasmuch as it prematurely supplies the child with the sexual object at a time when the infantile sexual impulse does not yet evince any desire for it. We must admit, however, that the infantile sexual life, though mainly under the control of erogenous zones, also shows components in which from the very beginning other persons are regarded as sexual objects. Among these we have the impulses for looking and showing, and for cruelty, which manifest themselves somewhat independently of the erogenous zones and which only later enter into intimate relationship with the sexual life but along with the erogenous sexual activity they are noticeable even in the infantile years as separate and independent strivings. The little child is above all shameless, and during its early years it sometimes evinces pleasure in displaying its body and especially its sexual organs. A counterpart to this desire which is to be considered as perverse, the curiosity to see others persons' genitals, probably appears first in the later years of childhood when the hindrance of the feeling of shame has already reached a certain development. Under the influence of seduction the looking perversion may attain great importance for the sexual life of the child. Still, from my investigations of the childhood years of normal and neurotic patients, I must conclude that the impulse for looking can appear in the child as a spontaneous sexual manifestation. Small children, whose attention has once been directed to their own genitals—usually by masturbation—are wont to progress in this direction without outside interference, and to develop a vivid interest in the genitals of their playmates. As the occasion for the gratification of such curiosity is generally afforded during the gratification of both excrementitious needs, such children become voyeurs and are zealous spectators at the voiding of urine and feces of others. After this tendency has been repressed, the curiosity to see the genitals of others (one's own or those of the other sex), remains as a tormenting desire which in some neurotic cases furnishes the strongest motive power for the formation of symptoms.

The cruelty component of the sexual impulse develops in the child with still greater independence of those sexual activities which are connected with erogenous zones. Cruelty is especially near the childish character, since the inhibition which restrains the acquisition impulse through the influence of others—that is, the capacity for sympathy—develops comparatively late. As we know, a thorough psychological analysis of this impulse has not as yet been successfully accomplished; we may assume that the cruel feelings emanate from sources which are actually independent of sexuality but with which an early connection is formed through an anastomosis near the origins of both. But observation shows that relations exist between the sexual development and the looking and cruelty impulses which restrict the pretended independence of both impulses. Children who are distinguished for evincing especial cruelty to animals and playmates may be justly suspected of intensive and premature sexual activity in the erogenous zones; and in a simultaneous prematurity of all sexual impulses, the erogenous sexual activity surely seems to be primary. The absence of the barrier of sympathy carries with it the danger that the connections between cruelty and the erogenous impulses formed in childhood cannot be broken in later life.

An erogenous source of the passive impulse for cruelty (masochism) is found in the painful irritation of the gluteal region which is familiar to all educators since the confessions of J. J. Rousseau. This has justly caused them to demand that physical punishment, which usually concerns this part of the body, should be withheld from all children in whom the libido might be forced into collateral roads by the later demands of cultural education.

The Sources of the Infantile Sexuality

In our effort to follow up the origins of the sexual impulse, we have thus far found that the sexual excitement originates (a) in an imitation of a gratification which has been experienced in conjunction with other organic processes; (b) through the appropriate peripheral stimulation of erogenous zones; and (c) as an expression of some "impulse," like the looking and cruelty impulses, the origin of which we do not yet fully understand. The psychoanalytic investigation of later life which leads back to childhood and the contemporary observation of the child itself coöperate to reveal to us still other regularly-flowing sources of the sexual excitement. The observation of childhood has the disadvantage of treating easily misunderstood material, while psychoanalysis is made difficult by the fact that it can reach its objects and conclusions only by great detours; still the united efforts of both methods achieve a sufficient degree of positive understanding.

In investigating the erogenous zones we have already found that these skin regions merely show the special exaggeration of a form of sensitiveness which is to a certain degree found over the whole surface of the skin. It will therefore not surprise us to learn that certain forms of general sensitiveness in the skin can be ascribed to very distinct erogenous action. Among these we will above all mention the temperature sensitiveness; this will perhaps prepare us for the understanding of the therapeutic effects of warm baths.

Mechanical Excitation

We must, moreover, describe here the production of sexual excitation by means of rhythmic mechanical shaking of the body. There are three kinds of exciting influences: those acting on the sensory apparatus of the vestibular nerves, those acting on the skin, and those acting on the deep parts, such as the muscles and joints. The sexual excitation produced by these influences seems to be of a pleasurable nature—a problem to which we will direct our attention later—and that the pleasure is produced by mechanical stimulation is proved by the fact that children are so fond of play involving passive motions, like swinging or flying in the air, and repeatedly demand its repetition. As we know, rocking is regularly used in putting to sleep restless children. The shaking sensation experienced in wagons and railroad trains exerts such a fascinating influence on older children, that all boys, at least at one time in their lives, want to become conductors and drivers. They are wont to ascribe to railroad activities an extraordinary and mysterious interest, and during the age of phantastic activity (shortly before puberty) they utilize these as a nucleus for exquisite sexual symbolisms. The desire to connect railroad travelling with sexuality apparently originates from the pleasurable character of the sensation of motion. When the repression later sets in and changes so many of the childish likes into their opposites, these same persons as adolescents and adults then react to the rocking and rolling with nausea and become terribly exhausted by a railroad journey, or they show a tendency to attacks of anxiety during the journey, and by becoming obsessed with railroad phobia they protect themselves against a repetition of the painful experiences.

This also fits in with the not as yet understood fact that the concurrence of fear with mechanical shaking produces the severest hysterical forms of traumatic neurosis. It may at least be assumed that inasmuch as even a slight intensity of these influences becomes a source of sexual excitement, the actions of an excessive amount of the same will produce a profound disorder in the sexual mechanism.

Muscular Activity

It is well known that the child has need for strong muscular activity, from the gratification of which it draws extraordinary pleasure. Whether this pleasure has anything to do with sexuality, whether it includes in itself sexual gratification, or can become a cause of sexual excitement, all these problems may be solved by critical reflection, which will no doubt also be directed toward the statements made above, namely, that the sensations of passive motion are of a sexual nature or produce sexual excitement. The fact remains, however, that a number of persons report that they experienced the first signs of excitement in their genitals during fighting or wrestling with playmates, in which situation, besides the general muscular exertion, there is an intensive contact with the opponent's skin which also becomes effective. The desire for muscular contest with a definite person, like the desire for word contest in later years, is a good sign that the object selection has been directed upon this person. "Was sich liebt, das neckt sich." ["Those who love each other tease each other."] In the promotion of sexual excitement through muscular activity we might recognize one of the sources of the sadistic impulse. The infantile connection between fighting and sexual excitement acts in many persons as a future determinant for the preferred course of their sexual impulse.

Affective Processes

The other sources of sexual excitement in the child are open to less doubt. Through simultaneous observations, as well as through later investigations, it is easy to ascertain that all more intensive affective processes, even excitements of a terrifying nature, encroach upon sexuality; this can at all events furnish us with a contribution to the understanding of the pathogenic action of such emotions. In the school child, fear of a coming examination or exertion expended in the solution of a difficult task can become significant for the breaking through of sexual manifestations as well as for his relations to the school, inasmuch as under such excitements a sensation often occurs urging him to touch the genitals, or leading to a pollution-like process with all its disagreeable consequences. The behavior of children at school, which is so often mysterious to the teacher, ought surely to be considered in relation with their germinating sexuality. The sexually-exciting influence of some painful affects, such as fear, shuddering, and horror, is felt by a great many people throughout life and readily explains why so many seek opportunities to experience such sensations, provided that certain accessory circumstances (as in fiction, reading, the theater) suppress the earnestness of the painful feeling.

If we might assume that the same erogenous action also reaches the intensive painful feelings, especially if the pain be toned down or held at a distance by a subsidiary determination, this relation would then contain the main roots of the masochistic-sadistic impulse, into the manifold composition of which we are gaining a gradual insight.

Intellectual Work

Finally, it is evident that mental application or the concentration of attention on an intellectual accomplishment will result, especially often in youthful persons, but in older persons as well, in a simultaneous sexual excitement, which may be looked upon as the only justified basis for the otherwise so doubtful etiology of nervous disturbances from mental "overwork."

If we now, in conclusion, review the evidences and indications of the sources of the infantile sexual excitement, which have been reported neither completely nor exhaustively, we may lay down the following general laws as suggested or established. It seems to be provided in the most generous manner that the process of sexual excitement—the nature of which certainly remains quite mysterious to us—should be set in motion. The factor making this provision in a more or less direct way is the excitation of the sensible surfaces of the skin and sensory organs, while the most indirect exciting influences are exerted on certain parts which are designated as erogenous zones. The criterion in all these sources of sexual excitement is really the quality of the stimuli, though the factor of intensity (in pain) is not entirely unimportant. But in addition to this there are arrangements in the organism which cause the origin of the sexual excitement as a subsidiary action in a large number of inner processes as soon as the intensity of these processes has risen above certain quantitative limits. What we have designated as the partial impulses of sexuality are either directly derived from these inner sources of sexual excitation or composed of contributions from such sources and from erogenous zones. It is possible that nothing of any considerable significance occurs in the organism that does not contribute its components to the excitement of the sexual impulse.

It seems to me at present impossible to shed more light and certainty on these general propositions, and for this I hold two factors responsible; first, the novelty of this manner of investigation, and secondly, the fact that the nature of the sexual excitement is entirely unfamiliar to us. Nevertheless, I will not forbear speaking about two points which promise to open wide prospects in the future.

Diverse Sexual Constitutions

(a) We have considered above the possibility of establishing the manifold character of congenital sexual constitutions through the diverse formation of the erogenous zones; we may now attempt to do the same in dealing with the indirect sources of sexual excitement. We may assume that, although these different sources furnish contributions in all individuals, they are not all equally strong in all persons; and that a further contribution to the differentiation of the diverse sexual constitution will be found in the preferred developments of the individual sources of sexual excitement.

The Roads of Opposite Influences

(b) Since we are now dropping the figurative manner of expression hitherto employed, by which we spoke of *sources* of sexual excitement, we may now assume that all the connecting ways leading from other functions to sexuality must also be passable in the reverse direction. For example, if the lip zone, the common possession of both functions, is responsible for the fact that the sexual gratification originates during the taking of nourishment, the same factor offers also an explanation for the disturbances in the taking of nourishment if the erogenous functions of the common zone are disturbed. As soon as we know the concentration of attention may produce sexual excitement, it is quite natural to assume that acting on the same road, but in a contrary direction, the state of sexual excitement will be able to influence the availability of the voluntary attention. A good part of the symptomatology of the neuroses which I trace to disturbance of sexual processes manifests itself in other non-sexual bodily functions, and this hitherto incomprehensible action becomes less mysterious if it only represents the counterpart of the influences controlling the production of the sexual excitement.

However the same roads through which sexual disturbances encroach upon the other function of the body must in health be supposed to serve another important function. It must be through these roads that the attraction of the sexual motive powers to other than sexual aims, the sublimation of sexuality, is accomplished. We must conclude with the admission that very little is definitely known concerning the roads beyond the fact that they exist, and that they are probably passable in both directions.

*   *   *

Freud's work was known in the United States as early as 1894 when James wrote a courteous note in the *Psychological Review* on an article by Breuer and Freud and, after the foundation of the *Journal of Abnormal Psychology* in 1904, psychoanalysis had a regular and sympathetic voice in America. But the ritual baptism of psychoanalysis into the American community took place in Worcester, Massachusetts, in September, 1909, under the direction of Granville Stanley Hall.

Clark University celebrated its Twentieth Anniversary in 1909, and Hall arranged intellectual festivities that were never again to be matched among psychologists. James, Cattell, Baldwin, Jastrow, Stern, and Boas were there; Jennings and Titchener delivered speeches; but the catch of Hall the "kingmaker" was the contingent from psychoanalysis—Freud, Jung, Ferenzi, Jones, and Brill. Freud's lectures on the origins of psychoanalysis and Jung's lectures on the association method were published in the *American Journal of Psychology* in the next year, together with papers by Jones and Ferenzi. The first full-dress treatment of a psychoanalytic theme to which academic American psychologists were exposed, therefore, was Jones' *Oedipus-Complex as an Explanation of Hamlet's Mystery;* it is interesting to speculate on the fate of psychoanalysis in the United States if it had arrived less thunderously.* James and Titchener and Baldwin were unmoved by the psychoanalytic view of man, but Boas was moved, and Holt, and Jastrow, at least to the point of examining its claims; and at that meeting in Worcester, psychoanalysis became an ineradicable part of child psychology. It was a moment of importance for Freud, too.

* Jones, Sidis, Putnam, Jung, and Prince had already published in the *Journal of Abnormal Psychology*, but the Hamlet paper was the first psychoanalytic document in the more conventional and presumably more influential *American Journal of Psychology*. Freud's paper was entitled, The origin and development of psychoanalysis, *Amer. J. Psychol.*, **21**, 1910, 179–218. Brill published his translated fragments of Freud's early work in 1909 [S. Freud. Selected papers on hysteria and other psychoneuroses (Translated by A. A. Brill). *Nerv. Mental Dis. Monogr.*, No. 4, 1909]. One of Hall's students published a dissertation on psychoanalysis in 1910. [H. W. Chase, Psychoanalysis and the unconscious, *Pedagogical Seminary*, **17**, 1910, 281–327]. It should be remembered, too, that American psychologists in the first years of the century had German as a firm second language.

In Europe I felt as though I were despised; but [in the new world] I found myself received by the foremost men as an equal. As I stepped on to the platform at Worcester . . . it seemed like the realization of some incredible daydream; psychoanalysis was no longer a product of delusion, it had become a valuable part of reality.[*]

As Freud pointed out, psychoanalysis did not lose ground in America. With good friends and polemicists on hand, Freud's ideas were well established in the United States when the Central European dispersion of 1933-1940 made psychoanalysis yet another American specialty. With the popularization of Freud's theory came some remarkable changes in its direction, particularly in regard to the behavior of children. Freud called the changes "watering down"; "transvaluation" may be more accurate.

In the hands of educators and advisors to parents, psychoanalysis was made part of the dogma of infant innocence and human perfectibility—the essential pessimism of Freud's view was hidden behind the thesis that permissiveness would free the child of conflict and neurosis. On this reading, psychoanalysis becomes a more subtle maturationalism; not only is infantile sexuality an obvious fact of life, but it is also a force for optimal growth that is hedged and blunted by ignorant parents. There can be no doubt that Freud's writings made it possible for parents to be more humane and more sensitive to the meaningfulness of the child's irrational behavior, but there is no Utopia in psychoanalysis. Unlike Watson, who brought the hope of Everyman pianist, poet, and king; or Gesell lauding Growth as essentially benign, Freud's picture of the child was uncompromisingly a picture of conflict. No matter how strong the forces of growth or how well-intentioned and informed his parents, Freud's child must inevitably face the confrontation of his wishes, unbearable to parents and eventually unbearable to him, with the facts of the world. With neither ultimate hero nor ultimate villain, the psychoanalytic theory of development is a complicated, often unsystematic, construction, but Freud was not escaping his usual modesty when he compared his "severe blow" to the "universal

[*] S. Freud, *An Autobiographical Study*, p. 95.

narcissism of men" with earlier assaults by Copernicus and Darwin.*

Psychoanalysis effected a transformation in the definition of the child that is comparable only to the transformation that Rousseau made. To be sure, the notion of infantile sexuality was a radical and productive idea, but the true novelty of psychoanalysis is its respect for the ambiguities and incoherence of childhood, both in the human exchange of therapy and in the constructions of theory. Freud was, sometimes in his own eyes and almost always in the eyes of his colleagues, a systematizer and theory-builder, but in the historical dialogue between the men who sought theoretical simplicity and the men who sought to understand the variety of man, Freud speaks for the psychologists of human variety.

The subtleties of human behavior that set Freud on the invention of his "science of unconscious mental processes" were largely those of man's relation to man and to his own impulses toward pleasure. In his elucidation of the war between instinct and society, Freud was remarkably unconcerned about the nature of physical reality; the world of things was there, to be sure, a surround for the development of man but not in itself a source of fundamental psychological questions. The hardheadedness that made Freud able to stare squarely at human irrationality was the hardheadedness of a nineteenth-century natural scientist; the world of physics was given and solid. Not so for Jean Piaget. Where Freud found revealing ambiguities in social encounters and in the expression of impulse, Piaget was to find revealing ambiguities in the development of the child's response to inanimate nature. For the Viennese, human development was a problem of being; for the Genevan, a problem of knowing.

During the epochal years of child psychology, which can conveniently be marked at 1905, Piaget was a child, younger than any of the men we have met so far by almost two decades, but he was already committed to the study of biological forms. He

* S. Freud, A difficulty in the path of psycho-analysis (Translated by J. Strachey). *Standard Edition of the Complete Psychological Works,* Vol. 17, London: Hogarth, 1955, pp. 137–144. Published first in Hungarian, then as Eine schwierigkeit der psychoanalyse, *Imago,* **5,** 1917, 1–7.

was an expert on fresh-water mollusks before his twentieth birthday and prepared, at least in his knowledge of biological variation, for the moment when his godfather opened the world of philosophy by telling young Piaget about Bergson. The conjunction of biology and philosophy was to be the continuing mark of Piaget's work, and he decided to "consecrate [his] life to the biological explanation of knowledge" long before he became interested in the behavior of children. But the search for origins that had made Watson and Freud theorists of child behavior drove Piaget, too, toward an examination of the beginnings of human knowledge in the mind of the child.

Human adults move with some reliability through space, deal with physical objects in a systematic way, orient in time. Moreover, they have quite complicated theoretical models for time, space, and object, even if most adults leave to the professional physicist the task of making explicit the assumptions of these models. There is, in the words that Piaget uses, an equlibrium between the organism and his environment and this equilibrium is represented by mental structures that are coherent and stable. The developmental question with which the psychological study of human knowledge opens is "How did these structures come to be?"

There have been two general ways of handling this enquiry in psychology, and the divergent answers have typically included two related but not logically entailed parts. One dimension of the divergence has turned on the issues of the priority of knowledge. The radical empiricists have followed the Humean line—that knowledge is constructed from contiguous presentations of events in nature and that no special assumption of innate categories or functions of knowledge is necessary to comprehend human intelligence and cognitive development. In psychology, the heirs and assigns of this philosophical position have been the radical behaviorists represented in his time by Watson and now, with consummate skill, by B. F. Skinner. In opposition to the empiricist tradition stands the far older and equally unyielding view, from Plato to Kant and beyond, that it is necessary to assign to human intelligence, independently of any particular brush with the environment, certain basic functions that impose structure and meaning on the world as perceived. Far less influential than their behavioristic colleagues, the psychologists of the Gestalt tradition have defended apriorism in human perception and thought.

A secondary argument about the nature of cognitive development, not perfectly parallel with the first, has concerned the form of thought. One attitude, again with its sources in the work of the associationistic philosophers, depended on the analysis of thinking into relatively discrete and initially independent units—association of sensations, conditioned reflexes, hierarchies of habits, and so on. The alternative attitude, again deriving from rationalistic epistemology and finding its psychological representation among the Gestalters, was based on the assumption that thought has structure and that no sense could be made of units without an understanding of the context in which the units were embedded. There is no logical or theoretical reason why there could not be empirical structuralists or aprioristic associationists but, in historical fact, such conjunctions have been uncommon in child psychology. Baldwin, from his philosophical vantage, made the first moves in a direction that Piaget has travelled throughout his career but, as we have seen, Baldwin's voice was hardly heard.

Piaget, with his predispositions toward a biological analysis, has been unremittingly on the side of the structuralists. The notion of an act independent of conceptual context—capable of description as "elicited" by some bounded aspect of the environment— is foreign to Piaget. Behavior is always structured, knowledge is always structured, and changes are not made in human cognition by adding or subtracting discrete units. More than that, if we are to understand the development of categories of space, time, and object, it is necessary to see the behavior of the child and his environment as a single system in a state of tenuous equilibrium. Piaget does not, in this way, abandon psychology's hard-won distinction between observer and observed (though he skates dangerously close to the hole in the ice), but he does block any analysis of development in terms of discrete physicalistically defined stimuli and topographically simple responses. The smallest "unit" in the Piagetian text is the reflex, but it is a reflex with properties different from those assigned it by Pavlov and Watson;

even so, reflexes give way very early to far more involved and clearly contextually defined "schemata" of structures of behavior and (later in life) conceptual knowledge. One of the chief obstacles to Piaget's acceptance among American psychologists has been their inability to fit his categories of description into any of the historically available definitions of response; it is an obstacle that shows no sign of eroding.

There is no doubt that Piaget is a structuralist. He is by no means so easily scored on the classic division between empiricism and apriorism. Knowledge is not achieved by the occurrence of adventitious event-pairings, certainly, but neither is knowledge given full in the newborn infant. Piaget proposes an inborn tendency toward adaptation which, in its encounters with the world as it is usually presented to the child, results in categories of knowledge that are remarkably similar among all human beings. The similarity is not necessary; it is the result of a common tactic—adaptation—and an environment very much alike for all of us. One can imagine a different world in which the same congenital equipment, the same tendency toward adaptation, will produce quite different epistemological results. It is unclear in Piaget's work what procedures might be used to retard or hasten the child's construction of the world and it is a problem in which he is not at all interested; unhappily the assignment of chronological marks to the child's changing understanding and the absence of experimental work in the Piagetian corpus have suggested that his position is that of an inevitable maturationalist. This interpretation of Piaget is made even more easy because of his failure to include specification of the ways in which the human being—parent or peer—is influential in the child's development. But it must be remembered that the postulates about adaptation permit the child to learn more and more about his world without any active didactic intervention of another person. In pointing out that increases in human knowledge, especially of early and fundamental categories such as object and time, may occur without social support, Piaget redresses somewhat the overemphasis on the active parental teacher that would, if taken seriously, make growing up impossible. Just as the child is not taught to walk, so he is not taught the dimensionality of time, space, and object;

Piaget presents evidence that nonetheless he achieves this knowledge, not by heredity, but by an active adaptive exchange with his environment. The Genevan research has described in some detail the course of the child's increasing comprehension of the world and of the surprising difficulties he has in achieving the adult's physics and mathematics and logic.* In the next selection, Piaget discusses in general terms the changes that take place in the thought of the child as he moves from his wordless organization of the world in the first two years of life to the intricate hierarchical thought of the adolescent.

* * *

Jean Piaget (1896–   )

The Growth of Thought

In order to understand the mechanism of the formation of operations, it is first of all important to realise what it is that has to be constructed, i.e. what must be added to sensori-motor in-

J. Piaget, The Psychology of Intelligence (Translated by M. Percy and D. E. Berlyne), London: Routledge, Kegan Paul, 1950, from the second French edition of La psychologie de l'intelligence published in Paris in 1947, pp. 119–153. Reprinted with permission of the publisher.

* Two recent books have summarized parts of Piaget's work: J. McV. Hunt, *Intelligence and Experience*, New York: Ronald, 1961; and J. H. Flavell, *The Developmental Psychology of Jean Piaget*, New York: van Nostrand, 1963. Representative of Piaget's varied interests are the following books: *Le langage et la pensée chez l'enfant*, Neuchâtel: Delachaux et Niestlé, 1924 [*The Language and Thought of the Child*, New York: Humanities Press, 1959, Translated from 3rd French ed.]; *La naissance de l'intelligence chez l'infant*, Neuchâtel: Delachaux et Niestlé, 1936 [*The Origin of Intelligence in the Child*, New York: International Universities Press, 1952]; *Introduction à l'epistémologie génétique* (3 vols.), Paris: Presses Universitaires de France, 1950; *Les méchanismes perceptifs*, Paris: Presses Universitaires de France, 1961.

telligence for it to be extended into conceptual thought. Nothing indeed could be more superficial than to suppose that the construction of intelligence is already accomplished on the practical level, and then simply to appeal to language and imaginal representation to explain how this ready-made intelligence comes to be internalized as logical thought.

In point of fact, only the functional point of view allows us to find in sensori-motor intelligence the practical equivalent of classes, relations, reasonings and even groups of displacements in their empirical form as actual displacements. From the point of view of structure, and consequently of effect, there remain a certain number of fundamental differences between sensori-motor co-ordinations and conceptual co-ordinations, with regard both to the nature of the co-ordinations themselves and to the distances covered by the action, i.e., its scope of application.

In the first place, acts of sensori-motor intelligence, which consist solely in co-ordinating successive perceptions and (also successive) overt movements, can themselves only be reduced to a succession of states, linked by brief anticipations and reconstructions, but never arriving at an all-embracing representation; the latter can only be established if thought makes these states simultaneous, and thus releases them from the temporal sequence characteristic of action. In other words, sensori-motor intelligence acts like a slow-motion film, in which all the pictures are seen in succession but without fusion, and so without the continuous vision necessary for understanding the whole.

In the second place, and for the same reason, an act of sensori-motor intelligence leads only to practical satisfaction, i.e. to the success of the action, and not to knowledge as such. It does not aim at explanation or classification or taking note of facts for their own sake; it links causally and classifies and takes note of facts only in relation to a subjective goal which is foreign to the pursuit of truth. Sensori-motor intelligence is thus an intelligence in action and in no way reflective.

As regards its scope, sensori-motor intelligence deals only with real entities, and each of its actions thus involves only very short distances between subject and objects. It is doubtless capable of detours and reversals, but it never concerns anything but reponses actually carried out and real objects. Thought alone breaks away from these short distances and physical pathways, so that it may seek to embrace the whole universe including what is invisible and sometimes even what cannot be pictured; this infinite expansion of spatio-temporal distances between subject and objects comprises the principal innovation of conceptual intelligence and the specific power that enables it to bring about operations.

There are thus three essential conditions for the transition from the sensori-motor level to the reflective level. Firstly, an increase in speed allowing the knowledge of the successive phases of an action to be moulded into one simultaneous whole. Next, an awareness, not simply of the desired results of action, but its actual mechanisms, thus enabling the search for the solution to be combined with a consciousness of its nature. Finally, an increase in distances, enabling actions affecting real entities to be extended by symbolic actions affecting symbolic representations and thus going beyond the limits of near space and time.

We see then that thought can neither be a translation nor even a simple continuation of sensori-motor processes in a symbolic form. It is much more than a matter of formulating or following up work already started; it is necessary from the start to reconstruct everything on a new plane. Perception and overt responses by themselves will continue to function in the same way, except for being charged with new meanings and integrated into new systems. But the structures of intelligence have to be entirely rebuilt before they can be completed; knowing how to reverse an object . . . does not imply one can represent a series of rotations in thought; physical movement along a complex route and returning to the starting-point does not necessarily involve understanding an imaginary system of displacements, and even to anticipate the conservation of an object in practice does not lead immediately to the conception of conservations affecting a system built up of different elements.

Moreover, in order to reconstruct these structures in thought, the subject is going to encounter the same difficulties, though transposed to this new level, that he has already overcome in immediate action. In order to construct a space, a time, a universe of causes and of sensori-motor or practical objects, the child has had to free himself from his perceptual and motor egocentricity; by a series of successive decentralisations he has managed to organise an empirical group of physical displacements, by localising his own body and his own movements amid the whole mass of others. This construction of groupings and operational groups of thought will necessitate a similar change of direction, but one following infinitely more complex paths. Thought will have to be decentralised, not only in relation to the perceptual centralisation of the movement, but also in relation to the whole of the subject's action. Thought, springing from action, is indeed egocentric at first for exactly the same reasons as sensori-motor intelligence is at first centered on the particular perceptions or movements from which it arises. The construction of transitive, associative and reversible operations will thus involve a conversion of this initial egocentricity into a system of relations and classes that are decentralised with respect to the self, and his intellectual decentralisation . . . will in fact occupy the whole of early childhood.

The development of thought will thus at first be marked by the repetition, in accordance with a vast system of loosenings and separations, of the development which seemed to have been completed at the sensori-motor level, before it spreads over a field which is infinitely wider in space and more flexible in time, to arrive finally at operational structures.

Stages in the Construction of Operations

In order to arrive at the mechanism of this development, which finds its final form of equilibrium in the operational grouping, we will distinguish (simplifying and schematizing the matter) four principal periods, following that characterized by the formation of sensori-motor intelligence.

After the appearance of language or, more precisely, the symbolic function that makes its acquisition possible (1½–2 years), there begins a period which lasts until nearly 4 years and sees the development of a symbolic and preconceptual thought.

From 4 to about 7 or 8 years, there is developed, as a closely linked continuation of the previous stage, an intuitive thought whose progressive articulations lead to the threshold of the operation.

From 7-8 to 11-12 years "concrete operations" are organized, i.e. operational groupings of thought concerning objects that can be manipulated or known through the senses.

Finally, from 11-12 years and during adolescence, formal thought is perfected and its groupings characterize the completion of reflective intelligence.

Symbolic and Preconceptual Thought

From the last stages of the sensori-motor period onwards, the child is capable of imitating certain words and attributing a vague meaning to them, but the systematic acquisition of language does not begin until about the end of the second year.

Now, direct observation of the child, as well the analysis of certain speech disturbances, shows that the use of a system of verbal signs depends on the exercise of a more general "symbolic function," characterised by the representation of reality through the medium of "significants" which are distinct from "significates."

In fact, we should distinguish between symbols and signs on the one hand and indices or signals on the other. Not only all thought, but all cognitive and motor activity, from perception and habit to conceptual and reflective thought, consists in linking meanings, and all meaning implies a relation between a significant and a signified reality. But in the case of an index the significant constitutes a part or an objective aspect of the significate, or else it is linked to it by a casual relation; for the hunter tracks in the snow are an index of game, and for the infant the visible end of an almost completely hidden object is an index of its presence. Similarly, the signal, even when artificially produced by the experimenter, constitutes for the subject simply a partial aspect of the event that it heralds (in a conditioned response the signal is perceived as an objective antecedent). The symbol and the sign, on the other hand, imply a differentiation, from the point of view of the subject himself, between the significant and the significate; for a child playing at eating, a pebble representing a sweet is consciously recognized as that which symbolizes and the sweet as that which is symbolized; and when the same child, by "adherence to the sign," regards a name as inherent in the thing named, he nevertheless regards this name as a significant, as though he sees it as a label attached in substance to the designated object.

We may further specify that, according to a custom in linguistics which may usefully be employed in psychology, a symbol is defined as implying a bond of similarity between the significant and the significate, while the sign is "arbitrary" and of necessity based on convention. The sign thus cannot exist without social life, while the symbol may be formed by the individual in isolation (as in young children's play). Of course symbols also may be socialized, a collective symbol being generally half sign and half symbol; on the other hand, a pure sign is always collective.

In view of this, it should be noted that the acquisition of language, i.e. the system of collective signs, in the child coincides with the formation of the symbol, i.e. the system of individual significants. In fact, we cannot properly speak of symbolic play during the sensori-motor period, and K. Groos has gone rather too far in attributing an awareness of make-believe to animals. Primitive play is simply a form of exercise and the true symbol appears only when an object or a gesture represents to the subject himself something other than perceptible data. Accordingly we note the appearance, at the sixth of the stages of sensori-motor intelligence, of "symbolic schemata," i.e. schemata of action removed from their context and evoking an absent situation (e.g. pretending to sleep). But the symbol itself appears only when we have representation disassociated from the subject's own action: e.g. putting a doll or a teddy-bear to bed. Now precisely at the stage at which the symbol in the strict sense appears in play, speech brings about in addition the understanding of signs.

As for the formation of the individual symbol, this is elucidated by the development of imitation. During the sensori-motor period, imitation is only an extension of the accommodation characteristic of assimilatory schemata. When he can execute a movement, the subject, on perceiving an analogous movement (in other persons or in objects), assimilates it to his own, and this assimilation, being as much motor as perceptual, activates the appropriate schema. Subsequently, the new instance elicits an analogous assimilatory response, but the schema activated is then accommodated to new details; at the sixth stage, this imitative assimilation becomes possible even with a delay, thus presaging representation. Truly representative imitation, on the other hand, only begins with symbolic play because, like the latter, it presupposes imagery. But is the image the cause or the effect of this internalization of the imitative mechanism? The mental image is not a primary fact, as associationism long believed; like imitation itself, it is an accommodation of sensori-motor schemata, i.e. an active copy and not a trace or a sensory residue of perceived objects. It is thus internal imitation and is an extension of the accommodatory function of the schemata characteristic of perceptual activity (as opposed to perception itself), just as the external imitation found at previous levels is an extension of the accommodatory function of sensori-motor schemata (which are closely bound up with perceptual activity).

From then on, the formation of the symbol may be explained as follows: deferred imitation, i.e. accommodation extended in the form of imitative sketches, provides significants, which play or intelligence applies to various significates in accordance with the free or adapted modes of assimilation that characterize these responses. Symbolic play thus always involves an element of imitation functioning as a significant, and early intelligence utilises the image in like manner, as a symbol or significant.

We can understand now why speech (which is likewise learned by imitation, but by an imitation of ready-made signs, whereas imitation of shapes, etc., provides the significant material of private symbolism) is acquired at the same time as the symbol is established: it is because the use of signs, like that of symbols, involves an ability which is quite new with respect to sensori-motor behaviour and consists in representing one thing by another. We may thus apply to the infant this idea of a general "symbolic function," which has sometimes been used as a hypothesis in connection with aphasia, since the formation of such a mechanism is believed, in short, to characterize the simultaneous appearance of representative imitation, symbolic play, imaginal representation and verbal thought.

To sum up, the beginnings of thought, while carrying on the work of sensori-motor intelligence, spring from a capacity for distinguishing significants and significates, and consequently rely both on the invention of symbols and on the discovery of signs. But needless to say, for a young child who finds the system of ready-made collective signs inadequate, since they are partly inaccessible and are hard to master, these verbal signs will for a long time remain unsuitable for the expression of the particular entities on which the subject is still concentrated. This is why, as long as egocentric assimilation of reality to the subject's own action prevails, the child will require symbols; hence symbolic play or imaginative play, the purest form of egocentric and symbolic thought, the assimilation of reality to the subject's own interests and the expression of reality through the use of images fashioned by himself.

But even in the field of applied thought, i.e. the beginnings of representative intelligence, tied more or less closely to verbal signs, it is important to note the role of imaginal symbols and to realize how far the subject is, during his early childhood, from arriving at genuine concepts. We must, in fact, distinguish a first period in the development of thought, lasting from the appearance of language to the age of about 4 years, which may be called the period of pre-conceptual intelligence and which is characterized by pre-concepts of participations and, in the first forms of reasoning, by "transduction" or pre-conceptual reasoning.

Pre-concepts are the notions which the child attaches to the first verbal signs he learns to use. The distinguishing characteristics of these schemata is that they remain midway between the generality of the concept and the individuality of the elements composing it, without arriving either at the one or at the other. The child aged 2-3 years will be just as likely to say "slug" as "slugs" and "the moon" as "the moons," without deciding whether the slugs encountered in the course of a single walk or the discs seen at different times in the sky are one individual, a single slug or moon, or a class of distinct individuals. On the one hand, he cannot yet cope with general classes, being unable to distinguish between "all" and "some." On the other hand, although the idea of the permanent individual object has been formed in the field of immediate action, such is by no means the case where distant space and reappearances at intervals are concerned; a mountain is still deemed to change its shape in the course of a journey . . . and "the slug" reappears in different places. Hence, sometimes we have true "participations" between objects which are distinct and distant from each other: even at the age of four years, a shadow, thrown on a table in a closed room by means of a screen, is explained in terms of those which are found "under the trees in the garden" or at night-time, etc., as though these intervened directly the moment the screen is placed on the table (and with the subject making no attempt to go into the "how" of the phenomenon).

It is clear that such a schema, remaining midway between the individual and the general, is not yet a logical concept and is still partly something of a pattern of action and of sensori-motor assimilation. But it is nevertheless a representative schema and one which, in particular, succeeds in evoking a large number of objects by means of privileged elements, regarded as samples of the pre-conceptual collection. On the other hand, since these type-individuals are themselves made concrete by images as much as, and more than, by words, the pre-concept improves on the symbol in so far as it appears to generic samples of this kind. To sum up then, it is a schema placed midway between the sensori-motor schema and the concept with respect to its manner of assimilation, and partaking of the nature of the imaginal symbol as far as its representative structure is concerned. . . .

Intuitive Thought

The forms of thought we have been describing can be analysed only through observation, since young children's intelligence is still far too unstable for them to be interrogated profitably. After about 4 years, on the other hand, short experiments with the subject, in which he has to manipulate experimental objects, enable us to obtain regular answers and to converse with him. This fact alone indicates a new structuring.

In fact, from 4 to 7 years we see a gradual co-ordination of representative relations and thus a growing conceptualization, which leads the child from the symbolic or pre-conceptual phase to the beginnings of the operation. But the remarkable thing is that this intelligence, whose progress may be observed and is often rapid, still remains pre-logical even when it attains its maximum degree of adaptation; up to the time when this series of successive equilibrations culminates in the "grouping," it continues to supplement incomplete operations with a semi-symbolic form of thought, i.e. intuitive reasoning; and it controls judgments solely by means of intuitive "regulations," which are analogous on a representative level to perceptual adjustments on the sensori-motor plane.

As an example let us consider an experiment which we conducted some time ago with A. Szeminska. Two small glasses, A and A_2, of identical shape and size, are each filled with an equal number of beads, and this equality is acknowledged by the child, who has filled the glasses himself, e.g. by placing a bead in A with one hand every time he places a bead in A_2 with the other hand. Next, A_2 is emptied into a differently shaped glass B, while A is left as a standard. Children of 4-5 years then conclude that the quantity of beads has changed, even though they are sure none has been removed or added. If the glass B is tall and thin they will say that there are "more beads than before" because "it is higher," or that there are fewer because "it is thinner," but they agree on the non-conservation of the whole.

First, let us note the continuity of this reaction with those of earlier levels. The subject possesses the notion of an individual object's conservation but does not yet credit a collection of objects with permanence. Thus, the united class has not been constructed, since it is not always constant, and this non-conservation is an extension both of the subject's initial reactions to the object (with a greater flexibility due to the fact that it is no longer a question of an isolated element but of a collection) and of the absence of an understanding of plurality which we mentioned in connection with the pre-concept. Moreover, it is clear that the reasons for the error are of a quasi-perceptual order; the rise in the level, or the thinness of the column, etc., deceives the child. However, it is not a question of perceptual illusions; perception of relations is on the whole correct, but it occasions an incomplete intellectual construction. It is this pre-logical schematization, which is still closely modelled on perceptual data though it re-centres them in its own fashion, that may be called intuitive thought. We can see straight away how it is related to the imaginal character of the pre-concept and to the mental experiments that characterize transductive reasoning.

However, this intuitive thought is an advance on pre-conceptual or symbolic thought. Intuition, being concerned essentially with complex configurations and no longer with simple half-individual, half-generic figures, leads to a rudimentary logic, but in the form of representative regulations and not yet of operations. From this point of view, there exist intuitive "centralisations" and "decentralisations" which are analogous to the mechanisms we mentioned in connection with the sensori-motor schemata of perception. Suppose a child estimates that there are more beads in B than in A because the level has been raised. He thus "centres" his thought, or his attention, on the relation between the heights of B and A, and ignores the widths. But let us empty B into glasses C or D, etc., which are even thinner and taller; there must comes a point at which the child will reply, "there are fewer, because it is too narrow." There will thus be a correction of centring on height by a decentring of attention on to width. On the other hand, in the case of the subject who estimates the quantity in B as less than that in A on account of thinness, the lengthening of the column in C, D, etc., will induce him to reverse his judgment in favour of height. Now this transition from a single centring to two successive centrings heralds the beginnings of the operation; once he reasons with respect to both relations at the same time, the child will, in fact, deduce conservation. However, in the case we are considering, there is neither deduction nor a true operation; an error is simply corrected, but it is corrected late and as a reaction to its very exaggeration (as in the field of perceptual illusions), and the two relations are seen alternately instead of being logically multiplied. So all that occurs is a kind of intuitive regulation and not a truly operational mechanism.

That is not all. In studying the differences between intuition and operation together with the transition from the one to the other, we may consider not merely the relating to each other of qualities forming two dimensions but their correspondences in either a logical (i.e. qualitative) or a mathematical form. The subject is first presented with glasses A and B of different shapes and he is asked to place a bead simultaneously in each glass, one with the left hand and one with the right. With small numbers (4 or 5), the child immediately believes in the equivalence of the two collections, which seems to presage the operation, but when the shapes change too much, even though the one-to-one correspondence is continued, he ceases to recognize equality. The latent operation is thus destroyed by the deceptive demands of intuition.

— — —

[The] difference between the intuitive and the operational methods may be pinned down still further by directing the analysis towards the formation of classes and the seriation of asymmetrical relations, which constitute the most elementary groupings. But of course the problem must be presented on an intuitive plane, the only one accessible at this stage, as opposed to a formal plane indissociably tied at language. To study the formation of classes, we place about twenty beads in a box, the subject acknowledging that they are "all made of wood," so that they constitute a whole, B. Most of these beads are brown and constitute part A, and some are white, forming the complementary part A′. In order to determine whether the child is capable of understanding the operation $A + A′ = B$, i.e. the uniting of parts in a whole, we may put the following simple question: In this box (all the beads still being visible) which are there more of—wooden beads or brown beads, i.e. is $A < B$?

Now, up to about the age of 7 years, the child almost always replies that there are more brown beads "because there are only two or three white ones." We then question further: "Are all the brown ones made of wood? "—"Yes."—"If I take away all the wooden beads and put them here (a second box) will there be any beads left in the (first) box?"—"No, because they are all made of wood."—"If I take away the brown ones, will there be any beads left?"—"Yes, the white ones." Then the original question is repeated and the subject continues to state that there are more brown beads than wooden one in the box because there are only two white ones, etc.

The mechanism of this type of reaction is easy to unravel: the subject finds no difficulty in concentrating his attention on the whole B, or on the parts A and A′, if they have been isolated in thought, but the difficulty is that by centring on A he destroys the whole, B, so that the part A can no longer be compared with the other part A′. So there is again a non-conservation of the whole for lack of mobility in the successive centralisations of thought. But this is still not all. When the child is asked to imagine what would happen if we made a necklace either with the wooden beads or with the brown beads, A, we again meet the foregoing difficulties but with the following details: "If I make a necklace with the brown ones," a child will sometimes reply, "I could not make another necklace with the same beads, and the necklace made of wooden beads would have only white ones!" This type of thinking, which is in no way irrational, nevertheless shows the difference still separating intuitive thought and operational thought. In so far as the first imitates true actions by imagined mental experiments, it meets with a particular obstacle, namely, that in practice one could not construct two necklaces at the same time from the same elements, whereas in so far as the second is carried out through internalized actions that have become completely reversible, there is nothing to prevent two hypotheses being made simultaneously and then being compared with each other.

[Piaget gives further examples of intuitive thought.]

This then is intuitive thought. Like symbolic thought of a pre-conceptual nature, from which it springs directly, it is, in a sense, an extension of sensori-motor intelligence. Just as the latter assimilates objects to response-schemata, so intuition is always in the first place a kind of action carried out in thought; pouring from one vessel to another, establishing a correspondence, joining, serialising, displacing, etc. are still response-schemata to which representation assimilates reality. But the accommodation of these schemata to objects, instead of remaining practical, provides imitation or imaginal significants which enable this same assimilation to occur in thought. So in the second place, intuition is an imaginal thought, more refined than that of the previous period, since it concerns complex configurations and not merely simple syncretic collections symbolized by type-individuals; but it still uses representative symbolism and therefore constantly exhibits some of the limitations that are inherent in this.

These limitations are obvious. Intuition, being a direct relationship between a schema of internalized action and the perception of objects, results only in configurations "centred" on this relationship. Since it is unable to go beyond these imaginal configurations, the relations that it constructs are thus incapable of being combined. The subject does not arrive at reversibility, because an action translated into a simple imagined experiment is still unidirectional, and because an assimilation centred on a perceptual configuration is necessarily uni-directional also. Hence the absence of transitivity, since each centring distorts or destroys the others, and of associativity, since the relations vary with the route followed by thought in fashioning them. Altogether then, in the absence of transitive, reversible and associative combinativity, there is neither a guarantee of the identity of elements nor a conservation of the whole. Thus, we may also say that intuition is still phenomenalist, because it copies the outlines of reality without correcting them, and egocentric, because it is constantly related to present action; in this way, it lacks an equilibrium between the assimilation of phenomena to thought-schemata and the accommodation of the latter to reality.

But this initial state, which recurs in each of the fields of intuitive thought, is progressively corrected, thanks to a system of regulations which herald operations. Intuition, at first dominated by the immediate relations between the phenomenon and the subject's viewpoint, evolves towards decentralisation. Each distortion, when carried to an extreme, involves the re-emergence of the relations previously ignored. Each relation established favours the possibility of a reversal. Each détour leads to interactions which supplement the various points of view. Every decentralisation of an intuition thus takes the form of a regulation, which is a move towards reversibility, transitive combinativity and associativity, and thus, in short, to conservation through the co-ordination of different viewpoints. Hence we have articulated intuitions, which progress towards reversible mobility and pave the way for the operation.

Concrete Operations

The appearance of logico-arithmetical and spatio-temporal operations introduces a problem of considerable interest in connection with the mechanisms characterising the development of thought. The point at which articulated intuitions turn into operational systems is not to be determined by mere convention, based on definitions decided on in advance. To divide developmental continuity into stages recognizable by some set of external criteria is not the most profitable of occupations; the crucial turning-point for the beginning of operations shows itself in a kind of equilibration, which is always rapid and sometimes sudden, which affects the complex of ideas forming a single system and which needs explaining on its own account. In this there is something comparable to the abrupt complex restructurings described in the Gestalt theory, except that, when it occurs, there arises the very opposite of a crystallisation embracing all relations in a single static network; operations, on the contrary, are found formed by a kind of thawing out of intuitive structures, by the sudden mobility which animates and co-ordinates the configurations that were hitherto more or less rigid despite their progressive articulation. Thus, quite distinct stages in development are marked, for example, by the point at which temporal relations are merged in the notion of a single time, or the point at which the elements of a complex are conceived as constituting an unvarying whole or the inequalities characterising a system of relations are serialised in a single scale, and so on; after trial-and-error imagination there follows, sometimes abruptly, a feeling of coherence and of necessity, the satisfaction of arriving at a system which is both complete in itself and indefinitely extensible.

Consequently, the problem is to understand what internal process effects this transition from a phase of progressive equilibration (intuitive thought) to a mobile equilibrium which is reached, as it were, at the limit of the former (operations). If the concept of "grouping" described earlier, in fact, has a psychological meaning, this is precisely the point at which it should reveal it.

So, assuming that the intuitive relations of a given system are at a certain moment suddenly "grouped," the first question is to decide by what internal or mental criterion grouping is to be recognised. The answer is obvious: where there is "grouping" there will be the conservation of a whole, and this conservation itself will not merely be assumed by the subject by virtue of a probable induction, but affirmed by him as a certainty in his thought.

In this connection let us reconsider the first example cited with reference to intuitive thought: the pouring of the beads from one glass to another. After a long period during which each pouring out is believed to change the quantities, and after an intermediate phase (articulated intuition) when some transfers are believed to change the whole while others, between glasses that are just slightly different, induce the subject to suppose that the whole is conserved, there always comes a time (between 6½ years and 7 years 8 months) when the child's attitude changes: he no longer needs to reflect, he decides, he even looks surprised that the question is asked, he is *certain* of the conservation. What has happened then? If we ask him his reasons, he replies that nothing has been removed or added; but the younger children also are well aware of this, and yet they do not infer identity. Thus, in spite of what E. Meyerson says, identification is not a primary process but the result of an assimilation by the whole grouping (the product of the original operation multiplied by its converse). Or else he replies that the height makes up for the width lost by the new glass, etc., but articulated intuition has already led to these decentrings of a given relation without their resulting in the simultaneous co-ordination of relations or in their necessary conservation. Or else, and this especially, he replies that a transfer from A to B may be corrected by a transfer from B to A and this reversibility is certainly essential, but the younger children have already on occasion admitted the possibility of a return to the starting-point, without this "empirical reversal" yet constituting a complete reversibility. There is, therefore, only one legitimate answer: the various transformations involved—reversibility, combination of compensated relations, identity, etc.—in fact depend on each other and, because they amalgamate into an organised whole, each is really new despite its affinity with the corresponding intuitive relation that was already formed at the previous level.

— — —

But what must be clearly understood if we are to arrive at the true psychological nature of the grouping, as distinct from its formulation in logical language, is that these various closely related changes are actually the expression of one and the same total act, namely, an act of complete decentralisation or complete conversion of thought. The distinguishing characteristic of the sensori-motor schema (perception, etc.), of the pre-conceptual symbol and also of the intuitive configuration, is that they are always "centred" on a particular state of the object and a point of view peculiar to the subject; thus they always testify both to an egocentric assimilation to the subject and to a phenomenalist accommodation to the object. On the other hand, the distinguishing characteristic of the mobile equilibrium peculiar to the grouping is that the decentralisation, already provided for by the progressive regulations and articulations of intuition, suddenly becomes systematic on reaching its limit; thought is then no longer tied to particular states of the object, but is obliged to follow successive changes with all their possible detours and reversals; and it no longer issues from a particular viewpoint of the subject, but co-ordinates all the different viewpoints in a system of objective reciprocities. The grouping thus realizes for the first time an equilibrium between the assimilation of objects to the subject's action and the accommodation of subjective schemata to modifications of objects. At the outset, in fact, assimilation and accommodation act in opposite directions; hence the distorting character of the first and the phenomenalist character of the second. By means of anticipations and reconstitutions, which extend action in both directions to ever increasing distances, from the brief anticipations and reconstitutions characteristic of perception, habit and sensori-motor intelligence to the anticipatory schemata formed by intuitive representation, assimilation and accommodation are gradually equilibrated. The completion of this equilibrium explains the reversibility which is the final term of sensori-motor and mental anticipations and reconstitutions, and with it the reversible combinativity which is the distinguishing mark of the grouping; the detailed working of operations simply expresses, in fact, the combined conditions of a co-ordination of successive viewpoints of the subject (with possible reversal in time and anticipation of their sequel) and a co-ordination of perceptible or representable modifications of objects (in the past, in the present, or in the course of subsequent events).

— — —

Formal Operations

Formal thought reaches its fruition during adolescence. The adolescent, unlike the child, is an individual who thinks beyond the present and forms theories about everything, delighting especially in considerations of that which is not. The child, on the other hand, concerns himself only with action in progress and does not form theories, even though an observer notes the periodical recurrence of analogous reactions and may discern a spontaneous systematization in his ideas. This reflective thought, which is characteristic of the adolescent, exists from the age of 11-12 years, from the time, that is, when the subject becomes capable of reasoning in a hypothetico-deductive manner, i.e., on the basis of simple assumptions which have no necessary relation to reality or to the subject's beliefs, and from the time when he relies on the necessary validity of an inference (*vi formae*), as opposed to agreement of the conclusions with experience.

Now, reasoning formally and with mere propositions involves different operations from reasoning about action or reality. Reasoning that concerns reality consists of a first-degree grouping of operations, so to speak, i.e. internalised actions that have become capable of combination and reversal. Formal thought, on the other hand, consists in reflecting (in the true sense of the word) on these operations and therefore operating on operations or on

their results and consequently effecting a second-degree grouping
of operations. No doubt the same operational content is involved;
the problem is still a matter of classing, serialising, enumerating,
measuring, placing or displacing in space or in time, etc. But
these classes, series and spatio-temporal relations themselves, as
structurings of action and reality, are not what is grouped by
formal operations but the propositions that express or "reflect"
these operations. Formal operations, therefore, consist essentially
of "implications" (in the narrow sense of the word) and "contra-
dictions" established between propositions which themselves express classifications, seriations, etc.

We can now see why there is a vertical separation between
concrete operations and formal operations, even though the second
repeats to some extent the content of the first; the operations in
question are indeed not by any means of the same psychological
difficulty. Thus, one has only to translate a simple problem of
seriation between three terms presented in random order into
propositions for this serial addition to become singularly difficult,
although, right from the age of 7, it is quite easy as long as it
takes the form of a concrete seriation or even of transitive co-
ordinations considered in relation to action. The following neat
example comes from one of Burt's tests: "Edith is fairer than
Susan; Edith is darker than Lily; who is the darkest of the three?"
Now this problem is rarely solved before the age of 12. Till then
we find reasoning such as the following: Edith and Susan are
fair, Edith and Lily are dark, therefore Lily is darkest, Susan is
the fairest and Edith in between. In other words, the child of 10
reasons formally as children of 4-5 years do when serialising
sticks, and it is not until the age of 12 that he can accomplish with
formal problems what he could do with concrete problems of size
at the age of 7, and the cause of this is simply that the premises
are given as pure verbal postulates and the conclusion is to be
drawn *vi formae* without recourse to concrete operations.

We thus see why formal logic and mathematical deduction are
still inaccessible to the child and seem to constitute a realm on
its own—the realm of "pure" thought which is independent of
action. And indeed, whether we are concerned with the particular
language—which, like every language, is learned—of mathematical

signs (signs which are quite different from symbols in the sense defined above) or with the other system of signs (i.e. the words expressing simple propositions), hypothetico-deductive operations are situated on a different plane from concrete reasoning, since an action affecting signs that are detached from reality is something quite different from an action relating to reality itself or relating to signs attached to this reality. This is why logic dissociates this final stage from the main body of mental development and is in fact limited to axiomatizing characteristic operations instead of replacing them in their living context. This always was its role, but this role certainly gains by being played consciously. Moreover, logic was driven to this course by the very nature of formal operations which, since second-degree operations deal only with signs, are committed to the schematization proper to an axiomatic. But it is the function of the psychology of intelligence to replace the canon of formal operations in its true perspective and to show that it could not have any mental meaning, were it not for the concrete operations that both pave the way for it and provide its content. Formal logic is, according to this view, not an adequate description for the whole of living thought; formal operations constitute solely the structure of the final equilibrium to which concrete operations tend when they are reflected in more general systems linking together the propositions that express them.

The Hierarchy of Operations and Their Progressive Differentiation

As we have seen, a response is a functional interaction between subject and objects, and responses may be serialised in an order of genetic succession, based on the increasing distances, spatial and temporal, that characterize the increasingly complex routes followed by these interactions.

Thus, perceptual assimilation and accommodation involve merely a direct and rectilinear form of interaction. Habit has routes that are more complex but shorter, stereotyped and unidirectional. Sensori-motor intelligence introduces reversals and detours; it has access to objects outside the perceptual field and habitual routes and so it goes beyond original distances in space and time but is still limited to the field of the subject's own action. With the beginnings of representative thought and especially with the growth of intuitive thought, intelligence becomes capable of evoking absent objects, and consequently of being applied to invisible realities in the past and partly even in the future. But it still proceeds by way of more or less static figures—half-individual, half-generic images in the case of the pre-concept, complex representative configurations, which are still better articulated, in the intuitive period—but they are nevertheless figures, i.e. "stills" of moving reality, which represent only some states or pathways out of the mass of possible routes. Intuitive thought thus provides a map of reality (which sensori-motor intelligence, bound up with immediate reality, could not do), but it is still imaginal, with many blank spaces and without sufficient co-ordinations to pass from one point to another. When groupings of concrete operations appear, these forms are dissolved or blended into the all-embracing plan and decisive progress is made towards the overcoming of distances and the differentiation of routes; thought no longer masters only fixed states or pathways but even deals with changes, so that one can always pass from one point to another and vice versa. Thus, the whole of reality becomes accessible. But it is still only a represented reality; with formal operations there is even more than reality involved, since the world of the possible becomes available for construction and since thought becomes free from the real world. Mathematical creativity is an illustration of this new power.

Now to picture the mechanism of this process of construction and not merely its progressive extension, we must note that each level is characterized by a new co-ordination of the elements provided—already existing in the form of wholes, though of a lower order—by the processes of the previous level.

The sensori-motor schema, the characteristic unit of the system of pre-symbolic intelligence, thus assimilates perceptual schemata and the schemata relating to learned action (these schemata of perception and habit being of the same lower order, since the first concerns the present state of the object and the second only elementary changes of state). The symbolic schema assimilates sensori-motor schemata with differentiation of function; imitative accommodation is extended into imaginal significants and assimilation determines the significates. The intuitive schema is both a co-ordination and a differentiation of imaginal schemata. The concrete operational schema is a grouping of intuitive schemata, which are promoted, by the very fact of their being grouped, to the rank of reversible operations. Finally, the formal schema is simply a system of second-degree operations, and therefore a grouping operating on concrete groupings.

Each of the transitions from one of these levels to the next is therefore characterized both by a new co-ordination and by a differentiation of the systems constituting the unit of the preceding level. Now these successive differentiations, in their turn, throw light on the undifferentiated nature of the initial mechanisms, and thus we can conceive both of a genealogy of operational groupings as progressive differentiations, and of an explanation of the pre-operational levels as a failure to differentiate the processes involved.

Thus, as we have seen, sensori-motor intelligence arrives at a kind of empirical grouping of bodily movements, characterized psychologically by actions capable of reversals and detours, and geometrically by what Poincaré called the (experimental) group of displacement. But it goes without saying that, at this elementary level, which precedes all thought, we cannot regard this grouping as an operational system, since it is a system of responses actually effected; the fact is therefore that it is undifferentiated, the displacements in question being at the same time and in every case responses directed towards a goal serving some practical purpose. We might therefore say that this level spatio-temporal, logico-arithmetical and practical (means and ends) groupings form a global whole and that, in the absence of differentiation, this complex system is incapable of constituting an operational mechanism.

At the end of this period and at the beginning of representative thought, on the other hand, the appearance of the symbol makes possible the first form of differentiation: practical groupings (means and ends) on the one hand, and representation on the other. But this latter is still undifferentiated, logico-arithmetical operations not being distinguished from spatio-temporal operations. In fact, at the intuitive level there are no genuine classes or relations because both are still spatial collections as well as spatio-temporal relationships: hence their intuitive and preoperational character. At 7–8 years, however, the appearance of operational groupings is characterized precisely by a clear differentiation between logico-arithmetical operations that have become independent (classes, relations and despatialized numbers) and spatio-temporal or infra-logical operations. Lastly, the level of formal operations marks a final differentiation between operations tied to real action and hypothetico-deductive operations concerning pure implications from propositions stated as postulates.

* * *

In the two centuries between Cadogan and Piaget, changes both subtle and profound have occurred in Western man's theory of the child. The skill of physicians and the zeal of reformers protected the child from the worst effects of maltreatment and neglect; the speculations of epistemologists and educators made him an object of serious intellectual interest; and science claimed him in the research of biologists and psychologists. More subtle than these changes in the child as object of professional study have been changes in the child's cultural position. At an apparently accelerating pace, he has moved from the periphery to the center of cultural interest, at least in the United States, and the commentators who sixty years ago hailed the "century of the child" little knew how prophetic they were. The men who have been heard in this book rarely saw themselves as reflecting a continuing change in the child's social locus but, for all their serious attempts to be dispassionate and scholarly, the history of the child is a history of social change as well as an intellectual history. In the face of so tight a coherence of society and human knowledge, it is difficult to make an uncontaminated description of the present state of child study and even riskier to predict its next directions.

Perhaps the most striking characteristic of child psychology in the mid-'sixties is the absence of professional singlemindedness. Child study is not an entrenched discipline with routine methods and a set of widely shared premises that prescribe the shape of research. Rather, the field of child study is in a condition of agitation and excitement that precludes accurate forecasts about the contents of a future child psychology but almost certainly insures intellectual novelty. Moreover, there is a decay in the emphasis on controversy among schools of child psychology that parallels the diminished interest of other behavioral scientists in conceptually inclusive and professionally exclusive theory. Psychologists, child psychologists among them, hope less than they once did for the unifying Newton—they probably also desire him less. Consequently there is an easier communication of problem, of method, and of hypothesis among child psychologists than has been usual in the recent past, and the distinctions among subdivisions of the specialty grow blurred. The result is not likely to be a loss of interest in building theories of the child—there will be more than sufficient sources in 2015 to put together a sequel to this book—and there is some promise that the new theorists will move from the grand simplicities of recent psychological theory to a view of the child that recognizes his intricate variety.

Name Index